RAGA'N JOSH

Stories from a Musical Life

for

Ishan and Nihal

SHEILA DHAR

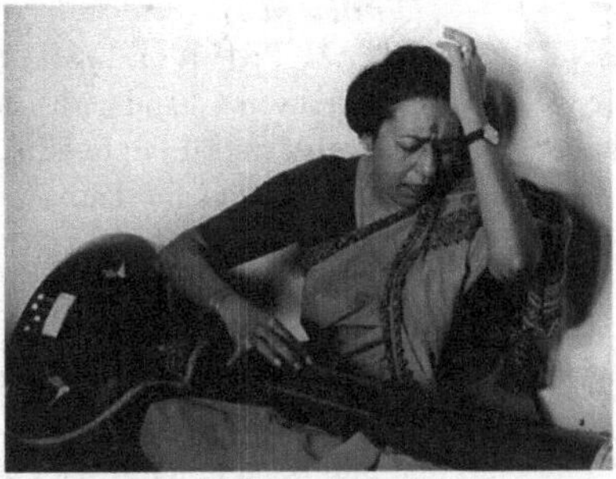

RAGA'N JOSH

Stories from a Musical Life

permanent black

Published by
PERMANENT BLACK
'Himalayana', Mall Road, Ranikhet Cantt,
Ranikhet 263645
Email: perblack@gmail.com

Distributed by
ORIENT BLACKSWAN PRIVATE LIMITED
Bangalore Bhopal Bhubaneshwar Chandigarh Chennai
Ernakulam Guwahati Hyderabad Jaipur Kolkata
Lucknow Mumbai New Delhi Patna
www.orientblackswan.com

Raga'n Josh was first published in hardback 2005
by Permanent Black, incorporating two books
by Sheila Dhar: *Here's Someone I'd Like You to Meet* (1995),
and *The Cooking of Music and Other Essays* (2002),
as well as two obituaries honouring her career.

First reprint in current format 2015

ISBN 978-81-7824-463-1

Printed and bound by Manipal Technologies Limited, Manipal

Contents

PART I

Here's Someone I'd Like You to Meet

Acknowledgements

I started writing this book when my son Madhav initiated me into the mysteries of his laptop with his characteristic confidence and enthusiasm. My elder son Abhinav also became a staunch supporter and on occasion an insightful critic. From my husband I expected encouragement as a matter of right but the extent of it surprised me. I owe much to my extraordinary family in this venture.

Only the luckiest people have editors who go so far beyond the call of duty that they are indistinguishable from good friends. I shall always be grateful to Esha for the depth of her understanding, for her enormous investment of time, effort and feeling, and for the infectious joy she brought to every reviewing session we had. I also want to thank Rukun Advani for his generous interest in the manuscript and for donating time even when he could not afford it. His many observations, suggestions, and comments were incisive and imaginative and always inspired me.

My computer illiteracy often landed me in terrifying situations where I thought I had lost the work of months. Whenever this or some other seeming disaster happened, I imposed on Madhu and Sanjay Duda, Nina and Rupa with pleas to bale me out of my many electronic impasses. I am indebted to them for making themselves available whenever I was in trouble and for patiently piloting me to safety every time.

My friend Shaista has no idea how much and in how many ways our long talks helped me. I am also grateful to Susan Lee for her tireless and cheerful assistance and to Shanti for simply being there.

Introduction

If a memoir needs a reason, mine is simply that wonderful things become even more wonderful for me if I can share them and dreadful things more bearable. The delightful and the bitter both seem more valid if I can believe that I am not the sole experiencer. Driven by this infirmity, I have over the years compulsively told and retold some of the stories that appear here. They have lived and become old in the minds of my friends. At some point Lalita and Zainub who are closest to me began to ask why I didn't write instead of talk.

That was a sobering thought because it implied a wider audience, which might not necessarily be as receptive. Clearly the writing venture called for a different kind of telling. For one thing, the vocal inflections and mimicry I used to rely on to draw character had to give place to descriptions, of both the people in these tales and of the setting in which they appeared in my life. For another, I had to render each experience from the Indian dialect in which it originally happened into its rough English equivalent. This exercise demanded more concentration and effort than relating anecdotes, but the heady feeling that many more companions might now wander into my world was reward enough.

On the whole I felt that in urging me to write, my friends had done me a favour. They had forced me down to a deeper layer of myself. I am a singer and unrolling the pictures in my mind through the written word felt exactly like singing. At any rate it took me to the very place I occupy in my head and heart when I try to express my whole self through the idiom of music. This realization made me ask myself, seriously for the first time, what it is that I am really saying when I sing. I knew from the accumulated lore of a lifetime in music that a conscious switching off of everything one has learnt is a necessary pre-requisite for a genuine musical performance. For me the act of singing ideally means recognizing and intensifying my own identity, and communicating it in the rigorous traditional idiom of an ancient musical language. This ideal is not always achieved, but when it is, my musical utterance inalienably carries within it the flavour of everything that has ever happened to me, and of all the emotional landscapes I have traversed. The feel of my grandfather's beard, the smell of the dank basement in our childhood home, the aroma of my Ustad's cooking, the sense of wonder I experienced at the pristine innocence of the Queen of Tonga, the sound of Siddheshwari's very musical but hearty belly laughs, the unbelievable simplicity behind Mohan Rao's eccentricities, the despair and the delight, the green chillies and black pepper of life itself are all within me and therefore a part of the body of my music.

If I were to take myself apart like a mechanical toy, and then try to retrieve the main parts from the debris of twisted wire and broken springs, I would at this point store them for possible reassembly in three bags clearly marked 'Home', 'Musicians', and 'Other People'. This is why I have retained these three labels for the reflections in this book. Most of the material has to do with Indian classical musicians and their world, which it has been my life's ambition to enter, but there are some accounts of unforgettable people and events outside it as well.

I love and admire the artistes that figure in this book. The eccentricities and frailties I have described do not diminish them in any way. On the contrary, they are intended to enhance the charm of their rich personalities.

As for the events I recount, they are the prisms through which I saw life and the transmitters of the cultural sounds I heard. In recalling them, I find once again the people, voices, and scenes that populate and nurture my spirit and the music within me.

The anecdotes that follow are not arranged chronologically but form a continuous narrative with overlapping threads. These are of different lengths and textures, and frequently break off, giving the whole fabric a random look. But for me that itself is the reality.

ONE

Number Seven, Civil Lines

The family dining room was the place where the final judgement on the state of the universe was available to both the adults and children of our family. It was the centre of the real world and there was no question that this real world was in the absolute control of my grandfather. He habitually surveyed his brood of sixty-odd people from his exalted position at the head of the table with a sharp but benevolent eye. If he smiled everyone knew that all was well with the world and life would soon shower exciting gifts on us. When he frowned the women looked funereal and the children apprehensive. The cue on how one should feel and what one should think came from him and was received with the utmost respect and willingness, at least for the entire period of my childhood.

We were used to incredulous exclamations about the size of our joint family from schoolmates and prided ourselves on both our numbers and our closeness. My grandfather had three sons whose wives and children were his responsibility as head of the household, and five daughters who though suitably married kept returning to the ancestral home on extended stays for one reason or another. Life was undoubtedly easier and pleasanter in their father's comfortable house in Delhi than in the smaller towns and humbler circumstances in which their husbands were placed. But the overwhelming official reason why Delhi tended to become their family headquarters was that the schools were much better in the capital city. In addition to the families of my aunts and uncles, we always had house guests and three or four children of distant relatives or friends living with us. This is how our household came to have more than sixty members at any given time, including the children whose number usually exceeded thirty.

Any visitor to the house was welcomed with great warmth and cheer by all. This came to be talked about as a wonderful trait of our family. We were very pleased with such praise and deliberately tried to outdo ourselves in devising little attentions and services for the comfort of our guests as this was sure to win the approval of all the adults. Another reason why we loved having people from outside was that even the smallest difference in dress, look, or intonation was an interesting novelty that lit up the comfortable sameness of our lives.

In the 1920s my grandfather, a barrister-at-law, spearheaded the move of three main branches of the extended family from the congested lanes of Chailpuri in the old city of Delhi to the Civil Lines, where a sizeable piece of land had been gifted by the British government to an ancestor, presumably for services rendered. There were subsequent family partitions and about twenty-four colonial-style houses surrounded by lawns and gardens came up in the spacious and elegant area, where highly-placed civil servants of the British government lived. Almost all the houses nestled among tall trees and were connected by winding lanes. It was an imposing and attractive neighbourhood. The relatives who still lived in the walled city and visited these houses occasionally were awed by the new Anglicized lifestyle that was the ideal of each of these units, and talked amongst themselves for weeks afterwards about the grandeur of the life they had seen.

It was noted with envy and admiration that breakfast in these households consisted of eggs, toast, and jam, instead of vegetable bhujia with paratha, and that even the women had begun to use spoons, though only little ones, to eat. There were many other amazing things. Guests to tea were served cakes and sandwiches instead of samosas and barfi. In the evenings there was Scotch whisky and soda in the living rooms instead of keora sharbat. The men played tennis, billiards, and bridge in clubs instead of chess and ganjufa in the courtyard. These were big changes and intimidating ones, specially for the women who lived there. They had been grappling with their improved, Westernized style of life for almost ten years when I was born.

We came of a long line of British loyalists. The title of Rai Bahadur conferred on my grandfather was a highly prized possession of the family and was used even more than his real name, Raj Narain, to identify him. His first son, born before this elevation could have been foreseen, was named Brij Narain, but the younger two had 'Bahadur' attached to their names, undoubtedly so that the advantage of the association could travel with them through life and ensure preferential treatment at every stage.

The refined but somewhat high-strung middle son was my father who remained a forbidding figure to me for most of my life. As a child I was much more comfortable with his elder brother, my uncle whom we called Tauji. Through my school years, Tauji had been a steady source of love and warmth, even though he did not live in Delhi for most of his working life. He was an engineer in government service and in his prime occupied various elevated positions in Bihar and Orissa, but he and his family spent every vacation visiting the family headquarters in Delhi. This time was like a joyful celebration that went on for the entire duration of his stay. It was understood by all that, of his three sons, my grandfather loved him the most and considered him more upright, generous, and able than all his other children. My grandparents dotingly called him Chaand. Strangely, none of my grandfather's other children seemed to qualify for a pet name. Sometimes I felt that he was the one with whom they had the strongest bond. It was almost something visceral that did not seem to enter their relationships with my other aunts and uncles. Tauji was like an extension of my grandfather and his very presence commanded the same kind of authority.

He always came loaded with gifts for everyone in the large joint family, specially the children. More than anyone else, he made us feel like individuals by trying to communicate with each child separately. This was a rare treat. The other grownups regarded all the children of the house as a collective entity, layered into several age groups. Tauji's personal and imaginative gifts were sharply aimed and did much to propel each child towards a sense of identity.

As a teenager, I was notorious for my lack of grace and beauty and therefore became a natural target for snide remarks from my father's sisters and my cousins. 'Whenever there is a loud bang and crash, it means that she has collided with something', they would say of me; or 'She should really have been a boy', or 'Who will ever marry this ragamuffin?', or 'Can anyone believe she is a daughter of this house!' When I was going through this stage, Tauji brought me a pair of extremely delicate silver filigree earrings from Orissa. I had never seen, let alone owned, anything so exquisite. It awakened something within me which helped me to cope with my physical awkwardness. My older brother got a train engine which his enquiring mind could study, take apart, and put together again. My younger brother who wanted to be a strong man got a toy gun that went 'bang bang' and sent the younger children scurrying away to his great delight. For each one of us, such reminders of Tauji's visits became landmarks which we associated with some important phase of growing up.

In those days it used to be a slow and hot twenty-four-hour train journey from Patna to Delhi, but Tauji and his wife Taiji always looked fresh and radiant as they got out of the old family Ford that brought them from the railway station. They used to bring several trunks, suitcases, attache cases, canvas bedrolls and dozens of assorted packages with them. These were first stacked on one side in the veranda while we danced and shouted with joy at their coming. Sometimes Taiji would bring along her khansamah Naggu as a special treat for the Delhi household as they considered him a wizard of a cook who could turn out cakes, puddings, and other 'English' delicacies quite outside the beat of the Delhi kitchen, where the skills were limited to more homely fare.

Taiji had a clear, ringing laugh which to me was a most reassuring sound. We would crowd round her as she gleefully unpacked, waiting for her to pull out her delightful surprises. There were always cartons of homemade biscuits and lozenge-shaped chocolates, undoubtedly the product of Naggu's skills and her forethought, imported tins of lemon drops and toffees specially chosen for the coloured pictures on them; golden-haired girls in pink, lacy frocks and pretty ribbons, fluffy puppies and beautiful but unrecognizable flowers. We cherished these tins long after the sweets were gone and they became the natural resting places for all our precious trinkets and mementos.

My grandfather expected each of his daughters-in-law to treat every child in the joint family as her own. This was the traditional ideal. Therefore he thoroughly approved of Taiji's attitude. So far as the world outside was concerned, he was a firm believer in being on the right side of the powers that be. He had studied law in England and the entire Mathur Kayastha community to which we belonged was awestruck by his knowledge of the ways of the British upper classes and secretly envious of his station in life.

I heard from my grandmother that his journey to England in his youth had become the subject matter of many ballads in the repertoire of professional folk singers of the old city who performed at weddings and festivals. From her demeanour I understood that some of the themes of these songs were satirical and highly improper. For instance there was one that referred to how he had learnt to ease himself standing up instead of squatting on the roadside like the other natives. According to the sarcastic refrain of the song, this was indeed a lesson worth crossing the seven seas for! I was amazed to learn that the song got permanently deposited in the local folk music repertoire of naughty material and was performed mechanically over the years by singers who had no idea who it was about. My aunts once got very flustered when they heard and recognized it at a wedding in the downtown area. The cleverest of them tried to divert the attention of the assemblage by babbling pleasantries in an unnecessarily loud voice. The strategy probably worked, but nobody could be absolutely sure.

My grandfather westernized himself and his family to a moderate extent for the benefit of his own career and that of his sons. He even employed an Englishwoman to come to the house and teach my grandmother some English. Her lessons seemed to be limited to practising some polite phrases which would enable her to be a suitable hostess at the garden party my grandfather might one day arrange in honour of the Chief Commissioner of Delhi. She went along with whatever her husband wished her to do, but the linguistic contortions she was engaging in so late in life were a source of great amusement to her. 'When Lady so-and-so collects her furs after the reception and prepares to leave, she will offer me her paw to shake and say "tank yoo" and I must answer "manshan not" ', she once told us, rocking with laughter at her own predicament. The English teacher also left her imprint on grandmother's style of dressing. Victorian ruffles gradually appeared on the neckline and cuffs of the blouses she wore with her traditional starched white voile sari and were recognized in the Mathur Kayastha community as a mark of the stylishly dressed woman.

Another revolutionary achievement of my grandfather was providing an English education for his two younger daughters who graduated from college, once again making headlines in the Mathur Kayastha community. However, enlightenment and modern ways of thinking did not help in getting them suitably married. This is not to say that matches were not found. They were, but the most stable tree of life for my aunts still remained the old family homestead presided over by their father. All my aunts, English-knowing or not, felt superior to their husbands and managed to tame their spouses to defer to their paternal home in all matters of style, taste, and values.

The house we lived in was a sprawling colonial bungalow that my grandfather designed and planned himself, without help from any architect, incredible though this may seem. His chief aide in the building project was an illiterate, wizened old master mason called Mangal, who turned out to be perfectly adequate for what he had in mind. Their partnership in the daily construction activity was an enjoyable sport, for my grandfather relied more on spontaneous common sense than any professional architectural skills. As a result, every door and window in the house was of a different width and height. The intended symmetries and finish of many features were just roughly workable. This was because the focus of my grandfather's life was the convenience and well being of his family. The design of the house had to echo the lifestyle of the family as well as the specific needs of individual members. Apart from the huge living quarters in the main house where most of the family were expected to herd together in loving harmony, there was a prayer room where my grandmother could put up a little temple of her own. My father who was romantic and artistic and liked his own private space away from everybody else was provided with an annexe. He was the only one who was indulged in this respect. For the rest, my grandparents considered privacy an alien and undesirable notion. There was a huge kitchen area with a pantry and storehouse and the longest dining room anybody could ever imagine. Its tubular shape was disproportionate but it adequately served its purpose which was to accommodate all sixty-two members of the household at the same time. However, we all thought the façade of the house extremely graceful. The colonial-style pillars were perfectly fashioned and successfully masked the crudities and arbitrariness of the internal structure. The house was surrounded by generous verandas, balconies, and terraces on all sides. There were many outhouses which were used as offices, guest rooms, servants quarters, and cattle sheds. Masonry stairways led down to a spacious cellar which always smelt of wet earth and mystery. Similar stairways led to many levels of the roof from where we got a clear view of the old bridge over the river Jamuna. Most of us children thought our home the most interesting playground we had ever been in.

The road on which our house was located was named after my grandfather, and we were all very proud of this. He was an eminent and respected citizen, titled by the government and obviously worthy of official trust. He served on a very large number of civic bodies and his voice carried weight. He arbitrarily chose the number seven for the family house because he liked the sound of it. The municipal authority never dreamed of questioning the decision. There was no number six at all and the house next to ours was called number sixteen because the occupants had followed my grandfather's example and chosen the number as though it were a name.

Our house opened in front to vast grounds which had two lawns separated by a hedge of sweetpeas. On both sides of the curving driveway that led up to the front veranda, there were fruit trees and flowering shrubs. Some of these trees were like special people in our lives and we loved to be near them and touch them. There was an old *ber* tree in the front lawn around which the family gathered on holiday afternoons in the winter and on summer evenings. This tree was definitely a member of the family for everybody. There was an enormous tamarind tree near the garages on one side of the grounds and several tall mango trees, the top branches of which were accessible to the more daring of us from the roof. The unripe fruit of these trees was the most coveted delicacy there could be, especially as we were told it would make us ill and ruin our throats.

There were so many interesting things to do and so many exciting places to play in that to be at home was always the best prospect. The house bustled with activity and rang with happy sounds. One could almost choose one's entertainment. The prize thing to do was to trail grandfather on his rounds and see the cows and buffaloes, the horse and the coachman, examine the fodder, listen to him instruct the gardeners and other retainers. If this was not happening one could go to the kitchen area and watch grandfather's valet Ishri churning the butter, which only he was privileged to do, or see my mother making pickles or supervising the cooking. My eldest brother would often be on the roof with his home-made telescope after dinner. The night watchman Bhola, who was supposed to have wonderful eyesight and knew something about stars, acted as his assistant and pointed out planets to whoever was interested. Grandmother's pooja room was yet another focus of fascinating activity. Besides her daily morning prayers, which were heartily but somewhat tunelessly sung to the accompaniment of votive bells and castanets, she observed numerous other cheerful and homely rituals which involved bathing, dressing, feeding, and decorating the deity. In addition there were frequent major or minor festivals which were observed with community singing of hymns, the serving of special food and social get-togethers afterwards. It was permissible for the women of the household to shed their routine chores on these occasions. They would dress up, wear shiny bindis on their foreheads and gather in the pooja room, smelling of sandalwood and looking festive. The children were welcome to come in and watch as a treat though the main participants were my grandmother, her daughters-in-law, and her married daughters.

My grandfather had cast himself in the role of a westernized gentleman, a sahib who pooh-poohed such observances as benighted superstition and never lost an opportunity to needle my grandmother about the hocus pocus she engaged in. He let it be known that he disapproved. But we all knew that this was only his official stance. In his heart of hearts he was relieved that his wife asserted the old tradition. This gave him a kind of safety insurance and enabled him to indulge in the luxury of denouncing all grandmother's fussy rituals as an enlightened modern Indian educated in English ways of thinking should. Only at one stage did this superior and distant attitude undergo a change.

My grandmother had adopted a religious guru whose centre of activity used to be a neighbouring temple on the banks of the river Jamuna. She would invite him frequently to the house, to give discourses, lead kirtan singing, or read the *Ramayana* to the assembled ladies. Apart from the dozen or so women of the household in attendance, my grandmother invited women from the extended family, distant relatives and neighbours. These invitations were greatly prized. Each such occasion, which was invariably arranged in the middle of a working day so that it did not disturb the hardworking men of the house, ended with an elegant vegetarian feast which was an exciting social high point for all the women present.

This guru, Swami Satyanand, was an extremely attractive personality. He was tall and had a smooth, serene pink and white face with penetrating brown eyes under gold-rimmed glasses. He looked quite spectacular in his flowing saffron robes. When he propounded some philosophical truth in his deep voice, the ladies would melt and sigh and almost fall into a trance. Once my grandfather unexpectedly came home in the middle of the day and ran into Swami Satyanand by accident. That day something changed. The Swami stopped being just a name that could be casually dismissed and became a person of whom my grandfather was distinctly jealous. I did not understand the psychology of my grandparents at the time but looking back I am sure that my grandfather was unprepared for the physical attractiveness of the Swami. The day he met him in person, he knew that this was someone who was used to commanding attention, just like himself. The issue, though not really a serious one, was my grandfather's exclusive right to his wife's attention.

His protest took the form of a pointed refusal to speak to my grandmother directly. This was particularly noticeable at the dining table. But she was a very self-possessed and confident matriarch and was not in the least fazed by his sulking in this fashion. She simply carried on her usual polite ministrations to him as though nothing had happened. This situation continued for about three days and then my grandfather began to break down. He started by announcing in a peeved voice to no one in particular that he was not feeling well. 'Oh I'm so sorry. What's the matter?' grandmother said, turning towards him with the utmost solicitude. 'Constipation', he replied, but he pronounced the word as though it was plague or worse, and still addressed the monosyllable to the middle distance. 'Oh really? How strange that I hear you flush the toilet many times each day as usual', she said sweetly. My grandfather's face became red like that of a little boy caught in a lie. And that was the end of that. The religious festivities presided over by the charismatic Swami continued as before and everyone's life was the richer for it.

The way the dining table was laid for dinner, when all the sixty-odd members of the household sat down to eat together, reflected the family's hierarchical attitudes. Grandfather, at the head of the table, was honoured with the most elaborate place-setting the household could rise to. There was a gleaming dinner plate and a side plate from an expensive set we owned, polished silver cutlery, a drinking glass of crystal and a starched white napkin. Grandmother who sat to his left on the long end had a dinner plate and side plate from the same set but no cutlery and no starched white napkin as this was somehow considered unfeminine from the Indian end of things. However, she had small Indian-style metal bowls to serve herself daal or curds and ate with her fingers. Next came the sons, daughters, and daughters-in-law. Their places at the table depended on their age and seniority. The eldest sat nearest to what was literally the seat of power. The other adult members of the household deployed themselves according to their own polite, self-denying interpretation of their status in the hierarchical structure. Frequently there were extra people who were persuaded to stay on for a meal and on these occasions it was not uncommon at the humbler end of the table for two family members to double up on one chair. Each place was marked by a dinner plate, but only the men seemed to be entitled to additional side plates as well. They also had forks and spoons but no knives or napkins. The only cutlery the women were entitled to was for some mysterious reason the versatile and low-profile teaspoon which could serve many unforeseeable purposes. In addition they had the optional use of the kind of metal bowls provided for my grandmother, except that at this distance from the head of the table these were stacked in the middle of the table and had to be reached for if desired.

In general, the services and trappings at the dining table declined sharply as the eye travelled to the far end of the long eating surface. This surface was made up of three structures placed end to end; the first was a fine piece of furniture, a regular dining table of polished teak wood. The second table was a much cheaper, rougher affair, bought from the local market by my grandfather's clerk, along with serviceable wooden chairs with crude cane seats to match. The third consisted of wooden planks on sturdy legs, the kind one could hire in any Indian town for large wedding feasts. This last structure was the joyous children's area and was flanked on both sides by long, smooth benches to sit on. This kind of seating arrangement was a wonderful, free and flexible idea and gave us the opportunity to have fun and eat at the same time. We would play at horse-riding, invent ways of weaving our legs into the runners of the benches and slide along their surfaces to make room for others to get in or out. The children's end of the dining surface had no resemblance to the elegant starting point at grandfather's end and did not even merit a table cloth. Here the basic food was plonked in the middle by a sweaty junior kitchen aide along with a stack of wet plates and everyone had to scramble for whatever else they needed. We loved the picnic atmosphere and considered it a treat to coexist with the grown-ups at mealtimes and listen to their 'real life' conversation. This was the only time when things were at rest, when every pillar of our lives was stationary and visible, and we could bask in the reassuring glow that radiated from the other end of the table.

Grandfather's benign but piercing eye never failed to detect an absence even from the gaggle of children at the far end of the table thirty feet away. He thoroughly disapproved of any member of his household going out for entertainment or pleasure and quite justifiably saw no need for it. 'A friend's house? What on earth for?' was a familiar and much feared expostulation. On the other hand we were free, in fact encouraged, to bring our friends to the dining table benches and present them to the family over a meal. As we moved into adolescence, there were more and more lapses and nervous explanations about birthday parties of friends; and special functions at school or college among erring absentees became more common. But everybody's best friends were inducted into the dining room at some point of time. Some continued to appear off and on for years and almost grew up with us on the benches. One of these was my elder brother's friend who brought his bride to dinner so that she could be introduced to the adults of the family. Two years later he got divorced and remarried and the new incumbent also ended up on the benches one Sunday at lunch. On this occasion, my grandparents were sharp enough to register that this person looked different from what they had seen in the same grid three years earlier. My grandmother could not help expressing her confusion and asked my brother directly and loudly for a clarification just in case she was mistaken. 'What I remember was tall and fair, not short and dark like this one', she said, tracing the remembered figure in the air with her hands, to the great embarrassment of the adolescents. She subsided only when one of her daughters repeatedly nudged her under the table.

My grandfather was both masterful and benevolent. His passage through the house was always significant for whoever he encountered. Whether it was a servant, a daughter-in-law, a house guest or a child, he would always greet them, ask them what they were doing and invariably offer suggestions on how whatever it was could be done better. In general, the household was divided into those who welcomed these encounters and were flattered by his attention, and those who shrank from the prospect of facing his well-intentioned scrutiny. For the first fourteen years of my life I was definitely in the first category. He had always had a special tenderness for me and my two brothers. I heard it whispered among my aunts that this was because he wanted to compensate for my father's much flaunted distaste for my mother and her offspring. Whatever the reason, I have a wealth of warm memories of times when I was given special treatment by my grandfather although no one including me and my mother thought I deserved it. I remember sitting on his lap and sharing with him a bowl of grapes which were meant only for him, while a number of hostile adult eyes glared at me for the impertinence. To this day the sight of fresh green grapes brings back to me the smell of grandfather's hookah, the feel of his not so silky white beard, and the reassuring sensation of a dependable and protective love. In later years when I discovered a world of my own through the windows of school, our relationship suffered somewhat.

I can trace the beginning of the deterioration to a particular incident. I had avidly started collecting photographs of film-stars and in the course of this activity fell hopelessly in love with Ashok Kumar, the popular screen hero. I saw his famous film *Bandhan* nine times along with similarly smitten school friends and we sent off an ardent fan letter requesting an autographed photograph, in the approved fashion of hero-worshipping teenagers. We didn't really expect a response and soon forgot the whole thing. One afternoon, as my cousin and I were getting off the horse carriage that used to take us to our Christian mission school in the Tis Hazari area, grandfather's clerk Chhail Behari came up to me and said that I was wanted in the legal office that had been set up in one of the annexes of the big house.

This was most unusual. Chhail Behari never spoke to us and we never visited grandfather's office when he was working there. Anyhow, when I tiptoed in on this occasion, he said in the voice of a stranger, 'Show it to her'. Chhail Behari silently held up a large photograph of my idol from the silver screen, with the words 'Best Wishes to Sheila from Ashok Kumar' scrawled across the bottom in green ink. He also held up the manila envelope in which it had arrived with my name in large type on it. From outside it looked like a serious official communication and they had been most intrigued that I was the addressee.

'Who is this young man?' grandfather asked sternly. 'Why is he writing to you directly? Are you by any chance under the impression that you are old enough to arrange such matters without consulting your elders?'

It was clear from his withering tone that he was truly outraged. No explanation on earth could change that. I realized in panic that neither he nor Chhail Behari had any inkling of such innocent pastimes as collecting mementos of famous personalities. It took several interventions from Tauji, who happened to be in Delhi at the time, to calm grandfather down. But after this incident he viewed all my projects and activities with scepticism and at least mild distrust. Though he continued to receive the greatest respect from everybody in the family, his control and energy began to wane during my adolescence. The fast pace of change in the lives of his growing grandchildren wore him down and a point came when he could no longer recognize the map of their world.

TWO

Persian Couplets and One Green Chilli

The Mathur Kayastha community were great believers in the good things of life. They were reputed to have provided the Mughal rulers at Delhi with executives and revenue officials for hundreds of years and had in turn imbibed the values of the courtly tradition. They appreciated Urdu and Persian poetry, classical music, good food, and refinement of manner. But as a community they had the additional gift of ready laughter which could often deteriorate into a collective reflex. Almost anything could provoke amiable guffaws from the typical Mathur Kayastha gentleman. These sounds reiterated the optimistic philosophy of the tribe which tended to regard every situation as a potential source of merriment. I had a cousin who had the reputation of being the life of every party. 'Jolly' was the adjective everybody adoringly used for him. He would enter a room, bend low from the waist, and pump an outstretched right arm up and down in the gesture of a lowly menial offering a salaam to a feudal lord, and ask in immaculate Urdu, 'What is going on here?' His own question was a cue for him to rock with laughter, in anticipation of the great amusement with which he was bound to be rewarded sooner or later. My staid and scholarly husband who was a Kashmiri Pandit used to regard this phenomenon with acute bewilderment and tried unsucessfully for years to get to the bottom of this intriguing trait among so many of my relatives.

Mathur Kayastha men were considered well bred and cultured if they understood Urdu and Persian poetry and the etiquette and manners of mushairas or traditional poetry readings. It was a distinct social advantage for the head of each family to be well versed in this lore in imitation of the Muslim nobility. The younger brothers and other less important male members of the family usually did not have to bother with it, unless they wanted to, because their seniormost representative had the voice that counted, and spoke for them all. Though he was not the head of a family, a cousin of whom I was very fond got interested in Persian poetry rather late in life and engaged a maulvi to come and teach him every evening. He did not want to share this information with other households in the neighbourhood for fear of being derided because he was making what would be considered a delayed bid for elegance. However he felt quite safe with my husband who was an outsider as well as a definite sympathizer. This was even more relevant than the fact that he was a scholar of Persian poetry.

Late one evening when we had just finished dinner, my cousin walked across to our house in high excitement. His eyes were shining and he looked radiantly happy. He said he wanted to talk privately to my husband. When the door to our small study was firmly closed, he almost burst out:

'I can't tell you how beautiful this couplet was! I was absolutely intoxicated when Maulvi Sahib explained it to me. I just had to tell someone! Wait till you hear it! You will feel like dancing, it is so exquisite!'

He was bursting with enthusiasm, like a pomegranate sparkler on Divali night. My husband who was normally a very reserved person waited politely with his hands resting on his lap, waiting for my cousin to recite the couplet that had sent him into such unbearable ecstasy. But the more he tried to remember it, the further away it went from his mind. Nor could he remember the name of the poet despite heavy prompting from my husband.

'Was it Hafiz?'

'No, no!'

'Urfi?'

'Oh no!'

'Do you remember any phrase or word from the couplet? Or what its subject matter was?'

'Let me see, now. *Saqi* was one word, I know. Another was *jaam.* No, no, not *jaam.* It was *saghar,* or *mina,* and perhaps *rind.* Anyhow, the meaning of the couplet was, "What are you doing here, Charlie?" ' he said at last, returning with relief from Khayyam's poetic world to his own bantering idiom.

Though my husband explained that 'here' probably meant 'on earth' and that the allusions were probably allegorical, the two of them could not get deeper into the business of enjoying the couplet for sheer lack of data. However, the impasse did not prevent my cousin from beaming happily at the thought that there were such wonderful things in the world.

This cousin had many endearing qualities—a warm, palpitating heart, staggering generosity, inexhaustible interest in all the refinements that life could offer, and a wry sense of humour. Like a good Kayastha, he loved good food and drink, and had a naturally sophisticated taste in music, clothes, people, and *objets d'art.* Throughout his adult working life, he supported a colourful younger brother called Pukkhoo who was an extraordinary character in his own right. Whatever his real age may have been at any time, he seemed to everybody to be permanently forty, too old for college and too young for retirement. He concerned himself with the minor problems of all the homes in our idyllic neighbourhood and had the reputation of being most helpful. He had all the time in the world because he neither was nor had any intention of being employed. In fact being a dependent younger brother was a wholetime profession to which he was wholly dedicated. I was aware that the younger brother was a clearly defined species in many Mathur Kayastha families and all counterparts had common characteristics which were utterly different from those of their elder brothers.

The main earning member of the typical joint family, the elder brother, could be recognized by the refined, Persianized Urdu he spoke and the elegant sherwani he dressed in for formal occasions. He had poise and could hold his own in English circles as well as in traditional soirees of classical music or Urdu literature. Of course, the family had to lavish most of their resources on making their main breadwinner as presentable as possible. He was singled out for the best education, the best wardrobe, and the best nutrition. Since the main inheritance of most Mathur Kayastha families was culture rather than money, they could usually not afford to extend such attentions to members who were not likely to bring in any returns on the investment. The younger brothers could thus be distinguished by their faint air of deprivation and self-denial and by their broad, unmodulated accents which resembled the speech of the unlettered household women more than anything else.

Pukkhoo did not own a sherwani like his brother, but dressed in kurta pyjamas, the starched snow-white look of which proclaimed his high birth. He was the vital link between the women's quarters (the zenana), and the men's area, or the mardana, in the family establishment. When official guests were entertained by his elder brother, he was not invited to join the party. Instead it was his business to lurk behind the door, transmitting intelligence to the women's centre of activity in the kitchen, so that the hospitality could be perfectly timed and tailored to the needs of the moment.

He was easily convulsed with shyness and stage-fright in front of outsiders but on his own turf in the women's quarters he was a lion and held sway as an important instrument of his older brother's wishes. He lived in the shadow of his elders but swelled with genuine pride at their skills and achievements. Though his elder brother was his idol, there was never any question in his mind of emulating him because the aims of their two lives were clearly recognized by him to be different.

His other duties were to buy the right cuts of meat for the household, to summon the cotton carder from the market and get the quilts for the winter stitched and stuffed, to supervise the catering of the halwai at wedding feasts, to escort the women and children of the family wherever they had to go, and to be available for all sorts of miscellaneous chores. He was on first-name terms with the barber, the washerman, the tongawallah and all the shopkeepers the family had dealings with, and could chat comfortably with them in their own idiom for hours with apparent relish.

The smallest sign of elegance, specially in snobbish guests, moved him to hoot with laughter secretly and sent him scurrying away into dark corners where he was safe from the need to respond with any polished manners or speech himself. He could understand English, but was too bashful to speak it. Once when we were both members of a baraat or the bridegroom's party, the Anglicized hosts of the bride's family began to direct their concentrated and high-class hospitality at him because he appeared ill at ease. He couldn't be ignored because he was the maternal uncle of the bridegroom. I had never seen him so uncomfortable. In fact he was like a trapped animal for the two days that we were forced to be guests at a five-star-hotel in Mussoorie. At the end of the luxurious festivities he was starving because he refused to consider the fancy dishes that were offered as genuine food.

'I can't put a single morsel in my mouth. Everything is dressed up to look like birds and flowers and even the sweet dish is set on fire when it is brought to me! I wish I could get a decent chapati with a bit of a kabab!' he sighed with some bitterness.

He managed to bully and astound a waiter by ordering him to fetch him some real food from the servant's kitchen. Just as he was about to lower a piece of chapati into his mouth, the most aggressive and impressive of the bride's uncles converged on him in alarm, aghast that this honoured guest had not been served the main European dish of the banquet.

'My dear Pukhraj, what'n earth huv they giv'n you?' he boomed solicitously, lowering the glittering naval medals on his breast almost in poor Pukkhoo's suffering face. By now he was resigned to his fate, ready for any extremity that was in store for him. His arrested morsel hung uneaten in mid-air. He took courage in both hands, looked straight into the naval commander's masterful eyes and spoke in colloquial Hindustani, in the desperate voice of a dying man.

'Listen, I have managed to get something I can eat after more than twenty-four hours, and with the greatest difficulty. If you are bent on doing something for me, please ask them to bring me just one green chilli.'

The naval commander looked as though he had received a blow in the stomach. There was absolutely no prospect of locating a green chilli in the splendid array of high cuisine on the banqueting tables. He backed off, expostulating and muttering, 'Yes, yes, of course, at once . . .' but no green chilli appeared. Meanwhile Pukkhoo lost his appetite and abandoned all hope of a proper meal. When at last we returned home, he told me that he felt like an escaped prisoner.

THREE

Baua

The saddest and most mortifying secret of my life and that of my two brothers when we were still infants was that our father did not like our mother, whom we called Baua. He treated her with the utmost disdain and usually did not speak to her or even answer her if she asked a question. Strangely, he made no effort to cloak this state of affairs from anyone, not even from his children. The living arrangements reflected the situation between my parents with a depressing finality. Ever since I can remember, my father had a sort of bachelor establishment in an annexe of the sprawling colonial house we lived in while my mother was allotted a small room in the main house where she lived with her three children. My brothers and I were very close to our mother and felt instinctively that our father's rejection of us was something to be ashamed of and to hide from everybody. We also felt guilty because somehow it seemed to be our fault. We envied our cousins for being able to approach their fathers and clamber up on their knees, prattling and laughing happily. They seemed to us to belong to a superior breed, privileged in a manner we could not even dream of.

We were too young to give a name to these feelings, but Baua understood and shared them, though she tried constantly to erase all negativity from our minds with her spirited optimism and warmth. Even so, an undercurrent of anxiety that she was deprived and troubled in some serious way was always present, even when we were enjoying our otherwise happy childhood. I remember an occasion when I tried to banish the pain I felt at Baua's unfortunate position in the household by telling totally unnecessary lies to my school friends about a visit to the circus with my 'mummy' and 'daddy'. I invented the fiction that I had sat on my father's lap when things had got too exciting. I went on about it until I realized that to my friends such a detail was nothing out of the ordinary and so not worth mentioning.

For my older brother, the main motivation for growing up was that he would be able to take care of Baua, me and his younger brother. We also began to wait for this day. We were sure that there was a golden future in which our mother would be cherished as she deserved to be.

The room my mother was given was an odd one in the centre of the house. It was probably never meant to be lived in as it had no bathroom attached to it or even close by. This was rather difficult for Baua, specially because her children were still small. She had to use the primitive facilities in a block of structures outside the house. My grandfather had had these built with his characteristic forethought in order to take the pressure off the attached bathrooms in the main house if need be. I remember my mother ferrying us across the veranda and the courtyard in the morning one by one to get us ready for school. When any of us were sick, or when it was too hot or too cold to carry us to the outhouses, which were a longish walk away, it used to be even more of an ordeal for her. But her hand when she woke us up was always cool and fragrant because she was already bathed and dressed.

A widowed aunt we called Shammo Bhua had made her home with us after her husband died. By nature she was not a particularly powerful personality but the joint family politics generated by my father's attitude of active indifference to his wife and children gave her an irresistible handle to exercise authority over us. She was always there to say 'no' to whatever any of us wanted or needed. Gradually this tendency hardened into a sort of instrument with which she thought she was giving shape to her brother's wishes.

Shammo Bhua had a huge, high-ceilinged room with six skylights which could be opened or closed by pulling at thick cords attached to the shutters above. Every time one tugged, the appearance of the room and the colour of the walls used to change in a magical way. It was a game we longed to play, but we knew, just from the way Shammo Bhua tightened her lips every time one of us reached for the inviting cords, that this was forbidden territory so far as we were concerned. Her bathroom was spacious and modern by the standards of those days and even had a bathtub and shower. She also had a dressing room almost as large as the room allotted to my mother and her children. Shammo Bhua's domain accounted for nearly one-fourth of the main bungalow and had been set aside for my grandfather's daughters whenever they or their families were in Delhi. However, Shammo Bhua was the most permanent and often the sole occupant of this accommodation. She also considered herself the local representative of what was thought of in the family collectively as 'The Sisters' and faithfully guarded the 'Sisters' rooms' against encroachments from undesirables like my mother even when the other claimants were not in town.

Although Shammo Bhua couldn't openly turn down her own mother's good-hearted suggestion that she share her bathroom with Baua, who was after all her own sister-in-law, she would make a sulky, sour face which my grandmother couldn't always see, partly because of her bad eyesight and partly because of her stubborn view that every member of her family was a decent person. But Shammo Bhua's hostile emanation punctured us, even when we were too young to be able to describe her attitude. Baua, on the other hand, never lost her robust optimism and had a sunny temperament which was practically egoless. She asked Shammo Bhua when she might use the bathroom without clashing with her timings or putting her out in any way. My aunt said 'seven o'clock' with a sullen face, but went out of her way the next day to keep the bathroom occupied at the very time she had given to Baua. She probably had to sit in the bathroom for several hours at considerable inconvenience to herself to make sure that it did not become available to Baua. The affair of the bathroom stretched out for about ten days in which my mother was given and vainly tried various timings—five o'clock, six o'clock, eight o'clock and nine o'clock. I remember her leaving our room, her towel and fresh clothes draped over her arm, and coming back almost at once because 'Shammo Bibi' was in the bathroom. This happened at least a dozen times before she finally gave up. Although my grandmother wanted everyone to be accommodated and accommodating, she usually didn't go into details. Baua never dreamt of complaining or making an issue of it, so things remained as they were.

Like a good dependent in a joint family, Shammo Bhua was going with the flow, not taking any individualistic position of her own. Her instinct was to reflect the attitude of the real centre of power in the family at this time, which was my father. It was usual for him to make pointedly unkind remarks about my mother's bulk, her lack of elegance and polish, about the unrefined family she came from, about the backwardness of Agra, her birthplace, about the way she talked, walked, or did anything at all. Most of the time he did this to entertain his fawning sisters, and of course to let the household know that she was no part of his life and therefore not worthy of consideration. When there was no audience, he just ignored her. The monthly allowance to run the kitchen and pay the servants' salaries was handed to Shammo Bhua, not to Baua. This was an unmistakable signal, if one were still needed, for the servants to know who the real boss was. Baua didn't protest or fight back or feel resentful. I know that this was not out of weakness but because of an extraordinarily generous disposition, and an inexplicable, unquestioning devotion to my father. Whether this last was a personal emotional condition or an entrenched cultural attitude, I was not able to tell.

My grandparents exercised a benign but loose control on things, but the actual running of the house was the financial responsibility of my father. Consequently Baua was expected to be physically responsible for all the family meals as well as for all hospitality. She was always in the kitchen supervising and assisting the servants and planning the next meal for the enormous household. I remember her as slightly out of breath from her exertions, her face pink and beaded with sweat, her white cotton sari which had been fresh and starched when she woke us up in the morning crumpled and stained with turmeric for most of the day. The other women of the house sat in cane chairs, sipping *nibu* sharbat and generally being animated members of my grandparents' durbar which admitted a constant stream of droppers-in from the neighbouring houses.

Baua would work hard and creatively in the kitchen trying to devise dishes to suit my father's delicate stomach and demanding palate. The special cup of soup before dinner which the family doctor had recommended for him was a major challenge that she took up every day. Even as a child it used to make me nervous because I felt my mother was on trial and might be sentenced to death. The steaming cup would be placed ceremoniously at my father's place on the table. When he lifted it to his lips there would be a hush in the dining room. All eyes were riveted on him as he took the first sip. My father was a deeply political being and quite simply relished the sensation of exercising power, especially psychological power, over people. So he would prolong the suspense of whether the soup had passed or failed by deliberately keeping his face expressionless for as long as he could. Then, after what seemed like ten minutes but was probably much less, one of three things could happen. He could nod his acceptance of the liquid and put it down, sipping it at intervals through the meal, causing my mother to glow with happiness. Or he could push it away and leave the room in a huff. The worst scenario was when he refused to take cognizance of it at all and acted as though neither the cup nor my mother who was responsible for it existed. Baua always looked stricken and bewildered when he reacted like this. To her meek 'Is something wrong with the soup?' she never got a reply. This business of her not getting any response at all from my father on the rare occasions when she ventured to speak to him made us anxious and miserable and dogged our entire childhood and adolescence. The rare occasions when he favoured her with a monosyllable in answer to a question such as 'Will you be back for dinner?' made news in the household that everybody commented upon without feeling in the least delicate.

My father's refusal to talk to Baua was not only an emotional difficulty, but a serious practical one too. The personal spending money that she needed for herself and her three children was supposed to be provided by my father. She was expected to present a list of her needs and what they would cost to my father every month for his scrutiny. He had the reputation of being an extremely generous man with a very cavalier attitude to money. The world of music and Urdu poetry was abuzz with stories of wildly extravagant gifts my father was in the habit of making to deserving artistes, in grand gestures of admiration. But so far as we and our mother were concerned he grudged every penny, and resented being forced to address himself to our problems. I remember my mother painstakingly making her list in Urdu, because that was the only script they both could read, on a page torn out of my old school copybook. It had items like hairpins, toothpaste, soap, ribbons, cloth and buttons for the children's clothes, occasionally shoes, socks and knitting wool. In the years between 1940 and 1950 the total was in the neighbourhood of sixty rupees.

Her monthly journey along the long back veranda to my father's rooms with this document was always a trial. Sometimes he just took the slip of paper from her without a word, dismissing her with a nod before she had a chance to sit down, and sent the money through his valet, Jai Singh, the next day. But at other times he would remain a stone behind his newspaper and Baua would have to retreat in confusion, her list still in her hand.

During our teens each of us individually tried to take up the cudgels on her behalf many times and confronted him with basic questions, unaccountably encouraged by our good school reports which my grandfather's legal clerk quietly publicized in the household. At the age of thirteen when I stood first in my class and won an arts talent prize, I also suddenly acquired the courage to address my father directly. Nothing worse than death could happen after all, and there were always my brothers to set right whatever went seriously wrong because of my foolhardiness.

Entering his rooms felt like being summoned by the principal of the school for a talking to, or like going into a dentist's clinic for an extraction. Everything smelt different, and everything looked exclusive and intimidating. There were Chinese vases and a white marble sculpture of a tragic Greek female figure lying on her face, her stony tresses in artistic disarray on the mantelpiece. In a niche in the wall was a four-and-a-half-foot high plaster of paris reproduction of the Venus de Milo whose torso Jai Singh used to cover decorously with a bath towel when there were visitors, even if it was someone like me. These and other artefacts, along with a good deal of crockery and cutlery, had been acquired by my father at an auction held by a hotel in Simla after it went into liquidation. He had been retained as a lawyer by the hotel during this process and the impression in the family was that for him the whole experience had been extremely advantageous in many ways. There were many reminders of this in the way his rooms were furnished. There was an upholstered three-piece sofa, with wood and chrome armrests of hideous design which proclaimed its modernity, a great assortment of occasional tables and knick-knacks, a roll-top writing desk and an antique dressing table. There was always a box of imported cigars and a jade green pack of some special brand of English cigarettes for guests from the outside world since my father was not a serious smoker himself. All this together gave off an aroma which I still consider the smell of fear, though physically it was clean and pleasant.

About the time that I felt confident enough to seek an interview with my father in a just cause, his own attitude to me had undergone a slight change. My academic prowess was not the only thing that claimed some grudging attention from him but also my passionate interest in music which the extended family attributed to his genes. He began to regard me as territory to be conquered and brought on his side. At any rate, he could no longer ignore the rebellion which he knew had now become articulate. He would let me sit and wait for a few minutes before he joined me, with a long-suffering and questioning look.

'I want to talk to you about my mother and ask you why you don't give her any spending money', I'd blurt out heroically.

'How do you suppose you are all clothed and fed? You go to school, you play games, you even learn music. You all have everything you could possibly need. I do not understand what the problem is', he would say, stalling like a lawyer.

'But she has to come to you so many times. She is so unhappy. You don't even talk to her properly.'

At this, a dark and tragic expression would come over his face and he would fall silent, looking as though he was trying to hold back his tears. I felt tremendous pressure from him to feel some sympathy but was just not able to.

'No one has control over happiness or unhappiness. I find myself in a predicament that is not of my asking.'

This was the sort of thing he would usually say and I never knew what it meant or what to say next.

'But if you didn't like my mother why did you have children, why did you have us?' I once dared to ask.

'You are too young to understand these things. One day when you are much older, you will have the answer.'

The operative part of the meeting was over very quickly but then he wanted me to stay and listen to anecdotes illustrating his sensitivity, his humility, his love of beauty, music, poetry and justice, his loneliness, and his generosity. He spoke softly, in a voice surcharged with emotion, but I felt totally unable to respond or even to warm to any of the unaccustomed disclosures. All I wanted was for someone else to come in and interrupt the session so that I could escape into the fresh air.

Both my brothers were familiar with this phenomenon and experienced it regularly themselves, but singly, throughout their adolescence and youth. The three of us were never summoned together. My father preferred to take us on one at a time. We discovered later that he kept notes of his conversations with us in separate files in which he entered remarks about our states of mind so that he would know better how to tackle us on the next occasion. My older brother and I also discovered random scribblings which really were a sort of homework he did in preparation for any issues on the anvil between him and his children. For instance, 'Am only criticising mother to fit them better for their own lives. If I say they are intelligent and can understand better than others their age, will they accept my bonafides? Can I tell Sheila that I want her to study medicine because she is not good looking enough to marry well? R cannot have cartridges for his gun unless he demonstrates responsibility. Must ask them what is the purpose of life', and so on.

By the time things took this kind of turn, we were already quite alienated from our father emotionally. Each session with him seemed an ordeal in which he was the stronger adversary, with nameless weapons whose impact we felt but could not describe or forgive, either then or even later when we were much older. My brothers and I were in our own individual ways overwhelmed by the quality of love and support that flowed constantly from Baua, so strongly, so unostentatiously and so selflessly. She really kept us alive and nourished our spirit as nothing else ever did. What she often had to undergo at the hands of our father only sharpened our awareness of what she meant to us.

Once the family was invited to a wedding in New Delhi and my father was going to drive one of the cars to the event. Baua dressed us and then dressed herself and we all waited on the cane chairs in the front veranda along with Shammo Bhua for my father to appear. I remember the rare and wonderful sight of my mother in her only 'going out' sari, a pale pink Mysore silk with a dull gold woven border of decorative leaves from Indore. It was a luxurious feeling for me that her clothes did not smell of kitchen spices this evening but of sandalwood. She looked happy like a child in fancy dress going to a party. She hardly ever went out anywhere except for kitchen and household shopping.

Finally my father took the wheel and all the children piled into the car, followed by Shammo Bhua while Jai Singh obsequiously held the car door open. Just as Baua was getting in, my father made a gesture asking her to wait. He reached out, pulled the door shut and drove off, leaving her standing in the driveway with Jai Singh, her face red with embarrassment. I watched her from the back window of the car, my heart pounding, and felt waves of nausea. But I knew instinctively that if I did get sick my mother would somehow have to suffer even more.

The strangest thing was that no one blamed my father for this sort of behaviour. My grandparents certainly wished things had been different, but treated the situation as an ailment that had overtaken their son. It was common knowledge in the entire community that my father was not nice to his wife and children though he was such a good man and so kind to everybody else. It was true that he never spoke to me or to my brothers during our early school years but lavished all his attention on the much better-looking children of his younger brother and his sisters. He would pointedly leave us out of the many activities and outings he planned for the children of the family—walks by the Jamuna river, trips to the Qudsia Gardens, picnics at Okhla in the mango season, elephant rides on New Year's day in the Roshanara Club and rowdy, improvised games in our own front lawn. Once he took all the older boys on a fishing trip to Kashmir but left my older brother behind, with no explanation. Nothing could have hurt my mother more, and as we reached adolescence we realized that that was precisely the reason why he did such things. It was only Tauji, my father's elder brother, who lifted us up in his arms, swung us around and hugged us, when he was there, which was at least once a year. When he went back to Patna, we felt like outcastes again. My grandfather's special consideration for us because we were neglected and needed compensation was somehow not visceral enough to count for much in our emotional lives though it provided a much needed support and reassurance to Baua.

I don't know why we never rebelled. I think there was a powerful, unwritten code that we followed without question. However, the sorrow about our mother's predicament and our own helplessness created a lifelong bond among the three of us. I also don't know how and when the story of why my father treated Baua in this unaccountable fashion became coherent to me. Some of the pieces came together through chance remarks Baua made to me in her old age when I was married and in my mid-forties.

Apparently, my father had fallen hopelessly in love with a distant relative when he was twenty years old and declared his intention of marrying her. My grandfather was appalled. He considered it extremely impertinent of my father to say anything at all about his own marriage while his elders, who knew what was best for him, were still alive. The fact that he had been to

England to study law and considered himself a person of modern views did not change this attitude.

'It's all because of the Parsee theatre and the romantic Urdu ghazals he has recently taken to. The boy has lost all sense of propriety', my grandfather had lamented.

But he stood his ground. So my father stopped eating, grew a beard, and lay down on his bed, speaking to none and sighing in the approved fashion of the classical lover. Women of the household were afraid that he would die unless he was united to his lady love. A kindly uncle intervened at this point and persuaded my grandfather to soften his position. Pundits were summoned to study the two horoscopes, and they gravely pronounced that this union was never to be because the stars of the girl were so malefic that they would kill the boy. The brief flash of hope was therefore quickly extinguished and my father took to his bed again, seriously prepared to die for love. Everybody watched helplessly. The kindly uncle said that since the boy was dying in any case, he had decided to take a second astrological opinion. This time the pundits peered at many more charts and came up with the same opinion, or almost the same opinion. The stars did not match, but the danger from the bad conjunction was to the girl, not to the boy. This slight shift in angle seemed to make a big and immediate difference to the attitude of my father's well-wishers in the family, though nobody said so.

In the mean time the news from the girl's home in Allahabad was not very different. She too was languishing, refusing to eat or speak and crying all the time. This was made out to be the immediate cause for the family's change of heart but the real clincher was of course that their own precious boy would be safe. The girl's parents didn't have much choice because her emotional state was already being whispered about in the community and physically she was already half dead. She was considered to be already committed and as such had virtually no better prospects to hope for. Both families kept their real feelings in their hearts but agreed with outward grace to celebrate the marriage as early as possible. My father left his bed, shaved off his beard and began to eat, drink, and laugh again. By the time he was dressed up as a bridegroom, the roses had come back to his cheeks. The rites were performed and a short, euphoric period followed. Exactly as predicted, the bride fell ill six months after the marriage and died, reportedly of typhoid, within a year, leaving my father an inconsolable widower at the age of twenty-one.

His parents couldn't very well allow him to weep away his life in sorrow. They badgered him unsuccessfully for two or three years and then forced an arranged second marriage on him. Reportedly, he abhorred the very idea but gave in to the relentless pressure in what must have been something like suicidal desperation: because of the structure of the joint family and because of the circumstances of the second marriage, he never felt personally responsible for his wife or children. Somebody or the other would take care of things, and it was not his idea anyway. He remained a sort of romantic, always thinking of himself as a victim whom life had caught in a web. He felt perfectly justified in taking his frustration and resentment out on his wife, my mother.

The most effective way of punishing her was to be harsh to her children and this was such an effortless exercise for my father that the three of us took it as normal and were never surprised. The more favoured children of the household took the cue from my father who was a natural leader in all the fun and games and tended to gang up against us. They delighted in manufacturing secrets for the pleasure of keeping them from us and tried to block our entry into their play activity. In fact this became, both for them and us, an exciting game in itself. Though it definitely made life more interesting for our own age groups, I know that it tortured my mother.

My grandparents were aware of the situation but they never spoke their minds to their son on this matter. They felt that their miscalculation and bad judgement was to blame for everything and that their son should not have to bear the brunt of their mistake. This attitude fuelled my father's predisposition to see himself as a martyr. In fact, as time went on, he armed himself with more and more grievances against my mother and her simple, affectionate family. I am sure that some of these were purely imaginary, but he clung to his half-truths because they justified him in his own eyes.

At the time when the family was looking for a suitable match for my father, now a widower and therefore expected to lower his expectations somewhat, a 'candidate' was pointed out by his eldest sister, whose comparatively humbler in-laws lived in Gwalior. This aunt of mine was an imperious and self-assured lady who considered that she had been married beneath her station. Possibly she did not see why she should be the only one in the family to whom this had happened. Her line of reasoning was that a humble background and low expectations or no expectations would be the best thing to seek in my father's second wife. She had sighted just such a person on the balcony across the road watching the Ramlila procession passing below and made enquiries about the family. Everything was satisfactory so she sent word that her parents could go ahead with arrangements for the wedding.

Her word carried a lot of weight and it all came about as planned. Years later, when she saw that it had really not worked out at all and that perhaps her brother blamed her in his heart for her part in the affair, she took the easy way out to clear herself and told him privately that the person she had been shown on the balcony, by arrangement, was someone else, not my mother, the implication being that there had been some kind of fraud. Ours was a very 'civilized' family and a matter like this could not have been brought out into the open, but my aunt's disclosure, which I am now sure was fictional, ensured that my father would never reconcile himself to his marriage or stop blaming my mother and his family for his misery. Baua would never have known this story but for a chance remark my father let drop much later in their lives. She put two and two together and reconstructed what must have happened. Although it was dreadful, it relieved her somewhat. She said it was better for her to know at least a part of what my father was simmering about than to be completely in the dark, always guessing, always trying and always failing to reach him behind his thick wall of emotional alibis.

Baua was fifty-three years old when my father died suddenly. Despite the kind of relationships that had existed between us, we were all devastated. There were big and bitter changes in our lives, including traumatic family partitions of property in which we had to give up the house where we had grown up and where Baua had lived ever since it had been built by my grandfather. She had to move to another old building which had fallen to our share, leaving Shammo Bhua behind in the main ancestral house. My husband and I decided to give up our quarters on the university campus and move in with her so that she would not be alone. This started a new phase in her life where she experienced freedom and respect for the first time.

My husband, whom most people thought cold and undemonstrative, developed a tender concern for her which I found miraculous and most gratifying. Soon he became her friend and confidant as well and the days soon began to pass happily and effortlessly for the three of us. The birth of my two sons enriched our lives even more and gave Baua great joy. Her presence was a tremendous support to me and I could pursue my music and my job without too much guilt or tension. She was a central figure in the lives of my children while they were growing up and they developed an independent and extremely close relationship with her.

Baua grew old as a part of my family. She had always been a most wonderful mother to me but at some point during this last phase of her life she and I became intimate friends. I felt I could tell her everything and ask her anything I wanted to.

Once when I had the use of a chauffeur-driven car, I asked her whether she would like to go out somewhere. She was most enthusiastic and said, yes, she would like to go and visit Shammo Bhua.

'Why on earth do you want to drive all those dusty and hot miles to see someone who tortured you for forty years?' I asked.

She made an impatient gesture and said that I had put my finger on it myself.

'In forty years, one can get attached even to a piece of furniture. She is a human being, not a table or chair. We have been associated for so long that I admit I am attached to her', she said with a shy smile.

It must have been about a month before she died at the age of seventy-two when Baua and I were talking about old times. I asked her a question that had troubled me the whole of my adult life. I had thought about it so many times that it came out with somewhat greater aggression than I intended.

'Baua, I really want to know why you stayed on in that house tied to my father's name when your life there was so unbearably humiliating. Were you afraid of what people would say if you walked out and went back to your parental home? Or were you afraid to hurt your parents with the disclosure that your marriage had not been a happy one after all? Or did you think that nobody except the house into which you were married would be willing to extend financial support to you and your children? Or did you want to ensure at any cost that your children did not lose the social and educational advantage of being brought up in a "high class" family?'

She was a little alarmed at the intensity of my tone and the unrelenting manner in which I threw all the possible alternatives at her.

'If you really want the truth, I'll have to think about it. Then I'll definitely tell you', she said in a matter-of-fact tone.

Other things claimed my attention and there was no further talk on this subject for the next three days. One morning when I was getting ready for office, she called me and said she had to tell me something important. At that moment our earlier conversation was far from my mind.

'I have been thinking about what you asked me. For three whole days and nights. You wanted the absolute truth. Today I think I can tell you', she said.

I put my files down on a table, abandoned the idea of going to the office altogether if necessary, and pulled up a chair near her.

'None of the reasons you suggested is correct. I made sure of that. I asked myself each of those questions many times most searchingly because I do want to tell you the truth about this.'

'What was the reason then? Did you discover it?'

'Yes', she said. 'The truth is that I loved him.'

FOUR

If Music Be the Love of Food

Because most Mathur Kayastha families were such staunch believers in entertainment, the first qualification they looked for in a prospective daughter-in-law was her ability to sing and dance. If she could also make conversation in English, it was an added and almost equally valuable asset. The ideal for girls therefore was to attend English-medium schools and learn Indian music at home. Most families were of the view that cooking and housekeeping were not as important because there were always servants to attend to all that. Accordingly, our household provided itself with a music teacher who constituted a regular and continuing service, just like the milkman or the vegetable hawker.

This was arranged for by Chhail Behari who lived in the heart of the city and knew everything about it. His identification with the family and his devotion to my grandfather was such that he took upon himself many tasks which could not remotely be his responsibility. He chose and bought cloth, shoes, utensils and spices for the house, initially arranged for the school admission of all the children—the girls to Queen Mary's and the boys to Modern School in New Delhi—and paid the bills. He was the only person who knew for certain which school and which class each child was in. The schooling plan created by him worked for many years. Some changes were made only when the children were almost grown up and demanded the direct attention of the elders.

The music teacher Chhail Behari arranged for the household was a kind and humble man whom everybody called Mohan Baba. He rode a bicycle from Neel Katra, a busy neighbourhood in the downtown Chandni Chowk area, to our imposing bungalow in the Civil Lines. The grandness of the setting and the presence of so many servants awed him somewhat. He would almost hide his bicycle in the thick hedge bordering one of the paved courtyards of the house and creep into the room which had been set aside for music. Every family in our community owned at least one harmonium, a pair of tablas, and a dholak. This was basic musical equipment which was used in the course of their normal life. Festivals, family dinners, religious occasions or even quiet times when nothing was happening could activate musical activity in which all these instruments were brought out and played as accompaniment to hearty vocal efforts by the women of the house. Many men too could play on the harmonium and the tablas. The advent of Mohan Baba somehow invested all musical efforts with official validity. The arrangement with him was that he would be available in the music room from four until half past five every single afternoon. The girls were specially enjoined to learn to sing, but whoever else wished to was free to avail of his services.

Mohan Baba could play and teach all instruments, sing, and talk about ragas and rhythm cycles with great earnestness. At times some of the boys would barge in to try their hand at the tablas which they found more attractive than the shrill singing of the girls. On at least one occasion my grandmother, who kept a vigilant eye on the proceedings in this room, came in and said she wanted to learn a new bhajan herself. I discovered later that this was a stratagem to point Mohan Baba in the direction of innocent lyrics about the love of God and away from what she considered unseemly texts describing the agonies and ecstasies of earthly love. When hints did not achieve the desired result, she told him outright one day: 'Masterji, it is not appropriate for young unmarried girls to sing about *piya* and *sajan*. Why don't you teach them songs about Rama and Shyama?' Mohan Baba could only say 'Yes, Ma'am'. Thereafter these two-syllable terms for 'beloved' so common in the traditional khayal material were summarily changed to Ram and Shyam, thereby ruining the metrical flow and snarling up the tala cycle.

This little music room was the starting point of a lifelong passion for me and for some others too. My own younger brother and two other boys became good tabla players and retained an intimate interest in classical music throughout their lives. Surprisingly, it was the girls who dropped out, one by one. In the end I was the only one left, waiting for something wonderful to happen. It didn't, but I could not abandon the feeling that it was just round the corner. Mohan Baba had a hoarse, unmodulated voice and a prosaic manner of utterance. Sometimes we were not quite sure whether he was singing or simply reciting the words of a song. The way he used to beat out the melody on the slightly squeaky and off-key harmonium was without joy or charm, but even his matter-of-fact renderings of various ragas gave me enough indication that there were hidden treasures to be discovered. We had a long association during which he slowly changed from a pedagogue to an ally in the search for beauty and depth in music. On the whole the association did not yield much except promise and mutual affection. Mohan Baba got greyer and more tired with every passing year, and my notebook of songs in ragas for different times of the day and for the festive season of Holi got fatter and fatter.

Family celebrations were a frequent happening in our house, something that we as children looked forward to with great excitement. A festival, a birthday, the arrival of a friend of the family in the city, or even the advent of the rainy season could be reason enough for a big feast in the house. All the sons-in-law and all the available members of the extended family who lived in neighbouring bungalows were invited to dinner. In preparation for the entertainment after the feast, the English-style sofas and coffee table in the drawing room as it was grandly called were pushed back against the walls. A freshly laundered and very large white sheet called chandni, literally meaning moonlight, was spread and the harmonium and tablas were placed ceremoniously in the centre of the room on the very large Kashmiri carpet. The sight of the servants carrying the instruments to the family arena always thrilled us children because it was a promise of pure pleasure. In addition to the variety of singing voices, there was much good-humoured teasing and laughing, some reciting of flowery Persian and Urdu couplets and the characteristic Kayastha whoops of determined and indiscriminate laughter, all ingredients of our idea of a good time. My grandparents and other guests of their age group sat on sofas against the wall. My grandfather's hookah stood by his side, and glasses of whisky for the men were placed on small side tables. Everyone else joyously slid to the floor on the chandni. One of my aunts or my father would act as master of ceremonies and each person who could play or sing, and sometimes even those who could not, were coaxed to perform for the entertainment of the rest. The warmth and bright informality of these interactions were always charming, and it hardly mattered that the rough and ready music that followed seldom had any merit other than coyness or enthusiasm. The tabla or dholak accompaniment was also usually provided by women of the family and there was boisterous applause at the end of each item.

Everyone's favourite performers were the bashful new brides who were trained for years to make their debuts on just such occasions and establish the cultural antecedents of the family they came from. They sat silently, smiling sweetly, weighed down with jewellery, heads decorously bent under the rich fabric of bridal saris, waiting their turn like sacrificial animals for the slaughter, or the heroic moment, as the case may be. In turn, the elder women of the household got their opportunity to grade the pedigree of the new entrants to the family. The first few notes and the enunciation of the first words of the song betrayed in a flash the social status and the quality of the musical training received, at any rate to the discerning. The bride on trial would be at pains to establish that she normally sang with a tanpura, as is the practice in the best musical circles, and not with the lowly, crude harmonium; that she had been taught by a real ustad, not just a run-of the-mill masterji; that she had studied English in school and was quite an up-to-date young lady with the best of both cultures at her command. It was not difficult to project this multitude of images through her song. At the end of this public examination, knowing glances were exchanged among the older women, and everyone knew instinctively whether or not she had passed the test. The daughters of the house were treated with far more indulgence and had much more freedom to suit themselves and could refuse to perform if they didn't feel like it.

I was always longing to perform and lapped up the grudging praise from my father's sisters, who did not think much of me otherwise. The general opinion was that my refined and sensitive father deserved a family far more graceful and elegant than anything my mother could be associated with. In some ways this view was accurate, because I was a gawky, boisterous, and clumsy person at that age, quite unlike most of my cousins. At any rate, it was a new experience for me to be singled out for praise and I got addicted to it with the greatest ease. In this phase, Mohan Baba's homespun songs began to shine with a new lustre and acquired magical properties behind his back, as it were. I sang them with great gusto at these family soirees and my renderings always ended in a glow of applause from unexpected quarters. 'What a wonderful, powerful voice she has!' they exclaimed, and I had no difficulty in believing them. I realized I was considered something of a prodigy and was in steady demand. I could be depended upon to establish a musical mood at the unruliest of gatherings and I loved this sensation of power, specially as my singing was the first and only evidence that my father accepted me.

Everybody thought of my father as a patron of the arts, with a great love of music. In his youth he had taken singing lessons from the legendary Vishnu Digambar Paluskar in the city of Lahore and was reputed to know a great deal about music. He volunteered his organizational and financial help very readily to all the well-known music circles in the city, and also in other places. I remember that he was deeply involved with the prestigious annual music conference that used to be held in Allahabad when I was a teenager. He was a pillar of many musical organizations in Delhi and did pioneering work in setting up several music and dance schools. He offered his home to put up visiting artistes invited to perform in Delhi and this is how we came in very close touch with many dazzling personalities who lived their fascinating lives in our household as honoured guests, sometimes for long periods.

During one of the annual music festivals of the Bharatiya Kala Kendra, of which my father was one of the founder members, Kesar Bai Kerkar, the famous singer from Bombay, was a guest in our home. In preparation for her visit, my father gave the entire family an intensive orientation course in how eminent she was and how artistes of the calibre of those we were likely to meet on a daily basis during the festival should be treated. Their every wish was to be our command and we should all consider ourselves fortunate if we could be of the smallest service to them. Apart from her, we had every prospect of being able to hobnob with luminaries like Bade Ghulam Ali Khan, the sensational singer from Lahore D.V. Paluskar, another great singer and the son of the famous Vishnu Digambar Paluskar, Ahmad Jan Thirakwa, the tabla wizard from the then princely state of Rampur, and Rasoolan Bai, a famous thumri singer from Banaras. All these names were familiar to me because of the two dozen or so records stacked in a worn cardboard box behind the sofa that had been there ever since I could remember. These must have accumulated in our home from diverse complimentary sources because nobody admitted to having bought them. My elder brother taught me how to play them on our ancient gramophone which had to be cranked and they became the solace of all my school holidays and vacations. It was a miracle that I was actually going to see and speak to some of the personalities that had so far existed only as badly printed faces on the rough paper of the jackets of the records.

In those days, polite speech and correct form seemed to be

as important as life itself. Our family was generally considered a rich repository of these. However, the thirty-odd youngsters in the household were never quite sure how to behave in any situation. They had been taught at least three different styles of good manners and etiquette, two at home and one in our English school. The chirpiness Miss Ashdown approved of as a sign of bright intelligence in class went down as impudence at home, more so in the presence of guests from within the community. But sitting down 'quietly and peacefully' which my grandmother was constantly exhorting us to do was not acceptable to everybody in all circumstances either. My father approved of it on some days but regarded it as bad behaviour when a literary or musical celebrity was present. When guests of this category made an appearance, my father became very tense lest we fail to express our deference and solicitude clearly enough through speech and action. In such a situation a new set of rules used to come silently into operation and depart only with the guest.

My father seemed very keen to expose me to the customs and manners of the music world. Perhaps he could foresee that in my adult life social ease with professional musicians would be an asset to me. Besides, he was always urging me to take more responsibility and help in whatever way I could, as a general rule of good breeding. I was about sixteen when he gave me the daunting job of welcoming Bade Ghulam Ali Khan, then a sensational young discovery from the Punjab, into the home of Nirmala Joshi where he was going to be a guest for the duration of the three-day music festival of the Bharatiya Kala Kendra. It was the usual practice in those days for interested citizens to offer the hospitality and warmth of their homes to the invited artistes. Since Nirmalaji had many organizational responsibilities, my father had offered her my services as deputy hostess.

My instructions were to welcome the guest with great respect on behalf of the host organization when the car brought him from the railway station, to wait in the house until he had bathed, changed, and eaten the dinner prepared in Nirmalaji's kitchen and to escort him in the same car to the lawns of Constitution Club in New Delhi where the concerts were being held. I was awkward and had no confidence that I could pull this off single-handed, but my father had said firmly that the only way to learn was to actually do it.

I had not even seen a photograph of Bade Ghulam Ali Khan, though I had heard some fabulous recordings. The power and magnetism of his voice had conjured up an image of him that I had been nursing in my heart for quite some time. However, what alighted from the car in Nirmala Joshi's porch had no resemblance whatsoever to the handsome singing star of my imagination. The real counterpart was huge, dark, unsmiling, and ungainly. His thin black moustache curved downwards at each end of a rather mean mouth, just stopping short of the jaw line. His small, beady black eyes which moved constantly made him look ferocious. Nor did there seem to be any connection between his speaking voice and his singing voice. The exchanges in Punjabi between him and the two disciples who had come with him were loud and rough. I was not familiar with the natural accents of the language, so even the pleasantries they exchanged sounded like angry outbursts.

I brought out the words of welcome I had been rehearsing over and over again, but in comparison with the sound levels established by the guests my voice was hardly audible. I managed to convey that hot water for his bath and dinner were both ready and that if he wished we could proceed to the pandal, where the music was in progress, as soon as he liked. He nodded enthusiastically and lumbered in for a bath with an enormous towel draped over his arm. To my consternation he backed out almost immediately and started an altercation with his disciples. One of them came up to tell me what was wrong. Apparently Khan Sahib was used to a particular brand of perfumed soap. The disciple suggested that we get him a cake of Mysore sandalwood soap at once. This was not difficult. It was only eight in the evening and many shops were still open in the Karol Bagh area where the house was situated. Half an hour later the interrupted bath was resumed.

After a while his huge, fragrant body clad in a pale blue kurta of embroidered silk appeared in the dining room where we were waiting. The old fashioned cook, dressed in a clean white dhoti, brought us four gleaming silver thalis one by one. Each had seven small silver bowls containing an assortment of dishes, all swimming in thin sauces of different hues—yoghurt white, spinach green, lentil yellow, potato brown, squash beige, beetroot red, and so on. The maestro scowled at the unfamiliar food and lowered the large and rather shapeless thumb of his right hand into each bowl in turn, hoping against hope that it would encounter a piece of meat on a bone. When the thumb met no resistance and sank clean to the bottom of each bowl, right through the thin gravies, the horrible truth dawned on him. He was trapped in a puritanical vegetarian household and there were no prospects of getting meat. That he was an honoured guest here was no consolation.

When the cook came in with freshly fried pooris, Bade Ghulam Ali Khan could not help saying witheringly in his native Punjabi, 'So you decided to cook every tree and every bush you could lay your hands on!' Fortunately, the poor man could not understand a word that was being said to him. I got the general drift, and was appalled at the terrible blunder that had resulted in such a glaring mismatch between guest and host.

I was the person in charge, so the maestro turned to me, pushing the thali roughly away. 'Such music as mine, and this food?' he thundered in a shocked tone. 'The truth is I can't manage with this at all. I'm going to cook my own dinner. I'll make a list of what I need. It's impossible for me to sing without proper nourishment. Even when we sit down to practise at home, a big pot of good food is always at hand, and we dig into it regularly to keep up our strength. Somebody told me that every note I sing has the aroma of kababs. Do you think I can sing the way I do if I have to feed on grasses swimming in fluids of various kinds?'

I was sure my father would think I had made some horrible mistake when we did not arrive even six hours after we were expected. The disciples had set off with a long shopping list that featured six broiler chickens, a kilo of khoya or solidified whole milk, a kilo of almonds, a tin of clarified butter, fifteen different spices, and a stack of tandoori rotis. A charcoal fire was lit and a portable stove set up in the open courtyard because no meat of any kind was allowed in the family kitchen. Full-scale cooking operations started at around nine with great enthusiasm and expertise and a delicious, one-dish meal was triumphantly produced within two hours. The maestro heaped vast quantities on to a china plate since the metal thalis were not available for this kind of depraved eating. Nor was any space inside the house, so the dinner took place outdoors and was all the more enjoyable for that. Three or four hearty belches announced the end of this phase of the proceedings and we finally set off for the site of the concerts.

Hearing him was pure and instant intoxication. My father was totally overcome. In those days he was adviser to All India

Radio and immediately proposed that they record him extensively. We noticed that Bade Ghulam Ali Khan was lukewarm about the project. My father had to use all his persuasive powers to convince him what a great public service it would be. The maestro reluctantly agreed to be taken to the studios of AIR on Parliament Street the next morning. I was allowed to tag along in the interests of my orientation, which was going rather well according to my father.

Our weighty delegation breezed into the studios importantly, according to plan. Everything looked shiny and clean and smelt wonderful to me. The studios had just been freshly painted. The master looked uneasy, his small black eyes darting this way and that, like those of a caged animal. Suddenly his vast frame swayed backwards and then shot forward again as he was convulsed by a gigantic sneeze which echoed through the whole complex. The waiting accompanists looked completely mystified as he turned on his heel and sailed out of the studio like a small mountain on wheels. He passed corridor after corridor like a man possessed. My father and his disciples trailed him in bewilderment, calling out to him to stop but he didn't come to rest until he was clear of the building and out on the small lawn in front of it. Here he collapsed on the grass, stretched himself out, and began to fan his face with his black cloth cap. When the rest of the party caught up with him and asked with the greatest concern what the matter was, he explained that he just could not stand the smell of the paint in the studios and that it would therefore be impossible for him to do any recording this time. It was incongruous that a man with as hearty and robust an appearance as his should be as delicate and sensitive as he was proving to be.

My father was not one to give up easily. AIR also agreed that Bade Ghulam Ali Khan simply must be recorded, no matter what they had to do to get over the problem of his allergy to paint. They did something unprecedented, which was to improvise an outdoor recording room on the front lawns of the main building, just about where the maestro's maiden flight from the fresh paint had ended. It could not be as perfect as they would have wished, but with the elaborate cloth canopy and arrangements for a live audience they hoped to offset some of the technical disadvantages. Three days later Bade Ghulam Ali Khan was invited to record outdoors. My father escorted him once again. At last he was seated on a raised platform inside a colourful marquee, flanked by an extensive ensemble of accompanists. There was a perfectly tuned tanpura on either side and the ravishing surmandal he strummed himself in front of him. A small and select but ardent audience waited hungrily as he tried out the instruments. We noticed that he looked uncomfortable and ill at ease again as he eyed the veritable jungle of wires, microphones, and other intimidating heavy equipment that had been pressed into service for this unusual event. The tanpura players started strumming and the rich tonics began to take hold of our senses. Just then there was a long, piercing, shattering sound as a car passed Parliament Street. The driver seemed to have had his thumb on the horn for the entire stretch. It certainly seemed to have destroyed the maestro's mood because he immediately heaved himself up from his place in the centre of the stage and started plodding purposefully towards the car that had brought him, like a man in a trance. My father practically ran after him and begged him to give it another chance. He hook his head and said in a distressed voice that he felt ill. The hideous sound of the horn had robbed him of every note he had in his system and filled the air with a horrible tunelessness that would take days to cleanse. Clearly the recording session was at an end and everyone was free to go home, however disappointedly.

My father went to him the next morning to commiserate with him and apologize for his role in putting him through such an ordeal. He suggested another try because it was too important a project to give up simply because it was proving difficult. He had made enquiries and there were some old studios in the outhouses which had not been painted, so if he would be so good as to give another date they could set up something very soon. At this point Bade Ghulam Ali Khan broke down and made his startling admission.

'I do not want to record for "Radio".'

He pronounced the word 'Radio' as if it was a proper name used for a much dreaded man-eating ogre.

'Why ever not?' my father asked, quite unable to understand his resistance.

'Because I don't want to lose my voice', he replied darkly. 'They tell me that "Radio" records on some kind of electric wire. This wire pulls out all the life and virtue from the voice, leaving nothing but husk. I have heard many voices after "Radio" has finished with them. There is no juice left. Just think what happens to chickens after they have been used to make soup! I don't want the same thing to happen to my voice. I have worked very hard on it and it is my most precious possession, as you know.'

My father was dumbfounded. It took many years of slow, gentle, patient work on the part of many music lovers in many cities for this great singer to be weaned away from his unreasoning distrust of 'Radio', specially its bad habit of making wire recordings. Inexplicably, the three-minute discs he did for HMV did not have the same dire consequences. Perhaps he considered that the shorter duration was not enough to squeeze out all life from a voice and that the benefits balanced out the dangers. I only know that twenty years or so after this incident, when our paths crossed again, he had completely overcome his fear and misgivings and had become one of the most frequently and extensively recorded artistes, not only of AIR but of many other organizations and recording companies as well.

Looking back, I see clearly that the circumstance which brought personalities like Kesar Bai and Bade Ghulam Ali Khan to Delhi and gave me a chance to touch the hem of their garments, as it were, changed my life in an important way. It definitely ended the first phase of my musical childhood and gave me a sense of the vastness of the ocean I was embarked on.

FIVE

Playing for the Flowers

I don't know exactly when my family adopted Ustad Bundu Khan as their favourite outsider. He had always been there as far back as I can remember, lending colour, variety, and a little bit of magic to our lives, specially on occasions like the Holi festival, a wedding in the family, or even a dinner party my father sometimes threw for the cultural elite of Delhi. A sarangi recital by Ustad Bundu Khan usually preceded or followed the eating and drinking and was regarded as a great treat offered by our family. Not many of the invitees had specially cultivated ears but the general view was that classical music was a good thing and should be sought after. The charm of the music was greatly enhanced by my father's fabulous introductions. He tended to romanticize and mystify the greatness of the artiste, his instrument, the raga, and the treasure-house of Hindustani music in general.

'Bundu Khan used to practice so hard and so long that blood would spurt from his finger nails, but he would still go on and on until his teacher asked him to stop.' Or, 'the only way to experience the raga Malkaus is to listen to it standing in cold, knee-deep water in a river on a moonless night.' Or, 'whenever he plays the raga Malhar, dark clouds gather and it invariably starts to rain.' My father made statements of this kind with a mixture of relish and authority which was characteristic of him. Whether what he said was literally true or not seemed irrelevant. My gullible aunts, the refined guests, specially the ladies, and some of us children listened wide-eyed, hungry for more myths and accounts of incredible musical feats which spoke of dedication, beauty, and the true meaning of things. After my father's stories, the music sounded even more magical than it would otherwise have done.

We placed Bundu Khan on a pedestal and grew up almost worshipping him. The welcome he received every time he came to the house was so intense that he seemed to shrivel up a little under its impact and look even smaller and more bent than he was. But his visits to us must have been a relief from the noisy and congested environment of his own large joint family establishment in Suiwalan in the Old City. He was not really concerned about the poor living conditions. What bothered him was having to deal with the world outside music. He once told us that when he was young, he was expected to do errands in the vegetable market for his mother and aunts. 'It seemed to take forever', he said with a tortured expression. We quite understood that the real hardship for him must have been the time he was forced to be away from music. To get over the problem, he designed a small bamboo sarangi which he could sling over his shoulder unobtrusively and use for practice with the fingers of his left hand without making any sound while he went about his extra-musical chores. He added that he would drape a light shawl over the left shoulder to hide the sarangi so that he didn't have to listen to casual comments from passing busybodies.

'I didn't want to go around telling the whole world that I was trying to perfect my finger-work. I arranged things so that they could neither see nor hear what I was doing. That way I felt quite free', he used to say.

Bundu Khan's occasional visits gradually became a regular weekly feature. He came every Sunday when my father was home and spent the whole day playing and explaining ragas to whoever cared to listen, and even to those who did not. Most of the time my father was the core of his audience, but even when he was not Bundu Khan's enthusiasm for his art continued to overflow. He would play for whoever he sighted—a child, a servant, giggling teenagers or serious adults. And when there was no one, he happily and compulsively played for himself. He always carried his sarangi on his person as though it were a part of his body. It was said about him that though he was a renowned artiste who had been court musician of the princely states of Rampur and Indore, he would just as happily accompany a lowly wayside villager reciting couplets from the Ramayana of Tulsidas or play at the Ramlila celebrations in the Parade Grounds in front of the Red Fort. He simply could not resist any opportunity to play, because he heard the possibility of beautiful music in everything and couldn't rest until he had found it.

One Sunday morning Bundu Khan got lost in our house. Dependable old Masoom Ali, my grandfather's chauffeur, had driven the family Dodge to Suiwalan and brought the maestro back in accordance with my father's standing instructions and deposited him on the veranda. After a few moments my father hurried out of his dressing room to greet him but he was nowhere to be seen. Not in the lavatory, not still in the car, not on the terrace, nowhere. My father's faithful valet, the smirking Jai Singh whom we all hated, was sent hunting everywhere without result. Half an hour after the panic set in we heard the faint, scratchy sounds of a sarangi. They seemed to be coming from the garden but we could not see anyone there. We followed my father in the direction of the sound and tracked it down to a tall, thick hedge of sweetpeas that divided the huge garden in front of our house into two sections. Ustad Bundu Khan was lying in the flower bed on the farther side, his instrument balanced on his chest and shoulder, his eyes closed, completely engrossed in the music he was playing. Even my father who prided himself on courtly manners did not know how to awaken such a great musician from his reverie, or how to call out such a revered name aloud. Anyhow, with much fake coughing and embarrassed clearing of the throat, my father managed to catch his attention. Ustad Bundu Khan opened his eyes, just a slit, and scrambled to his feet when he saw the concern on the faces of the small assemblage.

'It is spring time, and I was playing for the flowers', he said in complete explanation.

The sweetpeas were indeed in full bloom and that morning, for all of us, and for ever, the perfume of these flowers became a part of Raga Bahar, which he had been playing on this occasion.

Absolute, unquestioning respect for all artistes was a very early lesson that all the children of our household imbibed. In this matter it was my father who laid down the law. We had to learn a whole new set of manners and values which were quite different from good behaviour in other social situations. The normal standards of cleanliness and elegance that one had been taught no longer applied when it came to musicians and poets. However unkempt and ragged they might be, they were automatically entitled to almost god-like reverence, the kind of reverence my grandmother unquestioningly lavished on the unimpressive, raisin-like little idol that dominated her little prayer room at one end of the long back veranda. This idol, with its tinny, painted smile was swathed in brocade robes too big for its body and was offered wonderful gifts, flowers, and delicacies regularly. It was the most treasured and powerful focus of our lives. The same attitude was extended to Ustad Bundu Khan by all the sixty-odd members of the household and naturally by all the fourteen servants, regardless of whether or not they really understood the greatness of his art. My father was constantly instructing the women and children of the household in the etiquette of the mysterious world of traditional musicians. One could not stretch one's legs while sitting or change position while the music was going on. One's feet could never be visible, and even when covered could not point in the direction of the instruments. One could not speak a word, or eat or drink anything in the same room. The smallest slip could be construed as impertinence. Though fascinated by the proximity of this great master, most of the children thought the safest course was to hang their heads, crouch in a corner and pretend they did not exist.

My father did not consider this satisfactory either. It was important to him that his family make a favourable impression. Because I was considered to be more interested in music than my cousins, the heaviest weight of my father's project of educating the entire family in the norms of hospitality fell on me. Although far from being shy, I was nonetheless mortified when I was asked to approach Ustad Bundu Khan after a music session was over and serve him tea. I must have been about fifteen years old at the time. I now know that my father wanted me to perform this act of devotion both for my own sake and also to make the point that our extraordinary guest was too special to be served by servants. My father's expectations made me nervous. I was not sure that I would have the wits to say the right thing in the right accent at the right moment.

My mother poured a cup of tea for the Ustad and handed it to me encouragingly. Her manner told me that she had absolute confidence in my ability to offer it to our eminent guest in a proper way. Ustad Bundu Khan took the cup from me with a vague smile as though it were a bird that might fly away. I brought the sugar bowl next and asked him how many spoons he wanted. He looked mystified and said in his soft, hoarse voice, 'As many as you feel like putting in; it doesn't matter.' I started to add sugar to his cup, hoping he would stop me at some point; but when he didn't, even after I had put in six teaspoons, I put the bowl down myself. From the platter of hot samosas my mother prompted me to offer next, he picked up two and thrust them into the teacup, stirring the whole mess vigorously with a teaspoon, looking into the middle distance with faintly rheumy eyes. He did the same thing to the piece of barfi he accepted from the serving dish of sweets that was held out to him most deferentially. By this time there was no tea left in the teacup, only a thick, gooey pulp. The liquid had squirted on to the saucer, his clothes, and the floor. He seemed quite oblivious of this, and totally indifferent to eating or drinking. He took a couple of teaspoons of the unsightly mixture in his teacup to his mouth as a sort of reflex action, muttering something about the darja or degree of the komal gandhar in Raga Darbari to my father as he did so. All the other members of the family present at the tea were gazing adoringly at him as though he had just provided yet another proof of his otherworldliness.

I remember Ustad Bundu Khan as a frail man with a lined brown face and large, soft but sunken eyes that were usually half closed and fixed dreamily at something which was visible only to him. He dressed in chooridar pajamas and sherwani like most members of his community and profession. I never saw him bare-headed. On formal occasions he donned a colourful, oversized and elaborately tied Rajasthani turban and at other times a boat-shaped cloth cap. His footwear consisted of heavy, laced, Western-style walking shoes that seemed to have no connection with him or the rest of his outfit. His ears were large and stuck out just a little. This along with his sudden, childlike smile gave him the look of a pixie. It was whispered in our household that he was an opium addict. There wasn't the slightest hint of disapproval in this. Everyone completely understood that such a man must need to escape from the tediousness of daily life somehow.

Once in a rare mood he began to talk about the rigorous training he received in his youth from his maternal uncle Mamman Khan. The incident he described was not aimed at anyone. Perhaps he just enjoyed recalling it himself.

'I had practised fast runs in the raga Bahar for three years. Both the ascent and the descent of the raga are looped, so it is not easy to be fluent at speed. But I was determined to earn a word of praise from Mamu. I worked hard at a typical taan of the raga until it was perfect and then I confidently played it for him. He made a face and shook his head. It was not supple enough, he said. According to him, my taan in the descent was like the neck of a pig which is so thick that it cannot even look back. I went to work for another year, for several hours a day, just concentrating on the problem of the pig's neck. Finally, I managed to get it right. You see, the taan does not actually need to look back over its shoulder, but to be beautiful it must sound as though it could bend if it had to.'

'So, what did your Mamu say when you got it right?', my brother asked eagerly.

Ustad Bundu Khan smiled shyly, looking like a grizzled

elf. 'Mamu heard me go up and down many times. Then he said "Yes".'

That 'Yes' was apparently the highest praise Mamu had ever bestowed on his amazing protégé. The recollection of it still made his eyes shine though there had been so much achievement and recognition in the intervening forty-five years!

It was not usual for Bundu Khan to tell anecdotes. On the whole, he could not express himself in speech at all but was most eloquent in the musical language of the sarangi. When he sat on the floor with his instrument, bow in hand, he was inexhaustible. He could happily demonstrate, explain, and give examples of this and that all night long. Being without his sarangi was the only situation he considered uncomfortable. He seemed always to want the elaborate, long-winded hospitality for which our home was known to end quickly so that the business of life which for him meant the business of music could go on.

Those were times when there could be only one opinion on any matter in households like ours, though it could emanate from different sources in the family. In the matter of art and culture it was my father's opinion that prevailed. In the matter of what the women and children would wear or eat it was my grandmother's, and in all other matters my grandfather's. The reverence and awe in which Ustad Bundu Khan was held by my father was a clear signal to all, including my grandparents, the servants and the children, that they should follow his example.

This was not hard to do for anybody. He was so simple and unworldly that everyone loved him and felt protective towards him. In the 1940s, when we were in close touch with his life, it was my impression that people and organizations also valued his innocence. Nobody took advantage of him, or used him as they undoubtedly would have had he been part of the performance circuit in the music world today. His own family, his pupils, his princely patrons in Rampur and Indore, the music organizations that were springing up in Delhi and elsewhere as an expression of a new awareness of the old culture, the radio, HMV—the recording company—and the cultural elite of the big cities all treated him with unqualified deference.

Once a music circle in Allahabad invited him to perform and offered a thousand rupees as his fee in addition to travel and living expenses. He brought the original letter and the reply he had dictated to his son Umrao Khan for my father's approval. The reply said in polite Urdu, 'Unless I am paid at least five hundred and Umrao Khan is paid at least two hundred, I must refuse.' It took quite a lot of effort for my father to explain that the offer he had received was better than what he was asking for and that his son had not been mentioned at all in the invitation. Bundu Khan looked bemused, tried to count and add on the fingers of his hands but gave up after a while, his lined, childlike face wreathed in smiles.

He had the habit of breaking into song in his rough, cracked voice while he played the sarangi. There could not be a sharper contrast between two sounds. His bowing produced a clear, bubbling fountain of honey while his singing voice was gruff and toneless. The compulsive singing was interesting and informative when he was recollecting the bandish or composition and sharing the source of the music with connoisseurs in private baithaks, but it didn't go down so well with the radio authorities and the recording companies as it disturbed the flow of exquisite sound from his instrument. My father tactfully urged the Ustad to restrain himself during his next broadcast.

'Please, just let the sarangi do all the singing and explaining. Radio listeners do not really understand what you are saying', he told him. We all gathered round the large, battered Philips radio set that stood on a corner table in the drawing room of our house to listen to our idol. I remember thrilling to the magical strains of the raga Chandni Kedara. 'You have to hear this raga on a moonlit night to get its full flavour', my father whispered. When the programme was about to end, we exchanged smiles of relief because Ustad Bundu Khan had indeed desisted from speaking, singing and explaining in the middle of his recital as he always used to, even if it was a live broadcast. My father was deeply satisfied and took the entire credit for this bit of grooming. When the strains of the music died down after the allotted half-hour, and just before the announcer came on, we heard Bundu Khan's hoarse voice, clear and triumphant:

'See, I didn't say a word this time!' he managed to say just before he was cut off.

The partition of the country in 1947 was a terrible trauma for the Ustad who did not understand at all what had happened and why. He did not want to go anywhere, or change his life in any way. He must have been about sixty years old at this time but no one knew his age for certain. Soon after Partition, many members of his joint family went away to Pakistan, including his brothers, sisters, and son. He couldn't bring himself to go, to leave the courtyard in his old family house where he had practised, played, and taught for almost fifty years. So he clung to his old life for almost three years, depending for emotional support on the depleted household of cousins and nephews who had stayed behind. But we could all see the change in him. He would just come in and sit down quietly with his eyes closed as though he were dozing, instead of playing as he used to. When invited to do so, he would get into the music and drown in it completely, but this did not happen automatically as before.

One day my father asked him what was bothering him, and his eyes filled with tears.

'I have tried', he said, choking a little, 'but it is difficult. My children have gone. My wife has gone too.'

After much agonizing, he decided to uproot himself and follow his family. My father devotedly undertook to make all the arrangements for his safe travel and went to enormous trouble to ensure that he didn't have to worry about anything. I remember that he was very attached to an old radio set he had and wanted to take it, along with his large collection of sarangis. To arrange this was quite complicated at the time but with the help of friends in various offices and the army, my father managed to transport him quite painlessly and safely.

We never knew how he coped with his new life in Karachi. My father received only one extraordinary letter of thanks three months after his departure. He had dictated it to someone in Urdu and signed his name in his shaky, illiterate scrawl. The letter carried two sentences, the first said that he would never forget all that my father had done for him. The second was somewhat longer and said 'Here are the important taans of Malkaus.' About twenty note-patterns in the raga Malkaus followed. My father was so touched that he wept. He said he would never need to use the Malkaus taans in his life, but Ustad Bundu Khan's intention was to offer him what he considered most precious. This letter of Bundu Khan's reverberated through the remaining years of my father's life. He never tired of saying that this was the most graceful gesture he had ever come across.

We were hungry for news of Ustad Bundu Khan and used to try regularly to tune in to Radio Pakistan to catch his programmes, but never had any luck. Instead we stumbled upon many beautiful new ghazal singers who were marvellous and quite unlike anything that we had heard in India. Ustad Bundu Khan's relatives in Suiwalan said that he was doing a lot of recording for the radio in Karachi, but there were no live concerts or soirees, and that he was not very happy at the status of classical music in Pakistan. This was eating into him, they said. They must have been right because barely five years after his departure we heard that he had died. No one could tell us anything more to help us weather the blow. All we knew was that this beautiful life, which had nurtured us so long and so deeply, had been snuffed out behind a thick, black curtain.

SIX

Pran Nath: An Odyssey

We were a floundering yet opinionated group of music-lovers who considered ourselves more sensitive and more idealistic than most. It was taken for granted that we were in search of the highest and the best. Any music with ready appeal was regarded with suspicion. If it sounded pleasant, it was probably just a pretty trap that would hamper our quest. We were ashamed to be moved by music because that was something that happened to ordinary, sentimental, run-of-the-mill people, not to the chosen few like us. We were too sophisticated to be taken in by seductive voices and too intellectually demanding to accept any of the glib philosophies that our music world tended to dispense so freely. Though it didn't occur to us at the time, the truth is that we had an unduly high opinion of ourselves.

This 'we' was a multiple entity, a strange, shapeless alliance of four otherwise quite different personalities. It was this compound human entity that experienced the phenomenon of Pran Nath as a sort of joint spiritual venture. I was only an element in it. The other parts were my extended self and consisted of Madhu, the angry young economics genius of the campus; Krishna, the brilliant lecturer of English literature from Madras; and Zainub, the hypersensitive and discriminating wife of a professor from Hyderabad who had come to live on the campus as a young bride. We were actually in our twenties and thirties at this time, but the recollection tastes more like a teenage memory. The four of us had drifted into a very close relationship in the course of our search for the exquisite. For many years we functioned as a single collective mind, a single pair of ears, a single spiritual receiver that consolidated all our individual inputs into a single reaction. We could not savour a particular performance or recording fully until we had arrived at some sort of consensus. There was occasional straying from the party line but this was considered a betrayal by the others. Once, Madhu went into a serious depression that lasted more than a week because Zainub and I had irresponsibly been swept off our feet by a popular, people-pleasing idol at a music conference. This could not be set right without atonement. It took many evenings of incense burning to old recordings of unrelenting classicists like Krishna Rao Shankar Pandit and Abdul Wahid Khan to bring Madhu round and persuade him that we had really not meant to stab him in the back and that life was worth living after all.

Madhu and I were the ones who were actively involved in becoming classical singers, and were therefore the nucleus of the group in a sense. Krishna and Zainub were dedicated supporters who cherished and took pride in our talent. They were quite sure that one day Madhu and I would burst upon the consciousness of the country, leaving throngs of connoisseurs speechless with wonder at our achievement. In the mean time, we practised ceaselessly and showed off our voices to one another almost every evening. Each such session would end in a rich crop of compliments from already converted friends, and Madhu and I would fill up like hot air balloons and rise slowly heavenwards, quite sure that, though we were unknown, we had much more intrinsic quality and taste than many famous names.

It was at this point that Pandit Pran Nath came into our lives. So far as we were concerned, he was the discovery of Madhu's mother, a quiet, lonely, deeply musical lady from Maharashtra who used to listen regularly to classical music on the radio. Though her main interest was Carnatak music, she could tell that Pran Nath was a most impressive repository of the meditative Hindustani tradition. She pointed her son in that direction and I followed, with full faith in her judgement.

We sought him out and offered ourselves as pupils. He was badly in need of what he called 'tushans' and readily took us on. The first few encounters established that, apart from music, he was going to be a decisive influence in our lives. His tall, spare figure, his bright, burning black eyes and his radiant vitality compelled attention. His incisive intelligence was laced with an instinctive and extremely perceptive understanding of human affairs, at least our affairs. We found to our amazement that he knew our individual domestic situations and psychologies without having to be briefed in any way. For instance, he was aware that part of Madhu's anxiety about his pursuit of music stemmed from his father's publicly expressed but unrealistic expectations from his son of original research work in the field of economics. He also knew that behind my husband's courtesy and verbal support lay a deep-rooted hostility to the ambience of north Indian music and that I was trying my best to cover this up. Pran Nath had an infallible sense of who was friend and who was foe. In his case this was not a function of animal instinct but of sheer intelligence.

He told us at the outset that he did not come from a family of professional musicians. He had apparently run away from a disapproving home in his adolescence to learn music at the feet of Abdul Wahid Khan, an ustad he venerated greatly. But his dedication alone had not been enough. He was an outsider in every sense and had no money to offer as inducement either. He had spent a hard, rocky and arid ten years hanging around the ustad's household, tending his hookah, and pressing his feet in the hope of being rewarded with a lesson. Most of what he had imbibed was the result of association or of overhearing what the ustad taught to bonafide family members. Though Pran Nath did not say or even think so, it was clear to us that his ustad had not been too kind to him. It was equally clear that this was the model he had in mind for us as well. It was the only one in his experience.

Even before his musical gifts were fully revealed to us, we were struck by the clarity, economy, and power of his speech. Pran Nath had a gift for phrase-making which never received the attention it deserved because music always overshadowed it. However, we took great delight in it because it seemed to come from the same creative source as his music and required less courage to react to. Like the melodic lines his voice contoured, his spoken words too had the power to evoke a whole world of meaning and images. We used to hang on his lips and were always greatly affected by whatever he said. He spoke pointedly and briefly in a measured drawl which had a way of lighting up with meaning much later. He spoke with nostalgia of the beauty and grace of the music world that he had left behind in Lahore after the Partition. 'The faces, the voices, the warmth and the culture!' he would exclaim sometimes, without making his meaning clearer. He once likened the feet of a beautiful singer he heard in Lahore to fragrant sprays of the keora flower. His single-word comment on my husband's scepticism about our musical activity was 'Aurangzeb'. Once when the four of us were moved to tears by his rendering of a raga and started to sniffle self-consciously into our handkerchiefs, he dismissed the phenomenon as an 'infectious cattle disease'. His face would remain impassive, but there was just the suspicion of a twinkle in his eye and the faint beginnings of a crooked smile as he uttered his pregnant phrases.

His gaunt frame would stride purposefully across the campus from the bus stop to my house three times a week for my lessons. He had the same arrangement with Madhu. His lessons consisted mainly in demonstrations of heavy, serious ragas in his own voice. Most of the time we listened in hypnotized states of awe. He had a way of exploring a single note in such detail that it turned from a single point or tone into a vast area that glowed like a mirage. Each of us encountered this magic at different times. Whenever it happened, it overwhelmed us like a religious experience. There was no question of our even trying to repeat this sort of thing. All we could do was to drink it all in and wait for a chance to participate in some undefined way in the distant future. Needless to say we did not make much progress in the area of voice training. But something very important was happening nonetheless. We were learning about the musical values of an ancient tradition, almost by stealth. In those early days with Pran Nath, we seemed to concentrate on what not to do, what not to like. We were learning more about how not to sing than about vocal technique. It was as though we had enlisted in some gigantic project of purification which could never succeed or come to an end. Whatever it was, we found the activity it entailed totally absorbing.

The music Pran Nath carried within him spoke to me of the heights of human endeavour and of superhuman visions of great power and fierceness, not of love and beauty. Apart from the intrinsic difficulty of the material, Pran Nath just hated to teach. He also felt that it was not possible to transmit the quality of his music, at any rate to mixed-up romantics like us. We were too soft, too comfortable, and wanted too many things from life. Also, we had too much faith in the cerebral process, and believed that it could yield answers to most questions. Pran Nath thoroughly disapproved of this. He called us 'brain cutlets' and was frankly contemptuous of our naive, academic approach to the musical treasures that he carried under his rough, khadi kurta. He found most sounds unbearable and made no effort to hide the fact. After all, he had heard the music of the spheres from great masters and nothing that was produced in the present could compare with what was lodged in the memory of his soul. This attitude became the air we breathed. We were afraid to desecrate the atmosphere by producing any music of our own. We were even inhibited from trying out the phrases that he invited us to repeat after him on rare occasions.

I remember a fantastic exposition of the raga Multani, one of his favourites, in Madhu's house one afternoon. When he sounded the fourth note, the teevra madhyam, it seemed to expand, throb with tension and become luminous in a miraculous way that made my hair stand on end. As he outlined the raga, he sent the most powerful images through my mind. I saw an ageless mystic with a granite face and a flowing white beard, standing alone in the burning desert, his heart bursting with the agony of existence. He was looking up at the sky and shaking his fists at God, addressing him directly, as an equal. The raw and breathy way Pran Nath sang some of the phrases sounded as though the mystic was actually scolding God for the unspeakable things that were allowed to go on in life on earth. Both Madhu and I were overwhelmed by the power of the music. The lesson was really intended for Madhu. I had only been allowed to sit in on it. I could tell that Madhu was dying for a chance to sing a few notes himself. He sat quivering with intensity, clutching his tanpura with shaking hands, his knuckles white, his brow beaded with sweat and his mouth open in readiness. But no sound emerged. He was sure that nothing he could utter would be remotely like the accents of the master. And nothing less than perfection would do for either of them. So he just went on strumming the tanpura desperately, not even venturing to hum. This state of paralysis became a more or less chronic situation, for both Madhu and me. Pran Nath did not believe in encouragement. He had never had any himself. Nor had his teacher, as he often told us with deep satisfaction. He also told us as though it was an achievement to be proud of that his ustad had neither sought nor received public acclaim or even recognition. We knew that this was likely to be his lot as well.

We were perfectly happy with our struggles and convinced of our great good fortune in being owned by the dazzling musical mind of Pran Nath. We were used to thinking of music as colour and his rendering of ragas made us realize how beautiful black could be. It was natural for him to dive into the dark depths of early morning ragas like Lalit and Bhairav, where there was no sun. Sometimes we would hear the greys and dusky ochres of twilight ragas like Puriya and Marwa, the midnight blue of magical and mysterious ragas like Malkaus, and even the restrained gold of the majestic and courtly Darbari. We were most excited about this new way of listening which had evolved automatically because of the association with Pran Nath, though he never suggested it to us in words. Madhu, who used to paint, shyly and secretively, covered the walls of his messy room with pictorial representations of ragas. Graveyards, skulls and devastation figured prominently in most of his creations. His other themes were ageing courtesans looking back on their lives with resignation, and scenes of various kinds of desolation at sunset. He was committed to these intimate expressions and could not stand any difference of opinion in interpretation. A part of him was eager to display his paintings to us and another was most reluctant to do so. We always had to force him to share his visions with us, but once he got going it was difficult for him to rein himself in again. I once ventured to say that the skeletons he had strewn over the landscape were uncalled for in the intention of the raga Marwa. He was unwilling to dispense with a single bone and regarded me with pity because the obtuseness of my remark told him that I would never understand the raga.

Needless to say, Pran Nath gave Madhu no opportunity to paint pretty pictures in pink, green, and orange because his natural bent was for major ragas with a severe, architectonic quality. But even when he dealt with light, lyrical material, he tended to turn it into something awe-inspiring and monumental. Butterflies became elephants in his hands and love-lorn maidens lurking in ragas like Jaijaiwanti and Bageshwari fled, giving way to dignified, silver-haired prophetesses. We were enchanted.

He would dwell on the lower notes in his grave and gritty voice and slowly sketch a few short melodic lines to evoke the mood of the raga. There was no sweetness in his utterance at all. Only certainty and profundity. The lower register of the voice was where he believed the foundation of the musical structure had to be laid. After establishing the all-important base line of the raga, he would rise in the prescribed scale note by note in the unhurried and serene fashion of the singers of the Kirana school though he sounded like no one but himself. Slow development or alaap was to him the essence of everything. He never tired of telling us that the most significant and enduring music resided in the silences between notes and lines, not in the obvious sounds one made.

He considered the tabla a mundane intrusion and disdained teaching us anything conventional, including the basic rhythm cycles. As a result tala or rhythm remained our weakest area and the tabla gradually became a symbol of tyranny and failure to us. Though he was fanatical about the purity of a raga, he was unbelievably unorthodox and impractical as a performer. His entire concentration was on the spiritual and emotive intention of music. He could spend hours exploring and elaborating on the tonal nuances of the melodic phrase of a raga, but had only a fleeting interest in rhythmic accompaniment. As a result, his concept of presentation was considered wayward by all but research-minded connoisseurs. We faithfully imbibed his musical visions just as they manifested themselves, spontaneously. It was rather like learning to write poetry without first being able to spell or to recognize the letters of the alphabet. We often felt that he had skipped all the necessary preliminaries and gone straight to the heart of the matter, expecting that whichever of his pupils had the courage to jump in would do so and then try to keep afloat. Even if they couldn't, and drowned, he would not consider it a great tragedy, for he was not in the least bit ambitious, either for himself or for his pupils. Nor was he unduly weighed down by our talent, or by his own. Certainly he had no plans to do anything about either. 'This business is only for the contentment of your soul', he would say dismissively at regular intervals. This pronouncement, though suitably high-minded, made our hearts sink because we still harboured secret hopes of astounding the professional concert circuit one day.

Most of the texts of his khayals were from various Sufi traditions that overwhelmed us with their mystic devotion and made us feel unworthy and inadequate. These, and all the tales he reluctantly told us of his encounters with great masters and saints intimidated us even more. The realization that our singing was still 'green' and his ready acceptance of the probability that it would always remain unripe made us very humble and unsure of ourselves. We were living a kind of religion that we did not quite understand but were committed to absolutely. The music that we had started out to love became a sort of black vulture that hovered over our lives, threatening to demolish us. But we had no wish to escape from it because we were convinced that it was the 'real thing', the voice of divinity meant for the truly serious minded. Pran Nath abhorred ornamentation and sentimentality in musical utterance and transmitted his bias to us through the pithy sayings of his ustad. We became like critically charged balls of musical energy though we still could not sing a single note.

'I have first to clean your ears out. They are full of the garbage you have been hearing all your lives', he told us. 'You have to understand the tongue the ragas speak. If you look for rasagullas and tasty morsels in music you are lost. Even one moment of insight and enlightenment is worth a lifetime of toil and searching. This is what I am trying to prepare you for.' He said all this with an artless smile and a mischievous twinkle in his eye which made us wonder whether he was communicating something serious or amusing himself with a game in which he could now assume the role of the master, having been at the receiving end of such discouraging wisdom throughout his youth.

At last a day arrived, after six months of general orientation about values, when Pran Nath announced that he intended to start training my voice. I had a beautiful tanpura crafted in Miraj that had been a gift from Ustad Bundu Khan. The delicately carved woodwork with its elaborate inlay of ivory held a massive, resounding gourd. The beads for fine tuning were the shape of miniature swans, also carved in ivory. It was not just the spectacular good looks of the instrument that I gloated over but also its 'bol choral' or temperament. I had been showing it off for twenty years and everyone who ever examined it had admired its rich tone, its sensitivity and its long breath. If carefully tuned and played, it could set up a hypnotizing ebb and flow of resonance that was a completely satisfying musical experience in itself. Pran Nath delighted my heart by sharing my enthusiasm for this prize possession. He said with a sardonic smile that this instrument might really teach me to sing some day, even if he failed. That Pran Nath had approved of my tanpura was news. When I reported it to the group of four, Krishna promptly christened it Grandfather. The name stuck and in a way what Pran Nath had said did come true. The instrument was a tremendous support to me and nurtured my music throughout my life. There were many difficult performances in which it seemed to sing with me and uphold me as though it really was my grandfather.

On that first day, Pran Nath took nearly an hour to tune it. He had his eyes closed all this time and worked only with his ears and his fingers, feeling the bridge, turning the tuning pegs, adjusting the threads to get the right microtones. He was in such a high state of concentration that it was almost like a trance. He would stroke a string with his finger and listen intently until the last breath of sound had died away, lightly tapping the bridge, running his index finger lengthwise across the strings and gently coaxing the pegs, a hairbreadth at a time. Finally he began to stroke the four strings in a slow rhythm, pausing at the end of a set to give the low brass string enough time to breathe. Waves of tuneful resonance started to wash over us. Pran Nath gave me one of his rare smiles. I had never heard a tanpura sound so perfect. I realized for the first time how complex a process tuning was and that the cavalier fashion in which I had done it all my life was just a crude approximation.

We sat silently for a long time, just listening to this echoing, soothing, tapestry of harmonics. I felt as though the sound was weaving a comfortable nest for my soul. 'Try to join the instrument with your breath', Pran Nath said at last. 'Sing only one note, the tonic. There is a whole universe in that one note. In fact everything you have been looking for is there.' I sang the shadaja as I had done a thousand times before but it was unsteady and unconvincing in comparison to Pran Nath's example. 'This is the first thing you have to do. Find your basic voice and make it true', he said. 'I can teach you nothing until that happens.' He was most eloquent about the importance of the traditional early morning practice of shadaja or kharaj Marna, best translated as 'pouring oneself into the tonic'.

'Take the note and with your breath draw a line of sound on the silence. Think of it as a pencil of light. If it wavers and warps, discard it and start another. You have to do this all your life, for many hours every day, until you can draw a perfect line of sound. Slowly the line will gain body in your perception and seem to you to be a broad band with a middle and sides. The kharaj practice will help you to stay in dead centre, and this means being in tune. A tone is not a point but a melodic area to be explored. The more extensive this area becomes in the mind of a musician, the more evolved he is. You must learn to listen before you learn to sing. And you have first to listen to your own breath and then to the self it embodies.'

He showed me a few times how to do this, yawned with fatigue and boredom and stood up abruptly to leave. While I was still reeling under the impact of the profound things he had just said, he walked out of the front door, loudly cursing the broken-down public bus service of the city. 'Every bone in my body rattles and aches by the time I get home. I have to change routes three times and wait for buses for hours. And this after breaking my head trying to teach the fundamentals of music to various kinds of philistines', he said bitterly to the night air. Though I could understand and sympathize with the hardships he faced in his day-to-day life, I had a strange feeling that this man was not the person who had given me the lesson but somebody else.

I started the single note practice in dead earnest, every morning and evening. I had been strictly forbidden to sing anything else. Pran Nath had said firmly that he would not start me on any raga until my voice, ears, and spirit were ready. Theoretically this was meant to make me fit to receive the musical visions he carried. But I felt as though I was waiting indefinitely at a street corner for something to happen.

Though I was secretly frustrated, I boasted about Pran Nath's extraordinary teaching methods to my friends. They were all suitably impressed, specially Dharma, an economic historian who had herself started taking lessons in Carnatak music just six months earlier. She was doing it just because she thought it would be restful, and fun, but she was still most interested in comparing the techniques of our teachers.

'How many ragas has he done with you so far?' she asked me one day.

'None. Not a single one. He has just parked me on one note and I am supposed to stay put on it until he takes me off.'

'But you were already a singer when Pran Nath took you on! Surely it must be child's play for him to teach you songs.'

'I suppose so. But he seems to be laying some sort of underground pipes, so for the moment all construction work at eye level is at a stand-still. What about you? What have you been doing?'

'My vadyar has already taught me a dozen geetams, and four kritis', she said smugly.

'All in the same raga I suppose?'

'Not at all. Let's see now. Mayamalavagowda, Bilahari, Mohanam, Shankarabharanam. . . . There are lots of others. At least twelve. I can't remember all the names just now, but we are really making good progress.'

I was alarmed for Dharma's sake and explained to her that from any standards it was impossible to learn so many ragas in depth in such a short time. Any teacher of Hindustani music, however superficial, would take at least six months over one raga, not gallop merrily along like this. I treated her to an exaggerated account of Pran Nath's timeless project. 'Foundation weak, building fall', he would have told her himself if she had questioned him.

She quickly grasped the general idea and plunged into a state of dissatisfaction. Her vadyar was probably doing something wrong. He was definitely going too fast for her to absorb the spirit of the raga. She made up her mind to speak to him about it. When she did, he dismissed her fears without even giving her a patient hearing. Now she had no choice but to tell him about Pran Nath and the slow and steady way he was teaching her friend. She tried to strengthen her case by repeating this almost every time she had her lesson. Dharma's vadyar ended up loathing Pran Nath whom he had never seen. 'What do you think is the reason why these north Indians take years to understand a raga?' he had apparently asked Dharma. 'Everyone knows. Compared to us, they are rather dull', he is reported to have said with malicious glee, screwing his index finger into his temple. 'And their music is so boring. Nothing happens in it. Their alaap is enough to send me to sleep.'

Though I had been defensive of Pran Nath to Dharma, I had to admit that I envied her 'progress'. I had been standing on one note for six months and was now dying to be taught a proper raga. I mustered courage and spoke to Pran Nath about my south Indian friend who had done more than a dozen ragas in the same period of time.

'Couldn't I please start with something simple like Yaman or Bilawal?', I wheedled. Pran Nath was incensed by my request. 'Is this all you have understood of my efforts to mould your sensibilities?', he asked severely. 'Who is this jumped-up music master who is pumping songs into your friend at this indecent rate and creating so much din and turmoil? The trouble with these south Indian musicians is that they have no tranquillity, no serenity. Their music is so full of jerky movements and general restlessness that they cannot possibly know whether they are in tune or not. Since they are incapable of judging the depth of anything, they flit from song to song, from raga to raga without pausing to think. They have no sense of structure either. Listen to their first note, the *sa*! It sounds like a little earthquake. What kind of building can they erect on a foundation that is shaking so violently? Is this what you want?', he said, suddenly breaking into a withering parody of the Carnatak style.

His earlier tirade had unnerved me, but his take-off was hilarious, even good-natured. It diffused the tension and made me feel that he had forgiven me for my impudence. The most hilarious thing of course was that these two characters should loathe each other so heartily without ever having so much as seen each other.

Pran Nath was destined to have at least one more encounter with Carnatak music, though this was many years later. Mohan Rao, my boss at the Publications Division who later became a good friend, decided to take him to a recital of Madurai Mani Iyer, as a special treat. He had become an ardent admirer of Pran Nath and wanted, as a gesture of gratitude, to expose him to what he thought was a comparable quality of Carnatak singing. Madhu and I were also in attendance. There were nearly eight hundred people in the quadrangle of the Madrasi school where the event was held. It was the first time I had been at a live concert of Carnatak music though I had heard lots of recordings. This was a far more genuine and civilized affair than anything I was used to. There were no casual, poker-faced droppers-in who were there because classical music was in fashion. The front rows were not occupied by obviously affluent and influential sponsors but by ordinary, disciplined people who had spent their own money on tickets and obviously considered it well spent. There were no spoilt children weaving between the rows of people playing noisy games of their own and no bored women exchanging trivialities during the music. There was a much closer connection between the audience and the music they had come to hear than I had ever come across in public concerts of Hindustani music in Delhi. We remarked on all this and Pran Nath agreed with our observations. But this harmony did not last long.

The singer was in fine form and the opening Ganapati invocation, and the two shorter pieces that followed were beautiful, I thought. I sensed that Pran Nath was fidgeting a little bit but hoped that whatever it was would go away if we ignored it. Then came the major raga of the evening. Madurai Mani outdid himself and the audience was ecstatic. I heard an amazing new sound of appreciation, quite unlike the Hindustani '*wah, wah*'. Whenever the listener was smitten by something particularly wonderful that the performer was doing, he would raise his chin, bring his lips together in a protruding 'O', and make a series of little clicking sounds by striking the tongue against the back of the front teeth, gently shaking his head from side to side in mock helplessness. Difficult as it may be to believe this, these clicking sounds had a definite expression, as though their producer was prostrating himself before the performer in a state of abject gratitude and cajoling him to go on pouring his aesthetic bounty into the atmosphere. As the singer got into his stride, more and more people started to emit this sound periodically. I saw the alarm in Pran Nath's eyes and tried to soothe him but he was so deeply distracted by this sound that he just could not concentrate on the music. 'I cannot believe this. One or two noisy enthusiasts are bad enough. But there are rows and rows of them doing this together, like crickets in the monsoon', he said in a stage whisper. Mohan Rao managed to hush him up somehow but he looked as though he was in real distress.

The singer now introduced the kriti of the main raga of the evening. This was set in an eight-beat rhythm cycle into which the two percussionists literally exploded. The mridangam and the ghatam both let off the most vigorous rhythmic patterns to coincide with the beat of the melody. When the entire audience joined them by beating out the rhythm cycle on their thighs with the palms of their hands, Pran Nath could not stand it any more. 'I feel suffocated here', he said. 'They are driving the music out. How can music survive where a thousand people get together to slap their haunches?' He rose from his seat as though it was on fire and walked purposefully out without a backward look.

We knew that Pran Nath had an extraordinary mind and therefore could not understand his lack of interest or even curiosity about the work of fine musicians in different kinds of discipline. Madhu refused to accept that Peanuts, as he was now affectionately referred to amongst ourselves, could possibly be narrow minded or bigoted. I agreed that such a person could not have sung or talked the way Pran Nath did. So why was he so negative and non-committal about everything that was outside his own field? Madhu decided to find out. Pran Nath had grown attached to us and enjoyed the attention and adulation he received from the group of four, which had now swelled to twice its size. He used to visit one of our homes every Sunday just to bask, talk, and eat lunch. On these occasions, Madhu started to play recordings of his favourite Western music, mostly Bach and Mozart, whom he also considered the voice of God. He was sure that no human ear which was in the least musical could fail to respond to the pieces he carefully chose for Peanuts.

Pran Nath was interested but cool. He would point out the fleeting resemblance to ragas in the phrases of the orchestral pieces. His ears could not help picking out the melody from the rich harmonic fabric of the music, but before any one raga could establish itself, it would leap to another tonic and change into another one with an entirely different feeling. The way Pran Nath was listening to Western music was rather like the game we used to play in childhood of trying to find shapes of birds, animals, fishes and people in moving clouds. We saw everything except the cloud. Clearly there was something wrong about Pran Nath's approach. He simply could not give himself to this music totally. After several frustrating sessions, it dawned on us that his barrier was not intellectual but emotional. He was a sort of religious fanatic in music. For him there was only one beloved, and this beloved had only one face, only one voice. No one else, however beautiful, could entice him for even a moment. His entire being strained to hear the true voice of the loved one. Any other sound was untrue, and so not entirely welcome. Reluctantly Madhu accepted this theory and stopped harassing Pran Nath.

Pran Nath's uncompromising pursuit of the true sound was touching and impressive but we were intrigued by the fact that he was nowhere near as principled or sensitive in his other dealings. All the households he visited as a guru were divided into two clear camps. The devoted pupil to whom his word was law, and the rest of the household who regarded the pupil as a victim of the guru's extra-musical demands and were fiercely protective. There was always a silent tug of war between the two camps. Only the details of the deployment of forces varied from home to home. Madhu's father was a loud and dominating personality who believed firmly in 'results'. He expected Madhu to hit the headlines within months of starting music lessons and was quite indignant that Pran Nath was siphoning off all the hospitality their home could muster though Madhu had nothing to show for it. 'Do you know, he had twelve fried eggs with toast this morning! I get only one in a week! He looks quite healthy! But Madhu hasn't produced a single squeak so far. I don't know how long this will go on!' he complained to my husband who he imagined was a co-sufferer. He was, in a theoretical sense, but not being a father waiting to see his offspring's name in the papers, his contribution of animosity from the other camp was negligible. He was able to see from afar that Pran

Nath stepped on all our lives with a heavy foot but this did not affect him personally.

I realized that Pran Nath's predatory attitude to his comparatively well-to-do clientele was his way of dealing with the bitterness his own life had brought him. He felt that because we were comfortable, we owed him for all the deprivations he had suffered in the past. It seemed to be a matter of principle with him, not of actual need. If there was anything within sight that he could possibly use, he felt compelled to do so.

Once, Pran Nath arrived very early in the morning before anyone was out of bed. It could have been because his mind was on an early morning raga, or because he had been driven out that day by the dreariness of his own domestic environment which he regularly moaned and groaned about. He uttered a loud 'Hari Om' which was his usual way of announcing his presence and stationed himself in the living room. Just about this time Bacche Singh, our old and faithful servant who instinctively regarded Pran Nath as a threat, passed through carrying a tray with a steaming mug and the morning paper on his way to the master's study upstairs.

'What's that?' Pran Nath said. 'Bring it here. I am ready for some tea now.'

'It is not tea. It is sahib's shaving water', Bacche Singh said frostily.

'Bring it anyway. I need to gargle after all the dust I had to swallow on the bus ride.'

I had come into the room by now, and asked Bacche Singh to make tea at once. But Pran Nath took the shaving mug from the tray anyway. He also picked up the fresh newspaper which he could not read because it was in English. I winced because the virgin state of the morning paper was important to my husband. He hated having it handled, crumpled and refolded by someone else before it reached him. In fact he felt so strongly about this that he was willing to buy two copies, one for himself and one for everyone else, an extreme step for someone of such a frugal nature.

'I will look at the newspaper while you get ready', Pran Nath said walking out into the garden to gargle over the flower beds.

He then settled down on the cane chair in the veranda and started looking at the advertisements and photographs in the newspaper desultorily, humming Raga Lalit under his breath. Just then, my nine-year-old son passed through on his way to catch the school bus. He folded his hands dutifully to greet his mother's teacher as he had been repeatedly told to do. He was holding a small magnifying glass, a prize he had won in school a few days earlier for painting. As it was his first trophy, he carried it with him lovingly everywhere, not even putting it away during meals.

'What is that in your hand?' Pran Nath asked playfully. Abhinav shyly showed him the toy, for that is all it really was. 'Give it to me. It will help me to read the newspaper', Pran Nath said, reaching out for it and plucking it from the boy's hand.

Of course he could not have known what this meant to the child at the time but I doubt if he would have been able to curb the impulse even if he had.

About this time, Zainub started to take regular lessons from Pran Nath. She had no ambition to be a concert performer but loved classical music and wanted to be close to it, and now at last all the circumstances were conducive. She and I lived next door to each other and were in and out of each other's houses all the time. Pran Nath also treated her home as an extension of mine and would wander in periodically to savour the admiration and hospitality that was always available in abundance. Their's was a household of only two adults and Zainub often produced exotic delicacies for her husband who was an enthusiastic eater. Whenever Pran Nath appeared, she would bring out and serve whatever there was in the kitchen so that he was always assured of a delicious snack. The ayah of her two children on the other hand pulled in the opposite direction. She had a tendency to hide all left-overs and tidbits from possible predators and absolutely refused to disgorge the goodies until the coast was clear. She was an old faithful and saw no reason why bonafide members of the family should be deprived of their rights.

One afternoon Pran Nath walked in while Zainub was waiting for her husband to come home for lunch. She naturally invited him to join them for the meal which she had hurriedly prepared herself for two people, stretchable to three.

'No Bibi, I am really very tired. I will not stay. But if you can pack the food for me in a tiffin carrier, I will be able to eat in peace with my family when I reach home.' Zainub wordlessly did just that. When her husband arrived, he was given toast and tea, but no explanation.

Meanwhile, the music was going enchantingly for her. Pran Nath was baring before her dazzled eyes the reality of the ragas that had touched her in her childhood and youth. She had been too inhibited to share her nostalgic enthusiasm with Madhu and me lest we pooh pooh her favourite ragas as sweet and sentimental, not in keeping with our favourite adjective 'stark'. But Pran Nath, of all people, was most reassuring to her and gently led her through the fragrant gardens of ragas like Jaijaiwanti, though the route he followed was through a graveyard, as it were. She treated him with the deference due to a life giver and would have done anything for him, but he remained an enigma, an unpredictable and turbulent spirit who was equally and sometimes simultaneously at home with the divine and the base.

One cold and rainy day, Pran Nath left Zainub's house after a specially rewarding session, holding aloft a tattered and wholly inadequate umbrella. We saw his tall and splendid figure getting drenched, and Zainub cringed with solicitude. She rushed out after him and threw her woollen shawl around his shoulders. He nodded his acknowledgement of the gesture and walked on, ignoring our cries that he should turn back and wait for the downpour to stop. When he appeared a week later, he was still draped in Zainub's magnificent embroidered shawl. I felt responsible for him and hoped very much that he would return it to her. Instead, he reached into the breast pocket of his kurta, fished out a crumpled drycleaning bill and handed it to her with a twinkle in his eye.

'Bibi, the shawl had got completely wet and this is what you owe me for getting it in good shape again', he said, rearranging the family heirloom firmly around his shoulders.

He did not really need or care about any of the things he took. It was just his way of settling some private accounts of his own life. There had been so many debits in his past that he felt an inner pressure to reverse the trend and manipulate every situation that arose in such a way that he would be a gainer, no matter to how small an extent. Even though his actions seemed callous and crude on the surface, I know that he was not really motivated by selfishness. Deep down he felt that he was simply serving the cause of justice.

Because of this quirk of his, there was once a psychological confrontation between him and my husband who in his own way was equally principled. He was going on a trip to Kashmir and mentioned it in front of Pran Nath one day, just for something polite to say while he was waiting for me to get the music room ready.

'Oh, that is where the best saffron comes from, doesn't it?' Pran Nath said.

'Yes', replied my husband in his usual, non-committal tone with an emotional temperature well below zero.

'You must get me some saffron from Kashmir.'

'It is very expensive.'

'But I need it for medicinal purposes. I have been told by a famous hakeem that unless I drink hot saffron milk at bedtime regularly, my throat will never get all right. You know that I can't get it anywhere here.'

'It is very expensive.'

'But Dhar Sahib, don't you realize that this is a matter of my health? My throat is actually a matter of life and death for me. You should be happy to be able to get me some saffron.'

'It is very expensive', my husband said again, his face and voice both totally expressionless.

'Is money more important to you than my life?' he asked, now really incredulous.

'No, but saffron is too expensive', my husband said evenly, without the slightest trace of rancour.

Even Pran Nath was unnerved by the imperviousness he was up against. My husband could not be pressured in this way. But this seemingly casual exchange between the two resulted in the drawing of battle lines, to my great discomfiture. The fact that my husband, when pressed for his impression of a concert of Hindustani classical music which had been held on the campus, had said he could only describe it as 'organized hysteria' had already earned him the nickname of Aurangzeb from Pran Nath. The saffron episode was the last straw. I had to take care that the paths of these two men did not cross, or even touch. This became a difficult balancing act for me but I had no other choice if I wanted to pursue music.

Sometimes collisions between my two lives could not be helped. One winter we had Joan Robinson, the eminent economics guru from Cambridge, as a house guest. She used to enjoy sitting out in the garden with a book and was quite interested in all the social comings and goings in between her academic engagements. She was in her sixties at this time and had luxurious, snow white hair. She was a spectacular looking person altogether, well built and fair, and with regular features and warm blue eyes. Her lined, weather-beaten face had the innocent look of a baby. Pran Nath stopped dead in his tracks on his way to the music room when he saw her. He was sure she was a Western saint, a Mirabai from another world, and he instinctively bowed his head, folded his hands and closed his eyes in silent obeisance to a pure spirit. I had never seen anything remotely like this happen to him. He was normally too cynical to believe in the existence of good people, leave alone saints. She on her part was also struck by Pran Nath's appearance and guessed from other signs that he was no ordinary passerby. She smiled graciously at him while I told her that he was a great musician and my teacher. Goodwill flowed between them like invisible electricity even though they could not converse. Pran Nath said 'Hari Om' and sat down in one of the cane chairs near her, looking as though he had just entered a temple. He knew a few words of English and this he thought was the time to use them. He fixed his gaze worshipfully on her and asked with immense respect, 'At least eighty?'

This broke the spell. Joan drew herself up, and almost barked,

'I am sixty-four' in the indignant tone of one who is being undersold. Pran Nath could not understand her manner at all. As far as he was concerned he had said the most deferential thing he could possibly think of. In the world to which he belonged, to be eighty was nearly to be divine. But she obviously thought he had been uncomplimentary, so the pleasantries she had in mind for this unusual specimen froze on her lips. There was an awkward silence but Pran Nath was still unwilling to move away. I had quickly to find something to say which would interest both of them. It occurred to me that Madhu was someone they had both taught so I dropped his name into the pool of silence, and got ready to translate with vigour and speed. They both seized on this topic of common interest with enthusiasm.

'Tell her he is very talented, very bright. Understands everything and sees even what is not there', Pran Nath said.

I translated instantly.

Joan's face lit up with comprehension. 'Yes, yes, I know exactly what he is saying', she grunted in her characteristic British style of speech which consisted of almost inaudible murmurings evenly punctuated with sounds like gun shots.

'He was so keen to prove he had an original mind that he was even afraid to use words like 'the', 'an' and 'for' because so many others had used them before him. He carried this kind of thing to absurd lengths. You may have brilliant ideas, but you can't express them without framing them in well-worn phrases, can you?'

This was not so easy to translate into Urdu, but I did an impressionistic rendering which made Pran Nath nod repeatedly.

'What an intelligent lady!' Pran Nath exclaimed. 'How well she grasps the truth about our boy. This is his trouble with music also. He brings in his economics research into ragas and examines them from angles that nobody has ever thought of before. He wants to stand every raga on its head simply because it is a new thing to do. Even a bearded, respectable raga like Darbari is not safe from his experiments. What he does is no better than tickling the raga's chin to see how it will react. Who knows where respect ends and originality begins!'

Joan understood absolutely, though my translation was lukewarm and inadequate. My heart wasn't in it. I felt that the situation was forcing me to be disloyal to Madhu, and I didn't like it at all. Even so, I could not help marvelling at the depth and perceptiveness of this conversation between two heavyweights who had no common language.

Quite soon after this fairly close encounter with a person from the West, Pran Nath had many more, but with very different types of people. The late 1960s were the time when Indian cities began to fill up with naive young American seekers after truth, serenity, and spiritual enlightenment. Pran Nath acquired some instant followers of this type. They already knew what a guru was. What they learnt about discipleship was also a most attractive stance, at least in the short term. Two or three such devotees took to trailing after him in all his haunts. They obviously adored him and considered him a saint and a genius. Tradition, dedication, and total commitment were to them the most glamorous ideas there could be and he was someone who was reported to have these in abundant measure. Madhu and I met several of Pran Nath's new adherents at various times. Their faces, names, and concerns were constantly changing and only one survives as a clear memory because she stayed longer in Delhi than most of the others.

She was a thin, unsmiling, colourless young woman with haunted eyes who seemed to have been given rigorous lessons in how to visit an Indian home. Even if it was furnished in Western style, as many of ours were, she would discard her footwear outside the door, enter, and lower herself on to the floor in the lotus position with practised ease. She would close her eyes in meditation and keep her hands folded in a prayerful gesture until further instructions from Pran Nath, who was now referred to as 'Gurrujee' by everybody. He seemed much more solicitous about her welfare than he had ever been about ours and we were human enough to be jealous. Their communication consisted of hand gestures, nods, smiles and single words of English, such as 'eat', 'hot', 'good', 'tired', and so on. It seemed perfectly adequate, even when subtler expressions were called for. Once Pran Nath demonstrated for her benefit how magical a well-tuned tanpura could sound. At the end of what was a riveting experience for all of us he turned to her, smiled as though he was humouring a child, and asked, 'What? Anything?' She nodded vigorously and smiled back. 'Ya, ya, something's happenin' right here', she said hitting the top of her head with her hand. 'I feel a fantastic vibration, as though the whole of my kundalini is wakin' up', she confided to Madhu.

Not long after this we heard with sinking hearts that Pran Nath had been invited to America by a group of fans and that he had made up his mind to—what these fans called—'relocate'. It was true that he had not received the recognition he deserved in his own country, except from a handful of erratic connoisseurs. Now that he had a choice for the first time in his life, he had decided to take the plunge and seek fame and fortune elsewhere. Madhu and I were very worried about him, but felt helpless. It was also the sad end of a long and arduous journey for us, with the destination nowhere in sight. We felt orphaned and desolate. The frank relief our families felt at his exit was an added mortification. He on his part had no worries about what would happen to our musical dreams and advised us to carry on, repeating his depressing adage that this business was only for the contentment of the soul. I remember feeling that my soul would never be the same without Pran Nath to challenge and starve it.

The emptiness we felt the day he left for New York was like a first-hand experience of death. We knew that he was not coming back, even if things didn't work out for him. Madhu and I went to enormous trouble to ferret out vague acquaintances in the USA who would find out for us how he was and give us news of him. We knew him well enough to know that he himself would never look back or write to us. He had too neat a mind for that. The first news we got through a hotelier who had once taken lessons from him and was now studying journalism at Columbia was that he was surviving by giving concerts for the discerning few in artists' lofts and small art galleries in Soho. Another source informed us six months later that he had a small following of young American composers of New Music, but that he was still impoverished and that it was still a struggle.

A year later, I ran into the wife of an officer of the Indian Consulate in New York who was on home leave in Delhi. She had read an article on Pandit Pran Nath in *Village Voice,* an avant-garde weekly of New York, in which an admirer had thrown light on his theory of raga therapy. Apparently, every human ailment could be cured by treating it with the right musical intervals. The tranquil shuddha gandhar or the major third that occurred in all ragas of the Kalyan family had the power to reduce blood pressure. The flat second of the raga Bhairav could cure kidney ailments, and the two madhyams or fourths as used in Kedara could vanquish the most stubborn insomnia. Some lesser known ragas had intervals that could even dissolve gall stones. But this miraculous healing could happen only if the sound treatment was in accordance with the tonic '*sa*' of each individual patient. The pitch of the tonic was worked out with the aid of an electronic gadget invented by one of Panditji's new pupils. This contraption was placed on the navel while a stethoscope-like arm measured the natural sound of the prospective patient's humming breath and calculated the pitch of the tonic. It was stressed in the article that it was crucial to determine the correct '*sa*' in each case first, otherwise the body could easily mis-hear and misinterpret the raga or ragas that were dispensed, and things could get even worse.

News about the sensational success of the raga therapy venture continued to trickle in at regular intervals from various sources. His clientele consisted mostly of affluent American women who had been round the world at least once and were already familiar with Yoga, Taichi, and acupuncture. Within two years, Pran Nath had consolidated his financial position. He was able to abandon raga therapy and rent a small apartment where he both lived and gave lessons in vocal music. As I was to discover on my own a few years later, New York had a sizeable floating population of innovative young musicians who were fascinated by Indian classical music and the new ways it opened up for them of looking at sound. Many of these gravitated towards Pran Nath because they found in him a whole world of musical possibilities to be explored and studied. He on his part responded richly to the recognition, outdoing himself in insight and musical creativity, and offering a wealth of wisdom that answered their spiritual and personal needs. After some time it seemed natural for him to grow a beard. He was soon hailed as a rare 'happening' in New York and treated by several famous and influential art enthusiasts as a fantastic discovery. A close associate brought the incredible news that he was happy and that so far as material comforts were concerned, good times had been sighted at last. Though it was Pran Nath who had been the father figure, we felt the sort of relief and elation parents feel when a wayward child has done unexpectedly well at school.

It took us a year to pick up the threads of our musical life 'after Pran Nath'. He faded as a live presence but not as an influence which was for us synonymous with good taste in music. Every other year or so he visited Delhi, and when he was in town we would rush to his house in a state of high excitement. He seemed very different somehow though we could not put our finger on it. He was quieter, more tense, better dressed, much more businesslike in speech and not very comfortable in our company. After five or ten minutes he used to bring the meeting to an end by standing up, folding his hands in a namaste, and loudly wishing us the best. There was no doubt that he had entered a new life where all the rules were different from what we had known together. He had no interest in going backwards though we felt his attachment to us as a lifelong bond.

My next real contact with him took place fifteen years later, when my husband took up an assignment with the UNO and we had to move to New York. In the intervening years I had continued my search for a teacher and had found what I had been looking for. Every musical ambition I had ever nursed had been fulfilled many times over. I had appeared in the National Programme of All India Radio within a year of being accepted as a disciple by Fayyaz Ahmed Khan of the Kirana school, and had been invited to perform at the Harballabh festival for five years running. Things had been going pretty well for me until the move to New York which at first seemed both a break and a dead-end, though Grandfather had of course been transported to our flat in Manhattan in a huge coffin-like case. I slowly unpacked and tuned the instrument, my voice, and my spirit, and started working on music again. I was longing to see Pran Nath though I had heard that he had taken a dim view of my going to another teacher behind his back. Nor did he think much of my worldly efforts to succeed as a singer in the eyes of the public. His disappointment had been conveyed to me several times through the local grapevine in Delhi but I was sure that the affection we felt for each other would outweigh everything else.

It was easy enough to find his telephone number but to be able to speak to him was another matter. He was usually in the middle of his pooja, or meditation, or classes, or rest, and could not be disturbed. I was passed to several assistants and pupils and given a specific time two days later when I could ring again if I wanted to speak directly with him. Clearly he was now a celebrity and in the middle of a life he could not share. When I finally reached him, he sounded tired and spoke in a funereal tone, asking about the welfare of everyone in Delhi perfunctorily. I offered to postpone my visit to a time when it would be easier for him to accommodate me. This was not acceptable and he almost ordered me to come and see him at once. 'It is years since I have laughed, or spoken like an ordinary person. I am happy that I will see you after so long.'

I had never been inside such a large residential building in New York city. Coming from the mid-town area of small apartments it looked like the entrance to a private museum. I was screened by a receptionist and had to enter my name in a register. Then I was escorted in an old-fashioned lift to the fifth floor which was 'Gurrujee's living quarters'. The other floors were also part of his establishment. Classes, research, meditation, community cooking, and a permanent exhibition of mobiles and electronic tanpuras were some of the activities that went on in the house which had the atmosphere of an ashram—a haven to which one could retreat. I saw dozens of earnest young people, American, European, and Japanese, going about their business quietly, though I could not tell what it was. It was all quite overwhelming. I was asked to take off my shoes before being ushered into the presence of Gurrujee. About twenty pairs were already neatly lined up against the wall. My first view of Pran Nath in his own milieu in New York made an unforgettable picture.

He sat serenely on a divan in an enormous loft with a thick, snow-white wall-to-wall carpet. At the far end, about twenty tanpuras, obviously newly imported from India, lay side by side. The sunlight streamed in through tall glass windows. There was no furniture. On the wall behind him hung an enlargement of the only known photograph of his teacher, Ustad Abdul Wahid Khan, in which he looked like a ruthless executioner. I felt like falling at Pran Nath's feet and telling him how much I loved and respected him in spite of everything that had happened, but something told me that he would not appreciate such a display. I touched his feet and stood in front of him smiling weakly, unable to say anything. He rose from his seat, walked grandly up to me, and patted the top of my head. 'Cha', he said to the two pupils who were in attendance. They melted away dutifully to fetch the tea and then he gave me a smile which I can only describe as mischievous.

'I heard you on the radio. You are singing now. That is a courageous thing.'

'Did you think it was all right?'

'Well, I heard only a part of it. It is very difficult for me to listen to everything. You know that. I suppose for some tastes it would do. So long as it satisfies you. . . . What more can I say?'

The tea arrived and he fussily insisted on my tasting all the exotic snacks that had come with it. This was quite unlike him. After fifteen minutes someone came to take him to a class he was teaching and he told them to go ahead so that he could have a moment alone with me. I realized that I had been given a fifteen-minute audience, which was a very special thing.

'Regardless of how you sing, you will always be my daughter', he said with a catch in his throat. He took my hands in his and pressed a twenty-dollar bill into my palm. This was a shock to me and I began to protest loudly. He held a finger to his lips and looked furtively about him to make sure no one had seen what he had done.

'This is for your taxi fare. It is an old tradition, don't you know. A married daughter when she visits her father is always given her fare as a blessing. Say no more about it. You and I have long accounts to settle.'

I cried all the way back home in the taxi but I was also elated. After this it became a norm for him to telephone me and ask me to come and see him. I confided my frustration at being in New York where I thought I could do nothing in my field. He was reassuring and asked me to be patient. Our meetings were always short and always ended with his pressing money into my hands secretly. My husband simply refused to believe this when I told him. At this time, I really needed pocket money of my own and what he gave me was far more useful and valuable for me than he could ever have guessed.

A few months later, he asked me to come and give a recital in his loft. He sat on the same divan on which I had first seen him. There was a grave looking, silent and unsmiling audience of about sixty followers of Pran Nath who sat crosslegged on the thick white carpet, preparing themselves for the 'listening experience' they had been promised. Some had their eyes closed and some stared unblinkingly into the middle distance. I tuned up and plunged into the depths of raga Yaman. I felt I was baring my entrails for their inspection without being able to move them in the least. Nothing stirred in that space except waves of cold silence. In the shadow of the sneering expression of Ustad Abdul Wahid Khan's turbanned portrait, I felt like a mosquito with too much ambition. Pran Nath looked detached and non-committal. I was gripped by nervousness, my stomach suddenly a heaving blanket of fluttering butterflies. What if New York rejected me? What on earth was I going to do with myself if the music did not work?

I learnt within a month that I had not read my first audience right. They just had a different style of listening and did not feel compelled to share everything they felt with the entire community. My recital had been quite a success and Pran Nath was satisfied with my efforts. I was inundated with requests for lessons and invitations to perform. Very quickly my home became a sort of day school for advanced students of 'voice'. I had more than twenty students, some of whom were really talented. Many had been sent to me by Pran Nath himself. He rang me up and told me that I would enjoy my stay in New York. This turned out to be prophetic. An extremely intense and rewarding phase began in which I was thinking more deeply about traditional music than I had ever had occasion to before because so many well-informed people were asking me genuine questions which I had to find answers to. I was invited to seminars and lecture demonstrations all over the country. I gave concerts regularly, on the east coast as well as the west coast, and performed on the radio. I found the teaching I was doing most fulfilling, though there were some neurotic and hysterical women who regarded their lessons as a sort of therapy, a change from regular sessions with their psychoanalysts.

'I feel really strong after Bhoopali. I think there is something parental about the pentatonic ragas. They really wanna take care of you. The others are plain hostile and make me all weepy!' one of them whom my family called Barbara the Red had once said.

'Gee! I feel the colour of Bageshwari all over my skin, a sort of yellow-orange! It's ah-some, really. What I don't understand is the slow morning ragas that go on for ever and ever. They make me wonder whether the day in India ever picks up; if you know what I mean', was another memorable quotation, from Barbara the Brown this time.

Notwithstanding this sort of thing, my musical life in America had become a runaway success so far as I was concerned. It took me a year to get the full impact of what Pran Nath had set out to do for me and succeeded in doing. He now had everything he had ever craved—prosperity, fame, influence, and veneration. The struggles and frustration were behind him and perhaps for the first time he even had the leisure to love. He had simply decided to wave a magic wand which would change my life into something wonderful. He had that power. There was something maternal about his silent, undemonstrative concern. In the early days of our acquaintance, I could never have imagined him in this role. Nor could many other old associates who also had astounding stories to tell about the good turns he had gone out of his way to do for them.

After I returned from a concert tour which he had arranged for me in San Francisco and Los Angeles, he rang me up to ask how it had gone. As though this was not overwhelming enough, he insisted that I bring my husband to dinner at his house the next day. There was nothing for it but to comply. I made an issue of this with my husband who first hemmed and hawed but finally capitulated. I suspected that despite his protestations about how he would be out of place and have nothing to say, he had a certain involvement with Pran Nath, his old adversary. At any rate he was curious. They would be meeting after nearly twenty years.

When we were ushered into his presence, Pran Nath screwed up his eyes trying unsuccessfully to find the forbidding man he had once known in the mellow, greying figure that stood before him. He himself looked so much like a benign saint that my husband, who had always seen in him an unprincipled exploiter, stared in disbelief at the metamorphosis. Conversation was not easy but Pran Nath was the perfect host. There were dozens of devoted disciples waiting in the wings for the smallest sign from him, ready to do his bidding. We could not tell when the signal to bring in the wine was given. My husband was a connoisseur and I could tell as soon as he took a sip that he thought the Beaujolais quite marvellous. Neither Pran Nath nor I took any. He was really entertaining a son-in-law in the old-fashioned way. This suddenly dawned on me and tears stung my eyes.

We moved to another floor for dinner. Another lot of followers were working quietly in an enormous kitchen, cutting up fresh vegetables, tossing salads, stirring huge bowls, and checking the ovens. Wonderful fragrances filled the air. Two smiling Japanese girls brought in platters of delicately cooked chicken breast and fish and placed them on a vast dining table that could easily seat twenty-five people. There were yogurt raitas of many kinds, steamed vegetables that looked like a painting, and an unforgettable fruit drink called Machu Pichu. It would have been both an exquisite meal and an aesthetic experience if our minds had been on eating. We were both tongue-tied and uncomfortable. Pran Nath wore the intent expression of one who is piously performing a prescribed ritual. My husband still looked frankly incredulous that he of all people should be at the receiving end of such lavish hospitality from this source.

We took leave as soon as we could, and Pran Nath also looked relieved, though he patted my husband on the back and asked him to come again. My heart was full and I bent down to touch his feet. He raised me by the shoulders, took my hands in his and pressed the usual twenty-dollar bill into my palm so that nobody else could see what he had done. I wished fervently that Madhu and the other friends from the early days could have seen him in this incarnation. His face was inscrutable but in his eyes I saw the undemanding, all-giving love of a mother.

As we stepped out into the cold air of the street, I had the strongest feeling that he had been trying to say something to me. Perhaps it was that he had completed his account with life according to his own lights and was at peace with himself at last.

SEVEN

Begum Akhtar to the Rescue

'He is the greatest teacher of the Kirana style. There is no one like him. Of course, he is a little . . .'

This was everybody's opinion about Fayyaz Ahmad Khan. But the unfinished phrase 'he is a little . . .' at the end was always accompanied by a vague gesture and an inscrutable facial expression which were difficult to read, more so because they varied with each person who ventured a view. A little what, I used to wonder impatiently, because it was extremely important for me to know. The way it was said, it could mean eccentric, demanding, fussy, strict, hard to please, difficult to get on with or none of these things. In any case I gathered the impression that anyone who had ever learnt from him or worked with him had no choice but to reel under the impact of the experience for the rest of their lives. Judging from the accounts of many of his pupils and associates he was like an infection that started in a quiet way but gradually built up to an untreatable condition in which his view of music and its values dominated everything.

I was intensely interested in him because I was convinced, for a number of reasons, that at this stage of my musical life, only he could heal me and lead me out of the mire in which I had been stuck for so many arduous years. Music had started as a beautiful dream for me but had gradually turned into a sort of chronic despair, like the permanent loss of a loved one. I could neither have it nor forget it. It was not that I was particularly ambitious. But I did feel that unless I found a way of expressing myself through the singing style I had chosen in my mind, I would just stop existing altogether and fall to the ground in meaningless little pieces. I had passed through the hands of several dogmatic and frustrated teachers each of whom had been at pains to convey, one, how wonderful they themselves were though unappreciated by an ignorant and unfair world, and two, how unattainable professional musicianship was for someone in my 'position'. What they meant by this was that I was someone from a 'respectable' family with a husband and children to take care of and a whole-time job the basis of which was 'a first class English education'. This last specially made me an outcaste, tolerated and patronized only because of my addiction to music. I was allowed by the professional world of music to amuse myself with radio programmes and house concerts like many gifted amateurs but it was assumed that entry to the inner circle was not for the likes of me. 'The level you have achieved is really creditable considering all your other preoccupations. This is a difficult business even for us', I was often told by accompanists after a concert or radio broadcast. The superior tone used to gall me because I felt it was not a genuinely professional opinion, at least not all the time. The inspiration for such jibes was mildly trade unionist in nature and reflected the official stance of the mirasis, or practising professionals born to the trade, towards outsiders threatening to encroach on territory which had so far been their exclusive preserve. I knew at least a dozen other women from 'respectable' backgrounds who reported the same sort of resistance while trying to enter the serious concert circuit on the strength of their merit.

I practised hard and felt intense love for the music I had garnered from diverse sources over the years, but the skills required for the coherent expression of what was within somehow continued to elude me.

At one point in my life I was bullied into learning from a heavyweight Sanskrit scholar who compulsively pursued everyone who could possibly become a devotee. Once captured, his victims had little chance of escape. His energy was overwhelming and his technique was to bludgeon his coterie regularly with examples of his limitless knowledge and versatility and then declare, in effortless, colloquial prose, that only he could show them the right way. I had also been conquered and sat at his feet day after day learning his compositions. He worked tirelessly on these for many hours every day with pen and paper, exclaiming over their beauty and pointing out that they were not marred by imperfections like the traditional material of long ago. I remained in a state of stupefaction and paralysis for about a year. During this time I would enthusiastically treat my friends to the manicured and deliberate songs I was being taught. I had been so successfully brainwashed about the merits of these pieces that I was unable to exercise my own aesthetic and musical judgement. I was briefly intoxicated with the rhythm control I had newly acquired and bored everyone who was willing to suffer me with expositions of my teacher's latest masterpiece.

One of the people who humoured and encouraged me through this period of confusion was the great singer Begum Akhtar. She had been a legend and my idol all through my adolescence. I had had a chance to meet her personally a few years earlier, and felt an instant bond of friendship which I cherished beyond measure. I was drawn to her like millions of others but she became especially fond of me because I made her laugh. I was a good mimic and my stories about the different kinds of snobbery I came across in my life in Delhi amused her greatly. Her favourite piece was a depiction of the musical performance of a new bride of the Mathur Kayastha community to which I belonged. But she was also sympathetic to my aspiration to develop as a musician and listened with apparent pleasure whenever I sang for her seriously. I couldn't help unleashing the compositions of my scholar-teacher for her, parroting what he had said about their finer points. When I did that, she nodded and smiled indulgently, though without enthusiasm. This sort of music was really not her style but I knew that she wished me well. Every time she came to town she would send for me and we would have a long session in her hotel room along with her other friends and followers. There was always serious singing at first. This was invariably followed by uproarious stories and take-offs which we all enjoyed even more. Things went on like this for many months.

She was given to occasional attacks of melancholy which could last for days and were as much a part of her as her sparkle. During these times she was inconsolable though her friends never gave up trying to cheer her up. In this frustrating process, I discovered that the only role in which she felt really comfortable was that of the wronged woman. She was fully persuaded for the moment that her life was made up of unbearably tragic happenings and that these constituted reality. She lived each moment intensely, emoting inwardly, languishing like an exquisite orchid in a thick undergrowth of betrayals, never allowing the sun's rays to dispel her favourite disillusionments. Her heart remained permanently pierced by a dagger which some unfeeling and insensitive person was twisting. Devotees who had sworn undying loyalty had turned against her; men whose faithfulness was life itself to her had proved false; friends had tried to lace her drink with deadly herbs and secret concoctions that would cause her to lose her voice; relatives had used her and robbed her of her rights and possessions; and people who pretended to be worshippers had gone behind her back and made insulting remarks about her publicly. No one knew for certain whether or not any of these unspeakable things had happened. But if they hadn't, she would have had to invent them. It was an inner need which couldn't be denied though she rarely shared her alleged misfortunes with anyone. She just wore a sense of them like an exotic perfume. I am sure that this contributed in some way to her being a fantastic performer. The restraint and style with which she donned her mantle of grand tragedy added immeasurably to her image. Her confidences and disclosures were strictly only for those she wished to be close to. In a childlike way she needed proof of the love of her friends. The simplest test was to confront them with a set of misfortunes, wait for their sympathy and savour its quality. In the presence of casual acquaintances, she conducted herself with the greatest reserve and dignity. But whether she confided in them or not, people invariably succumbed to her potent charm and there were many stories afloat of poets and artists who were obsessed with her personality and wanted to die for her.

Her real name was Akhtari Bai. When I was a young girl, I used to listen again and again to the last few seconds of her commercial discs just to hear her announce in her then high-pitched voice, 'My name, Akhtari Bai, Faizabad', in accordance with the practice in the early thirties. Hearing her normal speaking voice at the end of the music gave me the sensation that I was meeting someone out of a story book because she was the subject of many romantic stories that I had caught snatches of in our home many times. Judging from the way grown-ups dropped their voices when retailing them, I guessed that most of these stories were not for the ears of children.

One of these concerned the head of an affluent princely state who fell so deeply in love with her voice and face that he carried her off to his palace and held her in luxurious imprisonment for many years. She was showered with gifts and allowed to wear the priceless heirlooms of the state, including a fabulous satlada, a seven-stringed pearl necklace, the last strand of which touched her ankles when she sat down. The nawab was rumoured to have said openly in the palace that the only thing brighter than the seven diamond pendants of the famous necklace was Akhtari Bai's smile. However, his fixation soon made her claustrophobic and she began to resent her gilded cage. Partly as revenge and partly as a game to test her power in the state, she ordered coins to be struck in her name and had them embossed with her profile. She was quite aware that here she was crossing some kind of limit but far from stopping her, the feeling intoxicated her and made what she was doing seem even more exciting. In any case, she thought it was time to bring matters to a head and this seemed a stylish way of doing just that. When the nawab's intense devotion began to turn into displeasure as a result of this incident, which she steadfastly regarded as nothing more than a lark, her mood changed to one of anger. She expressed this by decamping with the necklace, no doubt to teach him a lesson. The nawab's men were despatched in hot pursuit but could find her nowhere because she immediately stopped singing publicly and went underground.

When she emerged years later, it was as Begum Akhtar, the respectable wife of a lawyer from an eminent family of

Lucknow. The protection of such a husband made all the difference. The wild and now outdated allegations of the princely state seemed absurd. She gradually returned to the concert platform and took the country by storm once again, this time with much more class and sophistication than before. This was an often told story. If anything, her association with the affair of the fabulous jewels of the princely state further enhanced the glamour of her name.

There was another irresistible fairy tale which many people swore was true because they personally knew several eyewitnesses. This concerned a poet who literally went mad for love of her and began to spend his days and nights silently writing her name with chalk on the streets of Lucknow, the city where she lived. Her name, Akhtari, was to him the only poetic word he could think of. It was said that he continued his maniacal activity until he was too exhausted to move. One morning passersby found him lying dead in the middle of a main street. Once a friend indelicately asked her about this quite well-known story in my presence, and she burst into volleys of her characteristic laughter which we all loved so much. To her it was a perfectly adequate response to the friend's question about the identity of the mysterious admirer. Her laughter was a clear, intense sound, something in between a gurgling stream and a tinkling bell. If it went on too long, it could sometimes become faintly hysterical but on normal days it was a spontaneous, full-hearted acknowledgement of both the wonderful and horrible things that went on in her extraordinary life. There is no question that she was addicted to its highs and lows and would have been bored if things had progressed on an even keel. Her natural bent was to turn the most unremarkable event into something scandalous, hilarious, or dramatic.

A perfect example was a recital in Patna where she was sharing the evening's programme with the young and beauteous sitar wizard Rais Khan. This triggered off a series of extraordinary incidents which could have happened only to her.

'I was waiting in the green room looking through my note-book, trying to decide which poets and which ghazals I would present to this city of Urdu scholars and connoisseurs. And then my dear, what do I hear but Rais Khan trying to sing a ghazal instead of playing his sitar! I had never been so insulted in my life! I swore to myself that at my next concert I would not sing but play the sitar instead! That would teach the little colt a proper lesson. He dared to sing a ghazal when he knew that the audience was waiting for me to do that! Can you believe this?', she asked, fixing me with eyes still burning with indignation at the memory.

I could believe it. Piecing things together I knew that no insult had been intended but I didn't dare to say so as that would have been clear proof of my infidelity and would have brought on another emotional outburst. It was normal practice for the junior artiste to open the evening and for the senior one to end it. Apparently Rais Khan had opened his recital with serious raga elaborations on the sitar, but as the audience warmed up he began to sing the compositions in his attractive, tuneful voice. Soon the less cultivated sections of the house were clamouring for his brand of romantic, pop ghazals of the film variety, moment-arily oblivious of the high-quality fare of this genre that Begum Akhtar had in store for them. Obviously Rais Khan could not resist the chance to bring the house down and started to croon and throb with the crowd in the hope that he would floor them. It was easy to reconstruct what must have happened and perfectly clear to me that the poor innocent had intended no dagger for

Begum Akhtar's heart. But she was convinced otherwise and could not be deflected from her vengeful course.

'I decided to do something about this impertinence right away. I summoned Muhammad Ahmed and asked him to take a message from me to his friend Vilayat Khan saying that in all seriousness I wanted to become his shagird in order to learn to play the sitar. I had the music in me already. All I needed was a little guidance in playing technique. If I was going to learn, it might as well be from the greatest master there is, don't you think so?'

'Yes, yes, of course', I agreed tamely, wishing I had the guts to try and moderate her views.

'Vilayat Khan was quite excited at the prospect. I mean it was quite a scoop. Can you imagine what kind of headlines this partnership would have made in the verbal bulletins of the music world! Muhammad Ahmed came back with the glad tidings of his acceptance the same evening and demanded sweets! He told me Vilayat Khan's family couldn't believe their luck and were celebrating already. As for me, you know I have no false pride. If there is someone who can teach me something I value, I would gladly go to him in all humility. So I got myself a good instrument and started preparing my gifts and offerings for my new guru. When my initiation was only a day away, Muhammad Ahmed dropped in and told me sheepishly that Vilayat's mother had been making enquiries about what I intended to offer as nazar. She had hinted that the diamond ring I had made from one of the pendants of a necklace I had once received as a gift from a princely state would be a suitable offering for this great occasion.

' "And what did the maestro himself have to say to that?" I asked Muhammad Ahmed, beginning to lose my temper. When he said that Vilayat Khan had found the idea attractive, I flew into a rage. How dare anyone tell me what to offer as a gift? I might have given him ten times as much on my own, but to be led by the nose in such a delicate matter! It was insufferable. I made up my mind to never become the disciple of such a man even if he offered me a dozen diamond rings to do so. Not only that. I would teach him a lesson that he would never forget. I told Muhammad Ahmed to take himself off and go and tell him just that.

'And then I decided I would become the disciple of a sweet and mild vegetarian gentleman who was a pupil of Vilayat Khan. And I would widely advertise the fact. That would really gall and humiliate Vilayat Khan. He would never be able to forgive himself for his miscalculation. And I would never let him forget what he had missed!'

She was as good as her word. She turned up at the house of the mild and blameless pupil with the gifts that had been originally intended for his illustrious ustad and literally badgered him into accepting her as a disciple. He did not know what had hit him. She made it a point to fall at his feet in public places, specially where the maestro would see the spectacle himself. In cases where this was not possible, she made sure that it would be reported to him in detail so that he could burn with agony at what might have been and what had eluded his grasp because of his failure to treat her like the lady she was.

In actual fact she took only three desultory sitar lessons spread over a period of eight months in which lots of other more engrossing and important things were happening in her life as usual. Once she had taken action to redress the 'insult' to her person, she lost all further interest. Needless to say she never played the sitar on stage as she had threatened to do and when she accidentally met the much misunderstood Rais Khan at a wedding, she was charm and amiability itself, all grudges and complaints totally forgotten. The same was true of Vilayat Khan too. She had nothing but friendliness and goodwill for him at a function held in Delhi to celebrate his birthday. I remember watching her in amazement as she beamed at him. The duel was clearly over, and the fact that it had been a bloody one only enhanced in her mind the high quality of the sport.

On one visit to Delhi she fell into a deep depression and stayed in bed for three days, drinking and weeping uncontrollably about imagined tragedies that had overtaken her. When I went into her room to see her, she asked me almost mechanically what I had been learning from my scholar guru and demanded to hear the latest addition to my repertoire. It was a chhota khayal in honour of the god Ganesha in which the deity was addressed as Lambodar, meaning the one with the big belly, and the stress fell on the opening syllable, which was '*lam*'. The remaining two syllables, '*bo dar*', formed an independent melodic line. The name was fractured into two pieces to fit neatly into the beat. Every variation ended in the climactic, heavy and rather clumsy '*lam*', after which there was meant to be a pregnant little pause before the '*bodar*' took off again. I was hoping my singing would divert Begum Akhtar from her unhappiness, whatever its cause. Indeed, she wiped her eyes and turned her attention to the song. I sang two cycles without much reaction from her. And then it happened, in the third cycle. In the pause after '*lam*', she screwed up her eyes in an effort to concentrate, and a titter escaped this most cultured and polite person. Considering the state she was in she couldn't help herself. But once she let herself go, she couldn't stop laughing. Finally she let her remaining guard down and said, her words slurred but unmistakable, 'My dear, your music doesn't merely have a funny smell any longer. Now it just plain stinks!' Having brought this out, she burst into a fresh flood of tears and fell back on the bed.

I was devastated but I had to wait for her to be sober before I could find out what remedy if any she had in mind for me. There was no one whose musical judgement I trusted more. I had no choice but to wait it out. I sat in a dark corner of the room quietly sobbing into the palla of my sari. It took more than six hours before faces were washed with cold water and a big pot of coffee ordered. 'You have to tell me what to do, where to go', I said as soon as I could. 'Bitia, there is only one man who can take you where you want to go. It is Fayyaz Ahmed Khan of the Kirana gharana. He and his brother Niaz Ahmed teach in Bombay.'

To me this seemed an insurmountable difficulty. We didn't have the resources for me to be able to undertake frequent journeys to Bombay though there I had my most supportive younger brother with whom I could have stayed. I needed the job I had in the Publications Division and my children were still small. I mumbled all this to her.

'If he accepts you as a disciple, all these will be his worries, not yours. He will find a way. You will see.'

I felt like someone with an undiagnosed terminal illness. My only hope seemed to be to throw myself at this new pair of feet located more than a thousand miles away. I sent urgent messages to the proposed healer through friends in Bombay, requesting that I be accepted as a disciple. The reply I received was civil enough. 'She is welcome any time to come and learn whatever she wishes. There is no need for the formality of shagirdi.' The rejection in this message was unmistakable and this time I was really stung. I was no longer interested in buying music lessons by the yard. I wanted this ustad to take total responsibility for me. That is what discipleship meant. I honestly didn't think I was unworthy of it. I was deeply motivated, mature, hard-working, and sincere. My voice, ear, talent, musical imagination and spirit had always been acknowledged and praised by all. I considered myself well educated, broadminded, and intelligent. I had been trying to study music for over twenty years. Why on earth would any teacher turn me down?

I tried several times, hoping that the first 'no' had been just a cultural reflex, or a temporary stance. It was no good. He really did not want to take me into his fold at all. At the next opportunity I cried on Begum Akhtar's shoulder again. As usual, she was most sympathetic. 'I have some rights on the Kirana gharana, because I have been a disciple of its leading light Ustad Abdul Wahid Khan. I'll see to it that they accept you. Bitia, you have everything that is needed. Just leave it to me.'

Three months after this Ustad Fayyaz Ahmed, his brother Niaz Ahmed, and Begum Akhtar happened to be in Delhi at the same time for a music festival. I got an urgent message in my office that I should go to Begum Akhtar's hotel room at once. When I entered, I knew that this day would make a difference to the rest of my life. The two Khan Sahibs were in the midst of a formal social call. I knew that they regarded Begum Akhtar as a senior professional colleague who had had close connections with their family. They were very proper and polite, somewhat intimidating in their starched white kurtas, on the whole looking like two immaculate snowflakes. The moment Begum Akhtar introduced me by name, they exchanged glances and I felt them stiffen a little bit. 'So, this is the one who is after us', their looks seemed to say, although they were perfectly gracious to me.

'Have you ever heard Sheila sing?' Begum Akhtar said. 'She is really very good. If you teach her, well, *kya kehene*! Nothing better could happen. Bitia, you must sing for Khan Sahib just now. There is no tanpura but that doesn't matter, does it, Khan Sahib? Now, go and fetch the harmonium from the dressing room and give Khan Sahib a sample of what you can do.'

After this speech, she leaned towards me and whispered in my ear fiercely while the two brothers were talking amongst themselves.

'Do the take-off on the Mathur Kayastha bride's maiden performance. Don't say a word by way of introduction. Just do it. *Hamari qasam!*'

The last two words, meaning 'may I perish if you don't', were a trump card she often used to get her way and to cut through possible ifs and buts that she had no patience with.

My rendering of the Mathur bride's transparent efforts to impress her audience of assorted in-laws with her high musical taste was something that never failed to make her hysterical with laughter. I had first presented it to her as an introduction to some culturally pretentious sections of the community I came from. But she had asked me to repeat it so many times that the piece automatically became more and more evolved and subtle. In the friendly aura of her responsiveness I was able to add many telling nuances to my audio-visual efforts. It seemed to me that each time it was a new portrait. Normally I would have enjoyed doing it for her for the umpteenth time, but to subject Ustad Fayyaz Ahmed Khan to it without provocation or preamble was a daring, reckless act which could end in disaster. I was extremely nervous and self-conscious but she left me no option but to jump in and just do it, whatever the consequences.

Needless to say my performance this time was half-hearted

and mechanical. At first the ustad took it as a sample of my singing. He looked outraged as I negotiated a melodic loop in which every tone was just slightly off key. He couldn't believe that Begum Akhtar would subject him to such torture, such impertinence. Her own face was wiped clear of all expression. I plodded on, slowly warming to my theme. It was when I was punishing the high notes of the antara and belting out the words in rhythmic variations straight out of some unwritten textbook on How to Sound Classical Even When Not Musical that the ustad's expression changed. He realized that I was doing a take-off. At the same moment a giggle escaped Begum Akhtar, with all the force of something long suppressed. For a split second, Fayyaz Ahmed Khan wasn't sure whether he should be amused or enraged at the audacity of the whole thing, but then the scales turned in our favour and he added a giggle of his own to hers. Soon they were both rocking with laughter and holding their sides. I was truly amazed at the acuteness and sensitivity of the ustad's listening. He knew exactly what I was doing without having any background about who I was depicting. He also knew what Begum Akhtar's purpose was in dreaming up exactly the sort of trap he would find irresistible.

'All right, Begum Sahiba, I will accept her as a disciple. I must say she has demonstrated extraordinary musical skill today. It is really very difficult to stay out of tune for so long. The way she was able to settle on a note between *sa* and *re*, a note that really doesn't exist, is praiseworthy indeed. As usual, you win!'

This was the promise of redemption that I had been hoping for. I lost no further time and requested that my initiation be taken in hand before Khan Sahib went back to Bombay. He agreed to come to my house the next day to finalize the arrangements for the ceremony and to set up a long-term teaching schedule for me. I still didn't know how the spiritual power of discipleship could overcome the distance between Delhi and Bombay but I took Begum Akhtar's advice. I assumed the attitude of a new-born baby with no worries of its own. As it turned out, this was the perfect decision and worked beautifully.

He came with his brother whom everybody called Maulana because of his piety and another relative who was a tabla player. At this time we lived in a magnificent government house on Race Course Road in New Delhi because a year earlier my husband had been inducted into the prime minister's secretariat as Indira Gandhi's adviser. The most attractive feature of the elegant colonial house designed by Lutyens was a wide, pillared veranda opening on to a huge green lawn surrounded by tall flowering trees. The lawn was so big that the servants called it a park. It was a winter afternoon, and a large family of partridges was walking close to the shrubbery against the distant garden wall. The jacaranda trees were alive with green parrots. I had set up the session with Khan Sahib on the veranda because it was the loveliest place in the house. I had heard that he took pleasure in beautiful views and hoped that he would associate our first meeting with something pleasant. The instruments, the silver paan-daan, the cushions, the tray of tea and snacks were arranged on a huge Kashmiri carpet. As it happened, the group of elderly peacocks who sometimes visited the garden chose this afternoon to drop in. They picked their way gingerly through the flower beds and perched on the garden wall, their tails swishing and glinting in the gentle sunlight. I prayed for a dance performance but that didn't happen. Even so the setting for my first real music lesson was memorable.

Fayyaz Ahmed Khan was a frail, dark man with a serene

face, but the eyes behind the gold-rimmed spectacles were sharp. He had a quiet manner but everyone else fell silent when he walked into a room. Physically nothing in him suggested extraordinariness. It revealed itself gradually, incident by incident, phrase by phrase, expression by expression, like a winding staircase slowly spiralling upwards without any end in sight. His deep and silent enjoyment of the scene in the garden was apparent to everyone though he didn't say a word. After some time, he turned to me and asked 'Which raga is on your mind these days?'

'Puriya Kalyan', I said excitedly.

'We will use that in our work, then. But the raga itself is not so important. It is only the clay, the raw material which the musician tries to shape and mould until it begins to speak. What is important and what our family has taught for generations is the skill that enables one to do this. Now I need to hear you sing this raga that you like so much. That will tell me a lot about what is to be done next. Just relax, and sing as if you were singing for yourself.'

Obviously I couldn't do that, but I went through the motions. It felt like a medical examination. I wanted to postpone finding out the result though it was the most urgent thing in my life.

'Maulana, the trouble is that she has a very good voice', he said to his younger brother after an uncomfortably long pause. Both of them shook their heads with grave concern, and were joined by the tabla player who understood their predicament much better than I did. Had I heard right? Were they all really mourning the fact that I had a good voice?

I boldly asked Khan Sahib what he meant.

'Learning music means learning the art of expressing what is within you through the traditional language of the raga. If the natural voice is rich and tuneful to begin with, it confuses and dilutes the learning process. Physical beauty is not always an asset. I have known good looking women who felt that they need not say or do anything more to be valued because their looks were enough of an achievement. In the same way, if the singing voice is pleasant and agreeable without any learnt skills, the task of implanting those skills becomes much more difficult and tricky, not easier. That is our experience.'

I was the only one for whom this reasoning was a novelty. They all seemed to take it quite for granted. But now that we were on the subject of teaching, I decided to ask Khan Sahib why he had not accepted me at first. This had been gnawing at me even though it was no longer a problem. I was very curious to know.

'There were two difficulties. First, you have been taught by so many teachers in so many conflicting ways that it would have been a problem to clean the slate and start all over again. I could have done it but it might have extinguished your inner fires. And if I had succeeded in making a singer out of you, God knows which of your dozen teachers would have claimed the credit! I didn't want to go into it at all. Circumstances forced me to know you, and I love a challenge. So here we are. The second problem was that you are too much of an English-speaking person. I am told that you studied English in England and America and that in your job you think and write in English. This can have serious repercussions on what you consider to be the sound of normal speech. I was sure your beak or "chonch" must already be bent out of shape for the purposes of Hindustani music. My objection was not a bigot's prejudice, but the recognition of a practical disadvantage in this enormous endeavour. My ancestors and I have worked our whole lives to be able to round off and mute the jagged and jerky sounds which are the mark of correct English speech. In our style of music, every melodic line is an unbroken arc and you can't build arcs like that with English sounds. I think that music is just refined speech. It has to draw on sounds from the indigenous language of the region. To say that music is a universal language is sentimental, wishful nonsense. Someone whose mother tongue is Urdu or Hindi has better prospects as a khayal singer than say, someone from Japan, however ardently interested. You will understand better what I am saying as we go along. I am sure you can never be a Japanese singer either!'

I wanted to be accepted wholeheartedly, without reservation, so I made a decision to renounce English. I gave up my job in the Publications Division and made a conscious effort to speak only in Hindustani or Urdu. In our lifestyle, it was natural for me to be bilingual but when I turned off the English switch entirely, the sounds in my head really changed. I felt myself change as a person too. I became less impatient, more tolerant, more lackadaisical. My Urdu became much better. Earlier, I used to be self-conscious about reciting ghazals that I had heard from my father in my childhood. I slowly became more comfortable with them though it still felt a little like being in fancy dress. I thought that the *sa* I practised in the morning sounded more and more relaxed as the sounds of English leached out of my system. Above all Khan Sahib was suitably impressed with my rather melodramatic resignation from a job I had enjoyed doing for nearly twenty years. My purpose was of course to demonstrate my dedication to Hindustani music. But there was something more. I was a romantic and just liked the intoxication of flamboyant gestures. So was my new ustad, I discovered to my great delight.

A wonderfully happy, heady period followed, starting with an elaborate shagirdi ceremony to which the entire music community of the city was invited. It involved a performance by me in the presence of the guests who were all professional musicians, my offering of clothes, money, sweets, gur and *chance* to the ustad, his tying of the sacred red thread round my wrist as a token of his acceptance of me, community prayers for the successful outcome of this association, and finally the wonderful feast of qorma and khamiri roti for all the two hundred or so people who had gathered for the occasion. I was definitely entering a new and far more colourful world than anything I had experienced before and was all agog.

My husband used to spend all his waking hours in his office and did not witness any of the exciting new events in my life. But he sensed the beginnings of a cultural shift which he did not seem to welcome. He had always been sceptical about my enthusiasms and was sure that this time too something or other would come crashing down. He had been exposed to many of my music teachers before and had uniformly disliked them all. But they had been no more than unpleasant scenery to him. What was happening now went much deeper. I donned an attitude of old-fashioned veneration for my guru with all the enthusiasm of the new convert and this was accepted and shared by everyone else who was close to me —my mother, who lived with us at this time, my children, my friends, and my younger brother in Bombay who was more involved with my musical life than anyone else. The old servants in our home actually welcomed the idea of a guru, any guru. It was comfortable and familiar as a concept and took them nearer to their own roots in some way that I did not quite understand. They waited hand and foot on the ustads, trying to anticipate their every need, leaving me free to concentrate on my lessons. On the whole it felt as though something religious had entered the fabric of our lives. The most rewarding time of my life followed my initiation. It lasted, miraculously according to my husband, for nearly ten years until Khan Sahib's death. I enjoyed every moment and every aspect of this association.

That first time he stayed on in Delhi in our house for about twenty days. For me it was blissful in many ways. I got a running start with the music. I felt it was the most intense training I had ever received, though Khan Sahib was always easy, relaxed and gentle. I also unexpectedly learnt about the pure Mughlai cuisine of the Delhi Muslims because I discovered with delight that Khan Sahib was a gourmet and that his wife who belonged to Delhi was famous in the entire community for her culinary skills. While I was practising, my mother and Khan Sahib sat happily together on the magnificent veranda of our house exchanging recipes. Our old cook was sometimes asked to sit in on these sessions which were like an advanced course in meat dishes. Khan Sahib didn't care too much for vegetables, but my mother who was also a great cook and could make even grass taste delicious got him interested in what he called 'fodder'. The food in our house had always been good since eating well is both a Mathur Kayastha and a Kashmiri Pandit preoccupation, but now it suddenly soared to new heights. Khan Sahib would laugh and say each dish was like a raga. It had its own distinctive bouquet to which the chef must be faithful if it was to give pleasure to others. Nahari, qorma, pasanda, and aloo gosht, all delicious and all dripping with oil, were some of the new additions to the household menu. My husband made a rare appearance at dinner one evening and asked in an even, academic tone whether this kind of fare was really good for the health. His innocent rhetorical question deflated all concerned and effectively put an end to any further development in this direction.

At least a dozen people came from Suiwalan and Chandni Mahal in the walled city every day to visit Khan Sahib while he was staying with us. I realized that he was an important link in a vast network of families related by blood, marriage, or musical affiliation. Word that he was in Delhi and staying with me at Race Course Road had spread like wild fire through people who worked as accompanists in All India Radio. Straggling groups of callers started to arrive from far-off places in little three-wheeled scooter taxis, taking a lot of trouble, and at considerable expense, for no other purpose than to pay their respects. I was amazed that this activity did not seem to require the physical presence of Khan Sahib. Even if he was busy giving me a lesson, or out for a recording session, his visitors would arrange themselves on the veranda and sit silently for hours together, without any expectation. When he finally did appear, he simply acknowledged their muttered greetings with a salaam. Beyond that there was absolutely no conversation. The visitors sat on regardless, emitting respect and deference like an invisible gas while Khan Sahib pulled up a cane chair a little distance away and basked in the emanation. Essentially, this was the substance of the entire ritual. The long, patient faces of the callers wore the expression of devotees gathering merit through an act of piety. The longer their vigil, the greater the merit they earned. I overheard whispered exchanges between groups about how many hours they had put in, much as aviators might total up their flying time. They represented a culture in which one waited hand and foot on eminence and age, speaking only when, and if, spoken to. I had not encountered such an extreme example of this before.

There were new faces every day. When they stayed through mealtimes, I would courteously invite them to come in and share whatever there was. This they would steadfastly refuse to do. Khan

Sahib who understood them well didn't insist either. I got the distinct impression that suffering and doing without were a part of the ritual which was being observed and he didn't want to dilute their efforts by pressing hospitality on them. I couldn't bear it beyond a point and tried to sneak in a tray of tea and biscuits to them after Khan Sahib had retired for his afternoon siesta so that they would not feel bashful. I saw that every last drop of liquid had been drunk and every crumb demolished when the cups and plates were collected in the evening, but nobody actually saw the callers eating or drinking. It was as though some fairies had come and taken the nourishment on their behalf. Once I got the hang of the whole thing, I made the trays much more substantial and timed them more carefully so that everybody was out of the way when they arrived. This worked pretty well. There were more and more visitors who stayed longer and longer while the fairies continued to do their good work.

Khan Sahib's siesta was not a conventional one in any sense. It was simply a time in which he disengaged from interaction with other people. During his stay with us he would go into the secluded arbour in the back of the house with the great stack of kites and reels of glassed thread he had bought in the city and spread them out on the ground so that he could feast his eyes on his new acquisitions and gloat. He could spend a whole afternoon just sunning the kites and lovingly turning them around in his hands. He would finger the thread and mark each reel with special and secret information about which variety to use in which circumstances. He was cagey about disclosing this information even to our cook who was not likely to be his rival in kite-flying in a thousand years. Or he would sit in an easy chair by himself leafing through any book of coloured pictures that he could find. He could gaze at the same page for as long as half an hour, imagining himself entering the picture. Sometimes he used to carry into the arbour a worn old notebook in which he scribbled Urdu couplets, or phrases for the text of a khayal composition that might be dogging him at the time, or draw laboured and detailed pictures of idealized flowers that could be plucked only from marble friezes off Mughal buildings.

After twenty exhilarating days, it was time for him to go back to Bombay. He was sure I had enough homework to last me a year. He had diagnosed and tried to treat all my musical ills and shown me how to work on my own. 'If you can come to Bombay once a year, for about twenty days, we can do it', he said. To me this sounded as though he had said 'you will live'. I used to go once a year to see my brother and his family anyway, but now these trips became a many-splendoured thing. I went to him at least once a year, for ten years, until his death. This time was in many ways the happiest phase of my life. My brother Rajesh identified totally with my aspirations and opened his life and his home with a full heart to provide the perfect environment for my sessions with Khan Sahib and his entourage. His beautifully kept, Western-style flat was adapted to all their needs, including deep respect, a plentiful supply of paan, and overflowing hospitality.

My sister-in-law Leila spared no effort in transforming one of the bedrooms into a most welcoming and comfortable baithak. Before Khan Sahib arrived in the morning with his younger brother Niaz Ahmed Khan and Muhammad Khan, a friend of theirs who was a tabla player, the furniture was pushed back and clean sheets and bolsters placed on the carpet along with a newly acquired paan-daan and a decorous little silver spittoon. The extension wires for the tape recorder and the microphone which were my lifeline at this point snaked and wound incongruously round these elegant appurtenances. Leila cooked wonderful, aromatic curries and always invited everyone present at the music sessions to eat lunch. Each meal was a feast. In between were several tea breaks when a huge tray would be brought in quietly and secreted in a corner of the room by the cook who had been trained to tiptoe into the music room like a ghost. The sessions could last the whole day. The only reliable way of deciding how much food had to be prepared for a meal was to count the number of shoes and chappals outside the door. Sometimes there were twice as many people as Leila expected because these lessons were an attraction to our friends as well as to Khan Sahib's own music circle, including other disciples. Many times the session was still in progress when Rajesh returned from his office late in the evening. He would join us, bringing with him an extraordinary mixture of wit, camaraderie, warmth and respect which delighted the Khan Sahibs. Over the years he developed an informal, back-slapping relationship of his own with my ustads.

Bombay became a magic word. I worked on music like a maniac and that was heady enough. But following Khan Sahib's path through his own life was also full of excitement and laughter. I was introduced to the family and pampered by his wife. I went with him to the homes of many other disciples and was amazed anew at his skill in devising teaching techniques tailor-made to fit every temperament. We constantly talked like schoolgirls about his great musical mind and his sensitivity. When he was in a good mood he could keep us in splits for hours by imitating various kinds of voices—idols from the silver screen, professional singers of marriage songs in his community, modern ghazal singers, sentimental singers of Rabindra Sangeet, fashionable society women of the city, pretentious classical singers trying to throw the whole book at you, and so on. Even though this was very funny, it was also an extremely subtle lesson in musical values each time. He also loved to tell stories and to listen if someone had a story to tell, which was not often because there was something intimidating about his piercing intelligence.

I discovered that the sophistication and subtlety of his mind ended with music. Outside that he was like a child. After giving you rare insights into ragas that left you gasping with wonder, he would go off to watch a Tarzan film in an 'airconditioned English cinema house', even though he could not understand the language. Or get lost for hours in playing carrom with much younger nephews. Or go to the Hanging Gardens to fly kites. He was always deeply absorbed in something or the other and it was not always music. It could as well be a dish his wife was cooking or a photograph of a mountain peak. He could gaze at anything that caught his interest for disconcertingly long periods, his gold-rimmed glasses balanced precariously almost at the tip of his nose, his eyes half closed in concentration, a forgotten paan in his hand on the verge of being eaten. Time seemed to stop altogether when he was like this. Sometimes it was a sign that he was in the throes of composition and that a tarana or khayal bandish was about to emerge.

My musical education during the Bombay sessions, which were about a month long, had all the intensity of a crash course. He was tireless and I pushed myself to the limit. Things seemed to be coming together for me at last. When I returned to Delhi I was moved to write long, grateful letters to him. We now had a common language in which I could communicate with him about my musical problems, but we did not have a common script. I knew only Devanagari which he could not read since he had studied Urdu and Persian. I was sure there would be someone in his vast circle of followers who could read out my letters to him. I hoped for a reply, however short, however indirect. After waiting more than two months, I got a letter written in a childish scrawl in the Devanagari script which turned out to be Khan Sahib's own handwriting. He had first asked for help in deciphering my letters, but then decided it would be simpler if he learnt the script himself. He told me later that it was child's play for him and had taken him no more than a week. Within a few months he was able to write Hindi in a perfectly acceptable adult fashion. I was overwhelmed that he at his age should have gone to such trouble but he made light of it and said it was easy compared to the things they had been trained to do. I still haven't been able to get over the fact that my ustad thought nothing of sending himself to primary school in his old age just so that he could communicate with me directly.

It was an extreme thing to do, but it was typical of him. He did not really believe in moderation. At least it didn't attract him as a value. There was no limit to what he was willing to do for a friend, or a pupil, or a project. But this generosity could evaporate with very little provocation. He was extremely touchy and could take offence at unbelievably trivial things. Once, another musician who was visiting the same house as Khan Sahib failed to greet him or return his greeting because he was in the middle of an animated discussion about the resting places in a raga with his host. Although no deliberate insult was intended, Khan Sahib wrote the offending musician off for life and proceeded to boycott every home where there was a possibility that he might drop in. This involved giving up connections and relationships he had had for years but no amount of reasoning could move him to change his mind. According to him when something went out of tune, it was best to throw it away.

'Music, friendship, love and beauty have different rules!' he declaimed. 'They are not old socks which can be used after they have been repaired and darned. They either are, or are not', he said decisively.

As for me, I certainly felt like an old sock which he had repaired—though the thought elated me. Within a year of being under his tutelage I found the musical idiom I had been looking for for more than thirty years. It was like being able to fly, hear and speak as never before. He had illuminated and made meaningful all the work I had put in and all that I had learnt through many dreary and unfruitful years. The amazing thing was that at no point had he let me feel inadequate. He had not rejected anything that I had collected in the course of my long, misguided journeys. All he had done was to rearrange the chemistry of the cells I was made up of. This had been done with such delicacy and gentleness that I had no inkling that I was being totally reconstituted until after the process was complete. For the first time in my life I felt like a whole singer.

This was not just a subjective feeling. Suddenly I was invited to appear in the National Programme of All India Radio. Exclusive music circles in Bombay, Calcutta, Jaipur, Hyderabad offered me concerts. I even made it to the fabled Harballabh festival. To me this was as great a miracle as the birth of my first son. I even cut a small disc for an established record company, though they were more interested in ghazals via my voice than classical music. About the same time I was offered the first television engagement of my life and it was in Bombay. Though I was not at all sure I could handle it, I was too greedy to refuse. The temptation to look successful even if I didn't sound good was too great for me to resist. Khan Sahib requested his old and trusted associate Muhammad Khan to accompany me on the tabla even though he was far too eminent for me. His presence would be an insurance against any kind of musical disaster, Khan Sahib felt.

The two of us turned up on a sweltering day in the Worli studios of Bombay Television. I was far more eager than Muhammad Khan who was well into his seventies and ready to retire having experienced it all many, many times before. The stern Maharashtrian lady at the reception desk glared disapprovingly at my white cotton sari and said tonelessly that it would not do. It had to be 'dark coloured', she insisted. The project could be processed no further unless this obstacle was overcome. She sounded as unrelenting as a government clerk asking for yet another original document. I should have abandoned the whole thing and gone home but couldn't summon up enough character to do that. I begged Muhammad Khan to wait for me until I made a quick dash to my brother's house and came back in more suitable dress. He gave in although the whole exercise was a terrible bore for him.

An hour later I entered the studios once again in an unlikely purple outfit that had belonged to Leila when she was much younger. In the hectic taxi ride back from the city, I had slowly absorbed the fact that the borrowed petticoat and blouse were much too tight for me but there was nothing I could do about it. Even though I couldn't breathe freely in them, I wasn't willing to cancel the recording. Muhammad Khan was waiting as he had promised to do, yawning loudly on the chair in the reception room. We approached the stern Maharashtrian lady once again, but the lines of her face had not softened.

'You go to ladies make-up room', she said in a dry, antiseptic tone, without looking up from the untidy copy books and slips of paper on which she was busily scribbling with an air of great importance.

By now Muhammad Khan, who knew the ropes but had temporarily lost interest in the proceedings, was looking out of the window with his back to us. 'What about . . . him?' I asked.

She raised her eyes, and remembered without interest that a male specimen had been a part of this incompetent ensemble.

'Men's make-up room', she said exasperatedly, as if she was having to explain something obvious to an idiot. 'Other side', she added, with a gesture of dismissal.

I ultimately found and entered the aforementioned ladies make-up room. This area was ruled by yet another stern Maharashtrian lady. She wore thick glasses and a facial expression so sour that it would have curdled milk if she had so much as looked at it. She waved me in the direction of a stool in front of a mirror and switched on the lights, exuding resentful resignation. Then she picked up a long-handled powder brush and briskly started to dust my face with it, her unsmiling face just inches away from mine. It was humiliating to me that she should be so cold and impersonal while she was physically so near me, handling my face and touching my hair. I would simply have to break the ice and get a smile out of her, otherwise I would not be able to get in the right mood to sing. As she attacked my face anew with eye-liner and lipstick, I desperately reached out to her.

'You are working really hard on my face', I said with a friendly smile. 'I wish I had the looks to match.'

This was a perfect approach to induce a thaw, I thought. I was wrong. She set her lips even more tightly, and continued to paint my face as though it was a brick wall.

'We are not doing for beauty', she almost sneered. 'We are only doing for technical.'

I was so deflated at this snub that the Shuddha Kalyan I was trying to nurse in preparation for the recording started to ooze out of me and drip on to the floor. The make-up expert had totally crushed me. Even she began to wonder whether she had overdone it. She decided to make amends, to soften the effects of the blow she had just dealt me.

'Very, very bad looking ladies coming here . . . even worse than you', she said comfortingly.

Her repair work on my spirits left me feeling worse. As I emerged from her domain, I sighted the shocking visage of Muhammad Khan in the corridor. The furrows on his aged face had been smoothed over with some pasty pink stuff. His bald spot was heavily brushed with powder so that the studio lights didn't bounce off it. His white eyebrows had been partially blackened and there was greasy colour on his parched lips. They had managed to make this staid and conventional artiste of seventy-two look like a retired pimp. When we were settled in the recording studio, I caught a glimpse of myself on a screen and was shocked a second time. I didn't look in the least out of place in the company of a retired pimp.

It was important for me to find my own tranquil centre before the recording started, so I closed my eyes and tried to summon up the raga I intended to present. But someone nudged me and pointed upwards. The official director of the programme was sprawled directly overhead and was trying to catch my attention through the transparent glass ceiling. His feverish hand gestures indicated that he wanted me to move a little to the left and a little forward. The cameraman wheeled in his equipment and began to explain what he wanted us to do.

'I'll start counting and moving towards you from about here', he said, indicating a spot at the far end of the studio. 'Ten, nine, eight, seven, like that, until zero, and then roll', he intoned, moving towards us with his camera in the crouching attitude of a hunter stalking a wild animal. 'When you hear zero, you have to start singing.'

If I had to watch with wide open eyes and listen tensely to a count-down, Khan Sahib's lessons about how to find the inner voice were obviously not going to work, I thought helplessly. Muhammad Khan whispered that I should relax and not take it all so seriously. After a few false starts, in which I began either a few seconds too early or too late, causing the cameraman to yell 'cut' each time, it was clear that the main thing I was required to do was to act, not produce music. I made the necessary mental adjustment with what I think was superhuman effort and we finally began to roll.

The first five minutes of the half-an-hour recording were sub-human but by the time I reached the exposition of the third note in the raga, the tranquil shuddha gandhar, the prospects for managing a decent presentation seemed less bleak. I was slowly getting into it, swaying and gesturing involuntarily as was usual for me. What was not usual was the too tight clothes I was wearing. As I negotiated a spontaneous run across the scale, I heard the dreadful sound of my petticoat tearing. It was so unexpected and inexplicable that it had the impact of a fire-cracker exploding in the studio. Muhammad Khan who was most attuned to the music looked up in incredulous horror, and fixed an accusing eye at me because the ripping sound had definitely come from my direction. From his mortified look I guessed that for him the sound had visceral associations. I was dying to proclaim my innocence to him but couldn't because any interruption would have completely wrecked the recording. Fortunately no one apart from the two of us noticed the disturbance and the rest of the performance was uneventful.

When it was aired a few days later, I watched it with a group of friends, carefully chosen by me for their uncritical support. I waited with bated breath for the embarrassing part, hoping against hope that the unfortunate intrusion would have been edited out by the authorities. But it had not. There it was, quite unmistakable, about ten minutes into the programme. Of course I was being subjective but it sounded even louder to me than it had done in the studio. All my friends looked questioningly at me but I countered with an equally puzzled expression. I wondered how they could have let it pass unless they had put the make-up lady in charge!

When the incident was reported to Khan Sahib by Muhammad Khan, who still did not know what had caused the awkward interruption in the recording, he dismissed it as a triviality unworthy of anybody's attention. However, he commented on the spiritless and indifferent singing and analysed my state of being at the time with uncanny accuracy.

I now knew with absolute certainty that he was the only real teacher I had ever had. I also discovered that the ability to transmit musical skills was a highly developed art which had a long tradition quite distinct from that of performers. It was rare for musicians to be masters of both. He was such a complete teacher that even something like stage fright and other psychological problems faced by performers were within his domain. When I told him again and again that I was nervous about my broadcast on the national hook-up, he said it was just my ego worrying about how I looked.

'This is all much bigger than you. Just add your lamp to the myriads that have been lit before. Do you care what people think of you when you are really in a state of prayer? If you do, you are not in the right frame of mind', he said.

'It's not that', I countered. 'I just wonder whether I am equipped to light the lamp at all!'

'You should never feel you are perfectly prepared. There is a sort of crudity in that feeling which can destroy the perfume in the music.'

He didn't say much more and left me to work it out for myself. I was aware that this was a one-pill remedy for nervousness, a sort of mantra one could recite to oneself on stage and lean on for support. Khan Sahib had evolved many such formulae for various types of musical ailments. Most of them were like balls of suggestive words that could change colour and meaning so that each individual could cull from them the maximum support and guidance according to their needs.

He told me once that although what I had sung was correct, the image it created was that of a 'baseet', which in the language of the musical community meant a boring person who did everything according to the clock. 'To say something worthwhile, some rules have to be broken, but this has to be done with style and faith', he used to say. 'If you take everything I have taught you literally, you will turn every fragrant young note into an ugly old hag before you are finished with it.'

EIGHT

Siddheshwari: A Bird of Paradise

When I was about eight, it seemed much more important to belong to an 'old family' than to a good school. The term was used as though it meant an exclusive tribe, which it certainly did in a way. We took for granted that we belonged to this tribe. At the time we knew only a dozen or so other old families in the city of Delhi. They all greeted one another when they passed in their horse carriages or cars on the roads. But there was not much of what was called 'inter-dining' in those days, probably because each family was large and socially self-sufficient.

The only occasion when an old family might have to go outside itself and relate to the entire tribe was a marriage celebration. When my grandfather was invited to a wedding outside the community with all the members of his household, it was something of an event. It was a welcome acknowledgement of 'old family' status and therefore had to be responded to but it was considered bad form to take it literally. So there was no question of the entire brood going to a wedding outside the community. But if one or two children were taken along by the elders, it was usually seen as a token of genuine warmth in the relationship between guest and host.

In our household there was a rough and ready system by which its thirty-odd children took turns at treats of this kind. My cousin and her mother had gone to the last wedding with my father so this time it was my turn. As the outcome of some such calculation, I found myself holding my grandfather's finger and trailing behind him at a glittering celebration in Kashmiri Gate, dressed in an incongruous yellow silk frock with embossed gold patterns which my mother had stitched overnight out of a sari in honour of the occasion. The silk smelt of sandalwood and roses and I felt rather grand altogether. The shiny maroon shoes of which my grandfather's clerk had bought several pairs 'for the girls' at a Chandni Chowk sale fitted only approximately, loose at the back and pinching badly at the toes. But to me this was less important than the beaded brass buckles that adorned the shoes, making me feel like a princess. When my mother said she felt the shoes didn't fit, I vehemently denied it lest it jeopardize my chances for what was clearly a visit to fairyland.

The access to the scene of the festivities was through a narrow lane which fanned out into an enormous courtyard. I remember my amazement at seeing a caparisoned elephant standing comfortably in the area, greeting guests by lifting its trunk into a salaam and trumpeting occasionally. Huge silver platters of hot savouries and fragrant, freshly-made sweets were being passed around by a large number of harassed but still obsequious family retainers who seemed more involved in the details of hospitality than the senior members of the family. The only function of the hosts seemed to be to bow, smile, and fold their hands continuously as guests poured in. I was struck by the fact that though the newly married couple were the reason for the celebrations, no one seemed to be particularly interested in them. They sat side by side on a sofa in the vast pandal, still and silent, smothered in brocade, gold ornaments and flowers, heads bent and faces invisible. I was dying to lift the curtain of flowers from the bridegroom's face and the veil of gold cloth from the bride's to see for myself whether this was really the happy ending of a romantic fairy tale. I wanted it very much to be, but something, including the harrowed expressions of the overworked and sweaty halwais frying jalebis behind a colourful arras, told me it wasn't likely.

We were ushered into the main area of the pandal where at least fifty upholstered sofas and armchairs were arranged around a huge flowered carpet on which a striking woman in red sat apart, smiling and twinkling winningly at the guests. She was flanked by an emaciated drummer in a frayed achkan and a wizened old sarangi player with startlingly blue-black hair. There was also a modest harmonium player who had the air of a button waiting to be pressed. 'This is Siddheshwari Bai, the celebrated thumri singer from Banaras', someone whispered as the music began. She had been laughing and joking informally with whoever among the guests greeted her, but with the first strains of the sarangi her expression became more focused, more collected. She seemed to be weighing something in her mind, probably what she should open her concert with. She closed her eyes for an instant, then nodded her head in silent approval, bent towards the players to give them some instructions, and vigorously cleared her throat. She covered her left ear with the palm of her hand, stretched out her other arm in a gesture of appeal to the listeners, and began to sing. Her rich, resounding voice needed no amplification in that space. She established instant rapport by hitting some high notes which sent a ripple of excitement among the listeners.

The music did not mean much to me at this point but I was

hypnotized by her face and her voice. The two together sent such powerful signals of warmth and reassurance that I was reminded of my mother, to my great surprise.

The languorous beat of the thumri, and the passionate and persuasive words of the song in which Siddheshwari Bai begged Krishna, the apple of Yashoda's eye, to come home because night was falling, drew in the friendly audience immediately. Gradually her face and arms began to move as though she was acting as well as singing. The hand gestures and mime tried to paint different versions of the picture described in the thumri she was singing. I discovered later that this was no novelty but a routine part of the traditional 'mujra'. I had come across something like this in the performance of a dancer who had been invited to our school but this was the first time I had ever seen someone 'dance' while sitting down. It was also the first time I had seen one person exercise so much control, so effortlessly, over hundreds of people. I was sure she could make her audience feel whatever she wished.

Soon there was rapt silence, except for awed remarks about the excellence of the performer. 'She is no beauty, but my God how much salt she has in her face!' someone hissed from the row behind us. I asked my grandfather what salt in the face meant and he said 'Hush! We will talk later.' With each song, the atmosphere in the pandal became more and more informal. The audience expressed their appreciation with loud cries of *'wah wah, kya kehne; or jawab nahin hai'*; not by clapping. After some time, an uncle of the bridegroom called out to her with a request to dance. *'Baiji, zara jhumke ke saath ho jai!'*

She smiled radiantly, said something that made everybody laugh, and began to tie her ankle bells. This was obviously a stage of the entertainment which was most eagerly awaited because the audience hailed it with glad cries. She stood up and tried the bells by striking each foot on the ground. Now I knew why the white sheet which is invariably spread for musicians was absent. When the atmosphere warmed up, this was meant to turn into a dance recital. The sarangi player secured his small instrument to his waist with a padded, belt-like contraption and also stood up behind her, ready to follow her around the improvised stage as she danced. The tabla player did the same. The ensemble became mobile within minutes and was now able to address and delight each section of the audience intimately in turn. At long last Siddheshwari Bai came near us. I felt I was drowning. Her eyes were fixed on my grandfather but to my great discomfiture he was not responsive or appreciative enough, or so it seemed to me.

This time her song described a beautiful young woman drawing water from the well, filling her pot, balancing it on her head and walking home while the onlookers marvelled at her grace and loveliness. Siddheshwari Bai's mime, hand gestures, and body movements painted the picture for me very clearly. But for that I would not have been able to decipher the meaning of the words which were in an unfamiliar dialect and blurred for me by the musical embellishments. I was electrified by the sequences of brilliant footwork and explosions of sound from the tabla which peppered the musical story-telling.

In the middle of this number, when she was singing the intriguing words *jhama jham* again and again, trying to recreate the sound of overflowing water, there was a flurry of excitement at the far end of the marquee. All eyes and ears turned away from the performer and the magic she had woven evaporated. Some very special guests were being escorted in with loud and deferential exclamations by a group of the host party. They were led to the biggest sofa in the centre of the central row. When they were seated, and the fawning cloud of attendants and ushers dispersed, I was able to see that the special guests were an elderly British couple. He was dressed in a black suit which looked as though it had been fashioned out of metal. She wore a long white satin gown, furs and a gracious smile. 'It is the Chief Commissioner and his lady', our host told my grandfather as he bustled past, beaming with satisfaction at the superb eminence of the guests he had the power to summon.

The dancer also received enough signals from diverse sources to know that the occasion had now become even more grand than it had been. She decided to do something about it at once, and abruptly changed the song she was singing from *jhama jham* to 'my love is like a little bird'. I discovered later that this was the opening line of a musical hit in London. She sang the words with such a strong Indian accent that the British guests were none the wiser. However, many of the local people expressed their admiration and pride at such versatility and inventiveness. 'Like a little bird', she sang in many different ways, as though it were a traditional thumri. 'That flies, that flies, that flies from tree to tree e e e e e e..........' The last syllable stretched into a masterly taan that swept two and a half octaves, leaving the listeners gasping for breath. The style of the miming also changed abruptly. The languorous, elephantine walk of the village belle denoted by sinuous gestures and coy looks gave place to a high-heeled look and jerky, almost comic hand movements suggesting the erratic flight of the British bird. Siddheshwari Bai's impromptu confection in honour of the Chief Commissioner was clearly the highlight of the festivities and was talked about in Delhi for months afterwards. My earliest memory of Siddheshwari Bai is this childhood encounter. Her music had been inaccessible to me at this stage and the depth and beauty that I found in it later is no part of this memory.

The next time I heard her was twenty years later, by accident. I had been learning to sing all these years but somehow the effective influences in my life had led me towards the khayal form which I considered a more serious genre than thumri. We had gone in a group to a morning concert of the Bharatiya Kala Kendra in Delhi to listen to Ustad Amir Khan. Pandit Pran Nath, who was my teacher at this time and the last word on musical taste for me and all my friends, was with us. So was Mr Mohan Rao, the head of the office I worked in—he was the most enthusiastic and also the noisiest listener I had ever come across; and Krishna, my friend who taught English literature at Miranda House, whose favourite word to describe good music was 'stark'. Amir Khan was our idol, the ultimate khayal singer whose music always thrilled and inspired us. We had timed our arrival to make sure we didn't have to sit through anything else which would try our ears before he came on.

As it happened, everything was running late as it does so often at concerts of Indian music. As we took our seats in the huge marquee meant for the audience, we were told that Siddheshwari Bai was about to begin her recital. Mr Mohan Rao groaned with disappointment, and Pandit Pran Nath made some patronizing cracks about thumri being about betel-leaf chewing and little else.

The woman on the stage had no resemblance to my memory of the mobile singer in red. It was not only that she was much older and quite a bit heavier. Her attitude to the music and her projection of it seemed to me to be entirely different. She was definitely not trying to entertain anyone, but to share her own intoxication with the music in her, in an act of love. As she got deeper into the Bhairavi thumri she was singing, the powerful magic of her musicality and the seriousness of her musical intention enveloped and overwhelmed us all. Mr Mohan Rao was now emitting hoarse sounds of appreciation, and sighing in ecstasy. 'My God, I never knew! The big lady is fantastic! This music gets nine on ten, I tell you!' and so on throughout the hour for which she sang. Pandit Pran Nath also nodded his approval, though somewhat patronizingly.

I fell in love with her once again but this time I sensed more clearly what attracted me to her music. It is impossible to give it a name, but the main impression was one of boundless warmth and compassion, of perfect tunefulness, and something I can only describe as purity of spirit. Her ready good humour, informality of manner, and responsiveness to piquancy and spice in all things were evident to me from little gestures, little things she said and did on the stage. The way she demanded paan from her elder daughter who sat in attendance behind her, the disarming way she smiled at the audience when three of her glass bangles broke as she flung out her arms to enjoy a particularly rapturous note, the way her face, neck, and eyes moved to suggest and extract subtle meanings from the text of her songs communicated a puckish quality which did not in any way detract from the weightiness of her personality. The largeness of heart that everyone heard in her music seemed to include a knowledge of pain and the power to draw each listener into its own climate in an easy gesture of total identification.

I couldn't remember when I had been so moved. It was not just the music. It was also the person in the act of making music happen that fascinated me. I realized that though one could be more interested in one musical form than in another, the total impact of music had little to do with the form. In the course of my adult musical life I had become so enamoured of khayal that I had not seriously wanted to hear anything else. But now a recital of thumris had had such a tremendous effect on me that I could think of nothing but the voice of Siddheshwari Bai for days afterwards. I could hardly believe it. Though I definitely did not want to learn to sing thumri, I wanted more than anything else to get close to her musical aura, and to interact with it.

I hesitated to join the admiring crowds backstage after her recital because the contact with her was too important to me to risk her lumping me with other casual congratulators. What I felt deserved more earnestness than that. I wanted to go to Banaras on a sort of pilgrimage, just to see her. A colleague in the Publications Division who had connections in Uttar Pradesh arranged both the trip and the introduction and the day came when I was nervously knocking at an ancient wooden door in Kabir Chaura, a downtown neighbourhood of old Banaras which is almost a colony of musicians. A maidservant opened the door and the voice that had been haunting me for so many days came floating down the passage. This was a moment I had waited for for months.

As I look back, I can remember nothing except the voice, and later the face and the feeling that her personality evoked in me. I stood in the doorway, my ears on tiptoe, thrilled that the first sound I heard in her house was her voice. This time she was mostly humming to herself, but some full-throated words were interspersed too. '*Kya jadoo dara* . . .' she sang many times before I reached her. She was not performing and there were of course no instruments to embellish anything. For this reason the earthy, richly textured voice hit me with even more force. The maid who had opened the door led me to a courtyard where Siddheshwari Bai was sitting on a moodha, stirring a karhai over an open fire, singing to herself as she cooked. She wiped the sweat from her face with her crumpled and stained cotton dhoti and answered my greeting with a radiant and beautiful smile. She told me she was expecting me.

'I was just making some bhindi. A little tamarind in it is delicious. You must taste some at lunch-time and tell me how you like our Banarsi cuisine.'

I found her brand of informality captivating, though it did not surprise me in the least. The recital in Delhi had been very revealing to me. And she was exactly like her music.

We moved to the main room of the house where the only furniture was a large wooden takhat covered with rich tapestries and comfortable bolsters and cushions. A harmonium, tablas, and a tanpura lay on a thick red rug on the floor. She asked me politely, affectionately, to sing for her, banishing my diffidence with a mock grimace and an airy wave of the hand. 'You must be very interested in music to come all this way to meet me. How will I get to know you unless I hear you sing?' she said.

I fetched the tanpura, tuned up, and started a slow khayal in Mian-ki-Malhar which I had recently learnt from Pandit Pran Nath. My eyes were closed as I plunged in self-consciously. When I finished, and opened my eyes again I found that we had been joined by her two daughters who were regarding me noncommittally, waiting for a cue from their mother.

'Very good training! But you are so frightened! That will clog you up. You have to let yourself go. Without that you can't sing thumri', she said spontaneously when I finished.

I suddenly realized that she had taken for granted that I was at her door to learn. When I explained that I was concentrating on khayal and had not thought of learning thumri she became wary. I could see from her expression that she was puzzled and suspicious of my motives. That I had simply come to pay my respects because I admired her so tremendously didn't strike her as a possibility. She was on her guard for the rest of the day and kept screwing up her eyes in appraisal to try and make sense of my visit. The expansive mood with which she had first greeted me disappeared like a hurriedly lowered flag. But even in this I saw an endearing, childlike naivety. Her reflexes were those of an innocent person whose hard life had taught her to guard against the unfamiliar. Obviously not many people had approached her just to honour her and with no other purpose, and she didn't quite know how to handle this. She was amiable enough when she saw me off at the end of the day, but a little more tense and unsure. I found this very touching because it told me how difficult her life must have been and how defenceless and vulnerable she was.

About two years after this meeting, she moved from Banaras to Delhi to teach at Bharatiya Kala Kendra. She was housed in a couple of bare rooms in a barracks, a state-run hostel called Pataudi House. I enthusiastically renewed our contact and persisted in my efforts to get close to her. It took about a year for her to believe that I didn't want anything from her but the privilege of basking in her personality, and her friendship if I was so fortunate. When this did happen, she took me to her bosom as only a mother could and I began to call her Amma. I brought all the bits and pieces of my life to her so that she could be a part of it. She began to take great interest in my family, and established an independent relationship with my mother. She treated my husband like a son-in-law and always made a special trip to our house to press the customary silver rupee into his palm on festivals like Holi and Diwali, to his great consternation. She joined me and my friends in our attentions to Pandit Pran Nath, whose extremely lofty and uncompromising musical tastes she admired with as full a heart as we did. She also made friends with Mr Mohan Rao who continued to call her 'great lady, nine marks lady'.

This association was specially exciting to both. It was the first time in his life that Mr Mohan Rao had connected so closely with someone who represented the heart of the culture of the northern plains in such an uninhibited manner and with so much charm. She became the favourite target of his aggressive hospitality and was treated almost every Sunday to home-made Mysore rawa dosai, coconut chutney, pickles made of 'small small mangoes available only in our parts', stuffed arvi-ka-pasta, and the latest melodic gems in the raga Multani that Pandit Pran Nath had taught Ranna, Mr Mohan Rao's wife.

She for her part had never met such a good and simple man in all her life and lavished her special brand of affection on him and Ranna. She would often bustle in unannounced in a three-wheeler and enter the premises puffing and panting, always carrying some kind of treat for them, usually something elaborate she had cooked for them. Parathas stuffed with peas, sweet halwa, and the special 'ghuti-gobbi', the spiced and puréed cauliflower of UP that does not make sense to anyone even fifty miles away from the border. 'Just a little taste of something different for you', she would say, beaming happily. Then, to complete her offering, she would tease Mr Mohan Rao with a line from a song, a bait he never failed to swallow immediately. It was a signal that a long and leisurely music session could follow if he wished. For him there was no 'if' about it. He could never resist any such prospect. Besides Siddheshwari Bai's music had a double attraction. It was a novelty to him, and it was offered to him personally, specially for his delectation.

'Hai hai! What a voice! What a lady!' he would splutter helplessly because his words could never approximate his meaning.

They would both settle down on the durree on the floor, laughing, talking, exchanging anecdotes, and sharing their best musical memories. He talked about his Bombay days when he first heard Abdul Karim Khan, Kesar Bai, and Roshanara Begum and was dazzled beyond his wildest expectations. She told him how she as a young girl had started learning from Bade Ramdasji of Banaras by overhearing the lessons he gave to her cousin while she herself was slaving in the kitchen, like a Cinderella. When the guru heard her singing to herself while cleaning pots and pans, he was amazed and tried to move her tyrannical aunt to allow her to take proper lessons, but to no avail. So the guru taught and supported her secretly until she came into her own. These stories had all the gloss of fairy tales and nobody was ever tired of hearing them again and again.

Mr Mohan Rao once tried to reproduce the music of Roshanara Begum for the benefit of Siddheshwari, whose horizons he was trying to broaden. The trouble was that he had a thin, rasping treble by way of a voice. When he tried to sing, he sounded like a piece of rickety furniture being dragged across the floor. But he conducted the exercise with such ardour and concentration that nobody had the heart to tell him his efforts gave no idea whatsoever of the music he was so intensely trying to describe. Siddheshwari deeply appreciated his transparent but sometimes ill-fated sincerity and felt a great tenderness for him. It was a wonderful friendship in which teasing, clowning, laughter, food and music all played a part. I have an old photograph taken outside Mr Mohan Rao's house in which Siddheshwari, sixty years old and weighing more than two hundred pounds, is saluting like a soldier with a puckish grin on her face, just to amuse all those present and put them at their ease. She was perfectly at home in Mr Mohan Rao's Kannada-speaking household and he seemed always to understand her very local Banaras idiom. The truth was that their communication didn't depend on language.

Mr Mohan Rao had introduced many of the people he came close to in Delhi to Carnatak music. I began to appreciate musicians like Madurai Mani Iyer and Mahalingam for the first time in my life entirely because of him. Once when Mahalingam was in Delhi for a concert, he arranged for Siddheshwari Bai to meet him. He told us amid excited guffaws that it would be a fascinating experiment to watch the musical collision between these two great minds. She was one of the most responsive and humble people there could be, and was always game for anything. So one Sunday morning, she and her daughter Pappo, and Mr and Mrs Mohan Rao and I, set out to call on Mahalingam who was staying in a hotel suite in New Delhi.

'Mali' as everyone called him was not very prepossessing or communicative at first. She on the other hand poured her heart out in her own dialect, quite oblivious of the fact that Mali would not have understood a word even if she had used formal Hindi. Anyway, her face and demeanour did all the communicating that was needed. She folded her hands, pointed to the flute, thumped her heart, and looked heavenwards. An accompanist who was with Mali told him in Tamil that she was a celebrity in the North and was begging him to play for her. He nodded and picked up his flute somewhat reluctantly.

'Raga Todi', he said, in a joyless voice, looking down, keeping himself well hidden behind his glasses. He seemed half-hearted about sharing his morning with unknown fans though he had obviously been talked into it and had agreed. This is what Mr Mohan Rao meant when he said he had 'arranged' everything. How different Mali's attitude was from that of most Hindustani performers, I thought. He started to play. The very first sound had so much emotional weight that it overwhelmed us, knocked us out in fact. The melodies that began to pour out were like some magical winds that had been imprisoned and were now set free. The man behind the flute was also transformed. He was suddenly like a devotee in a state of rapture. He was improvising on a well-known traditional song invoking Krishna and though there were no words in his music, the meaning seemed to be piercing the hearts of all those present, including Siddheshwari Bai. The musical and cultural idiom was unfamiliar to her, but her sensitive ear and simple loving heart just erased the distance between herself and Mali. She was in ecstasy, listening with her eyes closed, tears glistening on her cheeks. She was a Krishna bhakta herself and was famous for her highly emotive bhajans. I knew that at this moment she was musically and emotionally entirely with Mali.

Even so I was not quite prepared for what happened next. Mali left a phrase hanging tantalizingly at the edge of a precipice because he was choked with feeling. In that instant, Siddheshwari Bai opened her eyes, looked lovingly at him, spread out her arms in a characteristic gesture and began to sing a beguiling bhajan as though she was simply upholding Mali's intention. She tuned her voice to his tonic and chose Raga Bhairavi, the nearest Hindustani equivalent of Mali's Todi. Miraculously, there was nothing incongruous in the two creating music together though they belonged to different worlds and did not even have a language they could talk to each other in. What followed was like spontaneous combustion. They inspired and provoked one another, spiralling to undreamt of heights, making the notes of the raga serve a new, urgent, and beautiful purpose which was the only truth in that moment. The flute and the voice alternated their entreaties in an extraordinary outburst, each making the other more poignant while retaining its own identity and idiom.

It was a freak musical event, a divine accident. One could not help wondering what the baithaks of Banaras and the pundits of the Madras Music Academy would have had to say about this duet, or rather about the possibility of such a partnership, had they been fortunate enough to witness it. But while it was happening it seemed as inevitable as an act of Nature. The two of them were airborne, gripped by the same musical energy and feeling, and intoxicated by the newness of this impromptu journey into musical outer space. It was unutterably moving, and soon tears were flowing freely down their faces and ours and no one was embarrassed by it or even aware of it. The devotional outpouring went on for more than an hour though it seemed much less. They stopped only because it became too overwhelming. They both started to exclaim loudly in their own ways, broken words and sounds of appreciation for each other, for the raga, for the compositions, for the wonderful chance that had brought them together. She called him son, and he cried out 'Amma!' again and again: they were in each other's arms, both visibly overcome. The rest of us felt that we had just witnessed a miracle. The glow of this incident lasted for a very long time and it was months before we returned to earth.

The relationship between Siddheshwari and me gradually developed into a really close bond. The wariness I had encountered in Banaras disappeared completely once she was convinced that I was not trying to take advantage of her in any way. She began to trust me and confide in me. We enjoyed each other's company greatly and her house became a haven for me, a place where I could always be assured of warmth, sympathy, and food, all three being high on my list of priorities. She was always interested in the details of the lives of all those she came in contact with, always ready to give whatever she could, sometimes even what she couldn't. Streams of lowly music jobbers and indigent relatives and acquaintances passed through her house to pay their respects, or to be remembered in case she needed an accompanist at her next concert, or in search of someone who would listen to their woes. She invariably fed them, called them bhaiyya, and pressed some money into their hands when they left. Whatever she gave she genuinely considered 'just a little something', not worth mentioning at all.

She told me fabulous stories about her life, about how she had grown up in an establishment run by a very strict aunt who threw her out because she had committed the unpardonable sin of falling in love. The object of her affections had promised marriage and she in a romantic dream was ready to follow him to the ends of the earth. She was only eighteen at the time. As it happened there was no marriage because the man in the story was already much married. It took him two years to tell her this. She now had a baby girl and nowhere to go because the aunt refused to take her back into the establishment. She had to fend for herself. The story was as old as the hills. What was new for me was that her spirit seemed to have remained pure and undamaged through it all. She never lost her appetite for life, which to her meant the ability to give herself entirely to whatever interested her at the moment.

Many years later when she was travelling with Rasoolan Bai to a music conference, a handsome man in a military uniform entered their railway compartment. They started to talk and she fell in love once again. She never reached her destination but got off at the cantonment station where the military officer was bound, fully expecting to live happily ever after. This time the idyll lasted only a year before the man went back to his wife and seven sons in the Punjab. After this she developed a sort of contempt for men and stopped taking them seriously. She used to caution all her pupils, at any rate the ones she cared about, against men generally. She hated the idea that her daughters should be dependent on men, even if they were their husbands, and went to enormous trouble and expense to see to it that they held their own in every way. All marital partnerships were found unsatisfactory and the final result of her exertions on their behalf was that both the daughters, along with their children, ended up at one point as a part of their mother's household.

She tried her best to ensure more comfortable and more respectable lives than her own for her daughters. The younger one was sent to college to graduate and as a result could converse in English. Siddheshwari was thrilled by this. She considered it a big leap forward in some vague sense, a marvellous symptom that would somehow raise the quality of life for the entire household. If she had had her way entirely, she would have prevented her younger daughter from having anything to do with music. But her own involvement with it was too powerful a current for anyone close to her to withstand. So both daughters did pursue music, after a fashion. The older one managed to imbibe her mother's manner after a lifetime of association. The younger one learnt to play the sitar competently. Neither of them became Siddheshwari, but then Siddheshwari was made of something else altogether.

Siddheshwari showed me albums of old photographs of herself and spoke uninhibitedly of her past. It seemed to relieve her to confide in someone outside her family that she could trust.

'It is true that I had to do many things for money, but I could never do anything unless it also gave me pleasure', she told me with pride.

She knew of my friendship with Begum Akhtar, with whom she seemed to be obsessed. They were two great names in the music world at the same time and circumstances made them rivals. No two artistes could be more different. Siddheshwari was robust and passionate in her artistic expression while Begum Akhtar was controlled and sophisticated. To look at, one was heavy, open and homely though full of 'salt', while the other was elegant, gracious, and intriguing. They admired each other's art but couldn't help making snide remarks against each other on principle. They were both on the same concert circuits and regularly ran into each other in cities all over the country, and for extended periods in the princely state of Rampur where the nawab held music festivals very frequently.

'She is so beautiful that everyone is smitten by her. Wherever I go, she is already being feted and made a fuss of and she laps it up as if the current admirer is the only thing in her life, although I'm sure she doesn't remember his name the next day! Who doesn't like being put on a pedestal and adored? I do too, but I can only deal with one such situation at a time. Only one at a time!' Siddheshwari repeated, raising her voice and thrusting her chin forward self-righteously. 'I know I am not very good looking and the effect of my kind of music is not instantaneous. I have to work hard at establishing the *sa* first. Do you know that every time I tried to do this in concerts in Rampur, Akhtari would make it a point to enter the hall late so that all concentration was diffused. And then she wouldn't just come in and sit down quietly. She would stand in the doorway facing me in her exquisite pink izaar-dupatta outfit, holding a beautiful silver paan-daan, greeting all her aquaintances one by one, bending her head demurely and lifting a hennaed hand to her forehead in the most beguiling salaam you ever saw, one for each individual she recognized in the assemblage. Each head in the audience turned to look at her while I was trying to sing. It used to destroy everything I had done before her dramatic entrance and I would have to start all over again. This happened to me so many times. But I have to tell you in all fairness that she is really quite beautiful! And her ghazal singing was nothing short of miraculous. I have to give her that.'

Akhtari was a subject that never failed to set Siddheshwari off. She admired her but was also maddened by her poise and exclusiveness. She would have dearly loved to be friends but suspected that Akhtari considered herself socially far superior and preferred to keep her distance. This was probably not true. The two just had very different styles of operation and were uncomfortable together because they knew too much about each other's early struggles. Siddheshwari was much more outgoing and whenever they ran into each other would warmly invite her to drop in. The response was always polite but cool and noncommittal. Siddheshwari's frustration at this sometimes expressed itself in uncharacteristic ways.

'She has lofty airs today but the Nata caste she belongs to were not even admitted into my aunt's establishment. If ever one of them visited, they had to sit on the floor outside, not on the durree. They were very particular about proprieties in those days. My aunt had a parrot in the courtyard who was trained to ask the caste and credentials of everyone who came to the house. "*Kaun jaat, kaun jaat*" the bird would screech and the visitor would have to fulfil some minimum qualification to enter. The women of our clan were the pride of Banaras. When they went to the Vishwanath temple in all their finery, crowds gathered to watch. It was really a splendid sight. So was the Budwa Mangal festival in which dozens of barges brightly lit with oil lamps floated down the Ganga river, each with a full-fledged music recital aboard, complete with enthusiastic audience. The Maharaja of Banaras himself presided over the festivities. I have been a part of it many times. Once when I sang a long taan while performing on my barge, I was thrilled to hear it echoing across the water because a sarangi player from the neighbouring boat had picked it up on his instrument and was repeating it, with loud cries of appreciation.'

Her eyes flashed defiantly as she tried to relive the glory. 'This should surely impress Akhtari' her look seemed to say. She was never to know that Akhtari's only known reaction to her was to nickname her '*tope*' or cannon, an unexplained epithet she always used for her and reinforced with an infectious gale of rippling laughter which rang across the room like silver bells.

Siddheshwari had a robustness of spirit which I found most endearing. It overwhelmed me, and many others too. Only once, in those years when Siddheshwari had become a part of my daily life, did I see her lose her temper. The object of her wrath was a compulsive ogler, a sarangi player of indifferent quality who was assigned to accompany her at a recording session in the studios of the radio station in Delhi. Siddheshwari had put on some weight and not being too meticulous about her clothes at this stage had not bothered to do anything about the fact that her blouses were too tight to hold her. As a result she was spilling over just a little bit though the pallu of her sari was meant to conceal everything. But as she moved or bent over to listen to the tanpura, the pallu would slip and the ogler would try to peer down the revealed area while perfunctorily scraping his bow over his strings. This happened several times. Suddenly she turned on him like a tigress, whipped away her pallu with a jerk, and said witheringly 'Come on and take a good look! Let us get it over with so that you can at least stay in tune!' He turned ashen and literally touched her feet, begging her forgiveness for the 'misunderstanding'. She laughed uproariously and was joined by the other musicians. It took her no time to regain her composure and in the end the recording turned out to be quite wonderful.

She once confessed that she was frustrated because she had never been asked to go abroad to perform.

'They all come and tell me how they danced and sang and played, here, there and everywhere! They show me little gifts and mementos from Europe and America to taunt me. Akhtari is about the same age as I am but even she has been to Russia and Afghanistan. She came back with exquisite carpets which were gifted to her by the high and mighty wherever she went. But no one ever thinks of me. I know it is because I am not slim and beautiful like "them"!'

This became a recurrent theme. The sense of being overlooked by the powers that be in favour of 'them' began to depress her more and more. Something had to be done about this but many of us who adored her art and loved her as a person felt as though an angel had expressed a desire to take off her wings and travel by public bus. She had clarified that she wanted to go by herself and not as part of a delegation or 'dagalaysan' as she called it because she had heard of the undignified things members were called upon to do at those jamborees.

Despite forceful reassurances by her large circle of followers that it was only the arbitrariness of official selection procedures that was to blame, she was convinced that she was being deliberately bypassed because of her excessive weight. I discovered by accident that she had secretly enlisted in a slimming programme called Figurette which had an outlet near her house and this pierced my heart like an arrow. I had been mystified by her unaccustomed outings in the mornings when she would normally have been at singing practice. One day she returned puffing and panting while I was waiting for her. When I asked where she had been, she blushed and didn't answer at first. Finally she responded to my concern by coming out with it.

'Somebody told me I have to be much thinner even to get on the plane. This place I go to will take all the extra fat off. I have to get on a plane once, even if I die afterwards. I have to know what it is like.'

'But what do they do when you go there?' I asked, really worried now.

'Oh, they have these big pattas they tie around you and then they stand you on a machine that shakes and shakes till you beg for mercy. Their puttee was too small to go round me so I asked them to do my upper arms instead. Phatar, phatar, phatar the pattas go as they massage you. It is an awful noise. The whole thing is very upsetting. They say it will take time. Do you think it has made a difference?' she said suddenly brightening and patting her arms and belly tentatively.

In that instant I dedicated myself totally to the cause of getting her on a plane for a concert tour, no matter what means had to be employed. There was a small-time Indian cultural operator based in London who happened to be in town to enlist victims for his next project. In normal times he would have been someone to avoid strictly. In fact I had once had to ask him to leave Begum Akhtar's room at her request when he was negotiating a tour in the UK with her. I was the interpreter and was listing for her the numerous responsibilities he wanted her to undertake for him. The last question I asked on her behalf was: 'What is the advantage to me?' To this there was no answer. He made self-righteous faces and said, 'You will be serving your country.' At this point she had said in a quiet and dangerous voice, 'Bitia, would you please ask him to go. Tell him I have nothing further to say or ask.' The memory of that last encounter with him two years earlier still rankled but I resolved to eat crow and go back to him with a request.

When I mentioned Siddheshwari's name, he almost embraced me. He had never been able to land an artiste of this calibre though he had been fishing for a long time. His main interest was transparently still himself but now I needed him desperately. I tried not to show it and after a surprisingly easy hour I had a proposal for Siddheshwari Bai's approval. A month's concert tour for her in England and Italy! I knew she would want to take her English-speaking daughter along and this was agreed to. The organizers would take care of all board, lodging, and travel. The rest of the terms were miserable, but that was not what she cared about at this point.

She was ecstatic at the news and hectic preparations for travel began at once though the tour was a month away. She was like a child about to be taken to the circus and could talk of nothing else. At last the great day arrived and a large group of devotees, including Mr Mohan Rao, who kept singing 'Great lady going to London' in his favourite raga Puriya, went to the airport to wish her and her daughter Pappo a happy journey. On the way back to the city we felt we were returning from the wars but the next day we all went back to our normal lives with a feeling of relief.

A week later when I was sitting at my desk in my office there was a phone call from Siddheshwari's house to inform me that she had returned and would like to see me as soon as possible. My blood ran cold. Heart trouble, accident, some other unspeakable disaster! I was sure she was dangerously ill so I dropped everything and rushed to her place, my heart pounding with dread. But she was fine, sitting calmly in the front room drinking tea. 'What happened? Is everything all right?' I burst out.

'Ram, Ram, Ram, Ram!' she exclaimed, holding her ears with her hands and shaking her head sadly from side to side. 'Such dirty people! I swear I'll never go to "Vilayat" again!'

'For God's sake, tell me what happened', I said. And she did, in her own inimitable Banarsi style.

'We were given a room upstairs in the house of a mean-faced English witch. After my long journey, I naturally wanted a bath. We hardly recognized the bathroom because it had carpets on the floor! I suspected right away that these people could not be very serious about washing themselves if they could have carpets in their bathroom. There was no bucket, no brass lota, no wooden patra to sit on and scrape one's heels clean. Nothing. Just flowered carpets. Along one wall there was a long white coffin-like tub which Pappo said one could fill with water and treat like a bucket. She said she would pour the water over me with a plastic mug we found in the room. But where was I to sit? What on earth did these people do themselves, I wondered. Pappo informed me that they simply sat in the tub and splashed their own dirt over themselves and called that a bath. Ram, Ram! We could never do that. I simply have to have clean, running water that goes *jhama-jham,* as in the song . . .

'So, I told Pappo to roll up the carpets and throw them aside. Underneath were wooden boards that could serve as a patra to sit on so I settled down and started to rub my special soap on my body and besan in my hair as I always do after long journeys. I ordered Pappo to pour water over me and had a nice bath. Soon there were loud screams and bangings from the ground floor. Pappo said the water from my bath had dripped directly into the witch's fish stew on her kitchen stove below and she was livid with rage, demanding to know what was going on upstairs. I was tired and in no mood for an argument through interpreters so I just pulled the blanket over my ears to shut out the din and went to sleep.

'The next morning I made a tobacco paan for myself and asked Pappo to get me a mug to take to the lavatory. She held up the same mug she had given me a bath with! I was appalled at how quickly she had forgotten basic proprieties. Not this mug, you fool! I meant the other mug, I told her. The air there is so corrupting that this little chit of a girl scolded me back, saying I was making an unnecessary fuss and generally carrying on as though we were still in Banaras and not in London. According to her it was all right for the same mug to do double duty in the bathroom and the lavatory! Did you ever hear anything so shocking? Listen, these are also human beings with the same needs, I said. Don't they need water in the lavatories to clean themselves? No, said Pappo. And then, my dear, she showed me a roll of paper, to enlighten me! That is what they clean themselves with! I could not believe it. I asked her to swear if that was all they used, and she did.

'Something happened to me from that moment onwards. I felt faint and couldn't even breathe properly. I was deeply uncomfortable with things around me and I am not used to that, as you know. I decided that while I was in this strange environment I must assert myself. I ordered Pappo to go down and brave the witch's wrath and boldly ask for a second mug because I insist on it. This time she went meekly enough, but her powers of expressing herself in English must have suffered a setback because the witch came bounding up the stairs to see for herself what was required. Yes, it was true that we already had a mug. What did we want a second one for? Pappo explained as best she could. We clean ourselves with water and our hands. This mug has to be different from the one we use for the body bath. The witch was trying to take in what Pappo was telling her but just couldn't believe that anyone could use their hands to clean themselves in the lavatory even with the aid of water. When light dawned at last, it was the witch's turn to feel faint and sick. She collapsed on a chair in shock. All I wanted was to go home as fast as I could.

'That evening I had a concert in Brighton. I tried my best to forget what I had been through but it kept coming back to me when I least expected it. Believe me, I couldn't even hit a pancham in tune because I was so distracted. I couldn't get myself in the mood to sing to these assorted pink, red, and white faces because the roll of toilet paper kept coming into my mind again and again. It was just hopeless. I simply couldn't establish any kind of rapport with people who had come to my concert after cleaning themselves in the way Pappo had described to me.

'I cancelled all the other concerts and begged the operator to release me from my contract because I was really sick. It will take me a long time to pay him back for the air tickets but I'll gladly do it. This is the whole story. I am so happy to be back again. Ram Ram, never again will I ask anybody to send me abroad. But I must tell you, I liked the plane ride!'

NINE

The Muse and the Truck Drivers

I had dreamed about this music festival ever since I first heard the famous singer Kesar Bai Kerkar speak of it at our family dining table when I was about twelve. In the following years, many more stories about Harballabh were added to my early impression. Almost every musician I came across spoke of it as though it was a religious experience. By the time I reached my twenties, the name Harballabh sounded like a magician's code word with a symbolic meaning. To me, it became the musical promised land, the ultimate criterion of true worth in music, a synonym for commitment and purity. All through my youth I longed to attend the festival but there was no practical way for me to go to Jullundur for three nights without an escort and without 'proper' arrangements. Nobody else in our large, joint household felt as intensely about this as I did, so it never achieved the status of a family priority. But years later, when I was forty-five years old and had almost forgotten my old dream, it came true in the most unexpected way.

Unbelievably, miraculously, absolutely unaccountably, I received in the mail an invitation to perform at the Harballabh festival. I was hysterical with joy and wanted to announce my big news to every passerby on the road. Many people I shared my excitement with deflated me by saying it must be a postal mistake. Some others were sure I had been asked only because my husband was in a very important position in the government. Yet others advised me not to worry about why the invitation had been sent but to just go there, get up on the stage, and do what they encouragingly called my 'stuff'.

Preparing for this performance was unquestionably one of the most intense things I ever did in my life. But all through those two months of vigorous practice, the things Kesar Bai had said about Harballabh so long ago kept coming back to me. Funnily enough, they had become associated in my mind with good eating because joint family mealtimes had been the natural setting for most of her pronouncements. I vividly remember her at the dining table, chewing a bone with great relish as she held forth on various topics. The women of the household had purred with delight at the informality of their special guest because to them it meant that she was quite comfortable and that she found the food delicious. 'The Harballabh people know how to listen. They know the difference between musicians and circus performers. You can't fool them. They are not like the puppet audiences of Delhi', she had declared, digging into the bone with a hairpin which she had deftly extracted from her coiffeur for the operation since no marrow spoon seemed to be handy. I also remember that we at the children's end of the dining table had stared in disbelief and gasped when the honoured guest slid the hairpin neatly back in the bun at the nape of her neck after its delicious work was done.

'But isn't this place, Harballabh, in the Punjab, near Jullundur of all places?' my father asked patronizingly, as though serious music and Punjab were incompatible. We had been brought up on this sort of prejudice and were quite innocent of the extraordinary esteem in which this oldest of all music festivals was held by all musicians. It was Kesar Bai who first educated our household in this matter, throwing some of my family's inherited notions such as 'Bengalis are artistic, Punjabis are practical, Sindhis are wily, and Lucknow-walas are delicate' into disarray.

'I could never have imagined how sensitive and sophisticated the musical tastes of the regular listeners at this festival are. And most of them are Punjabis', Kesar Bai had said with the air of someone who has witnessed a miracle. She had then gone on to tell us how this annual event had started. For some reason, I remembered vividly every single thing she had said although all of it was not equally interesting to me at the time. I was fascinated by the fact of her long train journey from Bombay to Jullundur every year and wanted very much to know what was at the other end. Apparently Harballabh was the name of the devotee of an old Saraswati temple that stood by the side of a lake called Devi Talao about three miles from the city. The story of Sri Baba Harballabh, as he reverently came to be called, was that he was a gifted musician who had spent his entire life singing, as an offering to the goddess. It was well known that he was oblivious of everything else, sometimes even forgetting to eat or drink. He died at the age of a hundred, sitting by the lake, his fingers still on the strings of his tanpura, his eyes closed in devotion as always. It was quite a while before they discovered that he was dead. Local musicians began to commemorate him and the small annual event, which first took place in the winter of 1875, became bigger and bigger with every passing year. At the height of its glory in the late 'forties and 'fifties, when Kesar Bai used to perform regularly, it had become an enormous undertaking which commanded the emotional and financial support of the whole of the Punjab.

Since Kesar Bai had first fired my imagination twenty-five years earlier, I had garnered a lot more information about Harballabh though I did not know from where. I knew that musicians and listeners came to the festival from all over the country as though it were a pilgrimage and the venue harboured a widespread superstition that whoever came to the shrine to pay their respects would become successful and famous. Ravi Shankar and Onkar Nath Thakur were often cited as examples. The current mahant or head of the Saraswati temple had the final say in all decisions and arrangements. Artistes were offered many times the fees that other musical events in the country could give, so the experience if one survived on stage was not only prestigious but also highly lucrative. A whole township used to spring up at the site of the lake by the original temple for the three days that the festival lasted. These three days had to be in the coldest part of the winter, the audience had to sit in the open, and there were no chairs. These brutal conditions ensured that only the most dedicated adherents would stay on. The resulting concentration and focusing of interest and the automatic weeding out of casual elements were believed to create special vibrations that changed the attitudes and indeed the lives of all those who went there. The audiences were huge and did not consist of the sort of elite one associated with classical music elsewhere. There were farmers, truck drivers, shopkeepers, fruit growers, small mechanics, big industrialists, journalists, and businessmen of all sorts. Most of them came with their families, bringing blankets and food, in the spirit of pilgrims on the road, happily prepared to weather all hardships, the bitter cold and the lack of sleep for three nights in expectation of the musical benedictions the festival offered.

Over the years, the Harballabh festival had developed a culture of its own. No light classical music was ever permitted, no matter how great. The ears of the local people, who were otherwise extremely simple, had been nurtured and conditioned since the origin of the festival to appreciate only the purest classical idiom of khayal and dhrupad. They were not receptive to novelty or innovation and dismissed any attempt to please as unworthy. But to their idols they showed unlimited indulgence, and a loyalty and constancy quite rare in the world of the performing arts. New talent was recognized only if it was in the direct tradition of any of the great names the Harballabh audiences had been brought up on. If it was outside their ken, the chances that the newcomer could establish communication with them were very slim. These audiences were not delicate in their responses. Their approval and disapproval were both clearly expressed. They insisted on a certain robustness of approach. As Kesar Bai had put it, 'They do not have the patience to wait while a musician crawls under the bed with a lighted matchstick looking for the exact nuance of a note! They want each sound to be explicit and healthy, like their own temperaments.'

On her way from Bombay to Jullundur she always stopped in Delhi, allowing something like two weeks to stay in our house. The period was shorter on her way back but the stopover was a regular feature. She enjoyed my father's urbane style of deference and he found her forthright, sharp Marathi accent an attractive novelty. Our household had always been wide-eyed and happy about house guests, but Kesar Bai's coming was like a festival in itself. My father reminded us almost every day how fortunate we were to have such a great star amongst us. She, who was the most widely acclaimed and sought after singer in the country at the time, overwhelmed us by offering to sing something for us every day. She would settle down on the big red Kashmiri carpet in the drawing room, resting her back against the seat of the sofa and ask for her tanpura to be fetched from her room. This was a cue for the servants to push all the furniture back against the wall. Everyone who was in the house at the time would hurry to the room and sit around her on the floor. She usually sang a devotional song for the benefit of my grandmother who was considered very pious. Bhajans were not really Kesar Bai's forte and she rendered them in a characteristically aggressive style which used to bring a startled though dutiful expression to my grandmother's lined face. The same style was absolutely magical when she sang khayals. She would choose her pieces carefully so that they appealed to the unsophisticated but strong musical tastes of my aunts. At the end of the not very long sessions, they would all be sighing with pleasure and whispering together incredulously at the undreamt of beauty of the experience. They loved the music as well as the fact that this wonderful thing was happening to them. Kesar Bai was shrewd and knew that her gracious attention to his family members would please my father.

Her style in public was quite different. She could be arrogant and sometimes nasty, without visible provocation. I once went with her when she was scheduled to perform for the annual festival of the Bharatiya Kala Kendra in Delhi. She genuinely believed that her khayal singing style was the best in the country and that there would never be anyone to equal her. She was right and there was no one who did not agree. Despite that, she felt insecure and was often ungracious to people who deserved better. As she swept regally into the green room in her diaphanous white chiffon sari, her head literally in the air, she saw Rasoolan Bai, the consummate thumri singer from Banaras sitting meekly on a rug on the floor, waiting to go on stage as soon as her tabla player had finished tuning up. It was well known that in order to hear herself better in concert, Rasoolan Bai had cultivated the habit of covering her left ear with the little finger of her left hand. This had become an idiosyncrasy that her many admirers loved. As a technical aid to perfect pitch she found it so invaluable that she used it in every recital. All concert-goers associated the gesture with her, and so did Kesar Bai, as I was soon to discover.

As soon as Rasoolan Bai sighted the great Kesar Bai, who was an awesome presence for all musicians, she courteously stood up and folded her hands in greeting. She not only respected the singer but also considered the khayal form she represented somewhat superior to the genre of the thumri and dadra that she herself specialized in. Besides, she was by nature a soft-spoken, cultured, and humble person with practically no ego. Far from appeasing Kesar Bai, Rasoolan's deference provoked her to bare her claws.

'Rasoolan, what on earth are you doing here? I am told it is a serious music conference. Can it be that you have come here to sing?' she asked haughtily, trying to disguise the dig as good-humoured banter.

'Baiji, when you have graced this city with your presence, it would be nothing but impertinence for me to claim that I have also come here to sing!' Rasoolan said, meaning every word. 'When you are here, how can I dare to sing?'

'Why not? Why not? Why should you not sing? Who can stop you? Unless of course your little finger has got too tired of working and needs a little rest!' Kesar Bai said.

None of the people who were witness to this exchange had the faintest idea what satisfaction Kesar Bai could possibly have got out of it.

At this time I was in the eighth class, and greatly interested in singing myself. I used to sing with equal relish the songs I had been taught by Mohan Baba, the family music master, and the hymns and English hunting songs our class mistress

Miss Ashdown sang every morning to the accompaniment of the battered piano in school. Normally I needed no encouragement to perform but I was intimidated by Kesar Bai and used to dry up when she came to stay in our house during her visits to Delhi. To my great mortification, my father coaxed me into singing for her so that she could give him an assessment of my talents. I knew it was a hopeless exercise. She couldn't possibly take me seriously, but I had no choice but to do what my father asked. I belted out my best song, trembling within under the delusion that my family's general rating depended on my performance, and at the same time feeling profoundly silly and self-conscious. She made the appropriate encouraging noises, spoke feelingly about my powerful lungs and said, with an arch smile directed at my father, that she would gladly teach me one or two things while she was in Delhi. I knew I was being offered the sun and the moon. My father made sure I squirmed with gratitude at the enormity of her gesture, but somehow I could not connect myself with it. I longed for the comfortable, humdrum musical activity of the community lessons with Mohan Baba. Instead of going to her room that evening when I was supposed to, I escaped to see the Disney film *Snow White and the Seven Dwarfs* for the sixth time, with some of my school friends. My father was speechless at such truancy and I still don't quite understand it myself. Nor did Kesar Bai. Needless to say the offer was never repeated and I was able to slide back into the familiar routine of my life with something like relief, though my father's disapproval hung over my days like a black cloud.

Kesar Bai had been dead for nearly twenty-five years when I started practising for Harballabh. During this gruelling phase I was transported into her awesome presence in spite of myself. She was my most vivid connection with Harballabh and now seemed to take possession of my mind. It was almost as though she was directing me, making sure I didn't fall on my face. I clung to this fancy because it diffused my nervousness like an anaesthetic and helped me to focus on the faults that she had said would not be tolerated at Harballabh. I had to move away from detail and nuance a little and look more at the broad outline and the shape of the total structure. The musical intention had to be much bolder than the tentative, delicate exploration I had been taught to idealize. I concentrated so much on these aspects that I felt a big change in myself, so much so that when it was time to go to Jullundur I felt like an athlete with rippling muscles getting ready for a wrestling match.

The two hundred-odd musicians who converged on the town were billeted in the homes of various local patrons who prided themselves on being chosen as hosts. The visiting artistes were regarded almost as messengers of the goddess, precious if not divine. Some of the older citizens treated their participation exactly as though it was a religious ritual which would earn them merit. The association of the occasion with the Saraswati temple definitely had something to do with this. On arrival at the railway station, garlands of marigold were flung around our necks by a disorderly but enthusiastic reception committee. While we were waiting for the other invitees to get off the train, I bought some oranges from a stall on the platform. The fruit vendor could tell from the garland that I had come to perform and absolutely refused to accept any money for the fruit. When I pressed it upon him, he got very upset. He touched my feet, folded his hands and begged me not to force him to commit sacrilege. There was nothing for it but to withdraw from the argument and accept the gift.

Kamalaji, the warm and hospitable wife of an affluent woollen garments manufacturer, was my hostess. Two of her other guests were so eminent that I felt I had no business to be under the same roof. The celebrated Bhimsen Joshi, with his wife, was another guest in the house. I nearly died of embarrassment when Kamalaji introduced me and said I had also come to sing. He did not change his deadpan expression and stiffly folded his hands in response to my greeting. 'And this is my jailer', he said stonily, jerking his head in the direction of his wife. I was intrigued at the time but Kamalaji told me later that he was passing through a very difficult time trying to stop drinking. His wife had become very concerned and taken to accompanying him everywhere. This explained his dig at her. Another guest was Rais Khan, the famous Adonis-like young sitar player who had once displeased Begum Akhtar inadvertently.

My ustad used to say he was the most talented player of the instrument he had ever heard. According to connoisseurs, he would have put all the more famous names in the shade if only he had had a little more discipline. Rais Khan was escorted by a glamorous English-speaking young woman in dark glasses who had obviously decided to take charge of his life, since he himself was 'so unworldly'. This was Rehana, who my hostess told me was a jewellery designer, political worker, and art lover. She was quite beautiful and moved with deliberate grace. In public she wore the intent look of someone who is constantly obsessed with worthwhile causes. Her present project was this beautiful, artistic creature whom she dotingly called 'Kaan Saab' and overwhelmed with her perfumed attentions. 'He is so humble! My God, he could take the whole country by storm if only he would let people hear him. That is why I insisted on bringing him to Harballabh', she gushed in her mincing convent accent, tossing her tinted curls in protest at the unfairness of life while the object of her infatuation smiled enigmatically, playing the role of the romantic genius he undoubtedly was to the hilt.

Rehana had designed a pair of versatile, flower-shaped eartops in which a changeable pin bearing the central stone could be passed through an unattached outer circlet of diamonds such that it held the whole ornament in place on the earlobe. There was a choice of five central gems: a larger diamond, a pearl, a ruby, a sapphire, or an emerald. In the glow of the instant intimacy that house guests feel amongst themselves she showed us how different the eartops looked after each change. Kamalaji and I both applauded the cleverness of the idea. That evening, when we all piled into a car to go to the festival, I noticed that she was wearing one of the eartops as a nose pin, while its companion glittered in the right earlobe of Kaan Saab. This was her childish way of savouring and announcing their special connection. The central gem this evening was a ruby and she wore a sari to match.

'Such a happy feeling, this red of the ruby! It is so right for the start of the festival. When Kaan Saab plays I will change it to suit his mood. If he plays Yaman, his favourite raga, it will be pearls. Pure white, you know! If it is Kedara, of course it will have to be blue sapphires!' she breathed. 'I'm carrying all the gems with me! One never knows!'

She was quite right. One really never knew. A special feature of the festival I discovered was that there was no fixed programme. The artistes could decide on the spur of the moment what and when they wished to perform. Since the music went on non-stop for three or four days, ragas for the oddest times of the day which never fall into any concert pattern, for instance three o'clock in the afternoon or the same time in the morning, got an airing at Harballabh. One was free to go up to the organizers and say exactly when one wanted to mount the stage. They set great store by spontaneity and simply scribbled in chalk on a crude blackboard placed near the entrance to the grounds what the next item would be. There was no need for setting formal limits to how long it could go on because the audience reaction here was very vocal. They would never allow anything to drag on out of politeness.

Nor did they leave one in any doubt as to who their idols were. They simply worshipped Bhimsen Joshi, who was lovingly referred to as Panditji, and would genuinely be unable to hear anyone else if they knew he had arrived on the scene. As a matter of fact he had, but before making a public appearance he disappeared with two disciples for a quick drink, giving everyone, including his wife, the slip. This led to a series of unforeseen situations. When he could not be traced anywhere, and twenty thousand waiting people had to be served something, a formal request was made to Rais Khan, who was considered by some to have the same stature, to fill in quickly. There was a readymade audience and it seemed the perfect time for him to make his debut. He was escorted to the tuning tent along with Rehana. She must have consulted him about the raga he was going to play and made the required switch in the central gem of his earring (and of course her own nose pin, for moral support) because when he made an appearance on the stage he was a pure white figure from top to toe, a lustrous pearl having replaced the earlier ruby. He looked like a young god as he settled down under the bright lights with his beautiful sitar, a straying curl playing artistically on his forehead. After a while the music began, and gripped the audience immediately with its unusual quality. Rehana joined us in the pandal, biting her lip and simpering nervously as though she was responsible for every note this genius played.

It was a huge stage, and the exquisite figure of Rais Khan looked a bit forlorn under the glaring lights. Nevertheless, he played with aplomb, his head bent dreamily over the frets. When he was midway through the performance, there was an unexpected uproar. The left half of the solid sea of people burst into hysterical applause. The artiste looked up, smiled triumphantly, bowed his head and touched his forehead with his fingers many times in salaams of acknowledgement, quite certain that he had succeeded in impressing this most discriminating of audiences. He could not see what was causing the commotion because it was literally happening behind his back. From the entrance at the right rear of the stage, the tottering figure of Bhimsen Joshi was seen slowly advancing towards the front edge of the stage with a fixed smile on his face. Before he came abreast of Rais Khan, he stopped under the lights with folded hands, swaying slightly in the act of granting 'darshan' to his adoring fans whom he had been told were clamouring for him. It was this vision that had caused the uproar, not the musical heights Rais Khan had achieved. He played on, quite innocent of what was sending the western side of the congregation into ecstasies. The organizers sensed that there could be a serious disturbance if something was not done forthwith to withdraw Bhimsen Joshi from public view until the sitar item was over.

An usher was dispatched to do something about this. He came up behind Bhimsen Joshi on tiptoe, making furtive gestures with his hands, holding a finger to his lips and generally pretending he wasn't there at all. He bent and squirmed so that his thin frame was hidden behind the solid body he had been sent to remove. He grasped the silk kurta at the back of the waist with both hands most respectfully, if such a thing can be imagined, and tried to pull the star backwards into the wings as though he were a kite on an invisible string. When he was swallowed by the black curtain, Rais Khan was still in full cry and continued to play with great ebullience for about five minutes.

Then, two things happened simultaneously. Rais Khan broke a string and had to stop playing while he set things right, and Bhimsen Joshi made another appearance, this time from the left rear of the stage entrance, so that the right half of the congregation should also be favoured with an opportunity to feast their eyes on his person. In his clouded state, he was troubled by the fact that he had been partial to the devotees sitting on the left side and had inadvertently denied a similar opportunity to those on the right. The purpose of his second appearance was to redress this wrong. When he was fully lit, teetering and smiling, and stretching his arms in greeting, there was a volley of thunderous clapping and another enthusiastic roar rent the air. Rais Khan turned ashen as he realized that this could not possibly be applause because he was still fixing his string and not playing. If only he had happened to look over his shoulder, the mystery would have been cleared, but he did not. The possibility that they could be booing him off the stage slowly hit him. He grabbed the microphone in panic and tried to make a winning speech in refined Lucknow Urdu in the hope of regaining the rapt attention he thought he had earned from this wild crowd in the beginning.

'I have great esteem for the name of Harballabh and I had come here with very high hopes. I want to offer to you the treasures that God has been kind enough to bestow on me, but only if you have any use for them. I will play on only if you wish. If not, I will go', he said in an injured tone.

'Now we want Panditji!' they roared in one voice. 'Only Panditji!' This time the usher did not have the guts to pull Bhimsen Joshi back. He weaved under the harsh lights with a vague smile on his bemused face until the whole area was chanting his name and demanding to hear him. The organizers looked resigned and defeated as Rais Khan stalked off in disgust, followed by a small train of indignant supporters led by Rehana.

The blackboard was wiped clean again and the name of Bhimsen Joshi written carefully across it in much larger letters than usual and without any spelling mistakes, which was something of a feat. Everyone was waiting. This was the highlight of the whole festival. The universal favourite was taken to the tuning tent to get ready to perform. There his doting followers apparently provided further refreshment disguised as soft drinks so that he did not get into further trouble with his 'jailer'. When he mounted the stage in a rich red and gold shawl half an hour later, there was ample evidence of the added inspiration he had received since his last stage appearance. To the regulars of Harballabh, he was nearly God and anything that he uttered would be a divine revelation. The time for judging was long past, buried in remote history. Now the deity had made an entry into the pantheon and the only relevant thing was faith and devotion.

The tanpura is a beautiful instrument in any case, but the pair that were carried to the stage for him were really spectacular. Two disciples stationed themselves on either side of the master and began to strum softly, directing obsequious glances at him so that they could stay in tune with his mood. There was a sarangi player to the left and a tabla player to the right. Behind one of the disciples sat a harmonium player. Two other attendants, one with a thermos and the other carrying a flowered bath towel, flanked the ensemble. Each one in the group was draped in a coloured woollen shawl and the whole looked like an exotic flower arrangement with Bhimsen Joshi as the bouquet's centre. He covered his legs and feet with his red shawl and cleared his throat, his characteristic signals that the recital was about to begin.

Another characteristic dear to the heart of his admirers was his passionate body language when he produced the first note which was supposed to emanate from the solar plexus. To find it, he used to stretch his arms sideways, with the palms turned outwards, and bend his body forward at the waist, nearly touching the floor with his forehead. Apparently this posture was most effective in locating the centre of his being from where the note had to be fetched up to an audible level. This is what he did now while we all waited in a fever of excitement for him to surface. The dive seemed longer than usual, and we could now hear the expectant breathing of thousands of people. But he did not rise. A whole minute went by and then another. Nothing happened. Slowly, the outstretched arms went limp. The tension went out of the body which was now resting comfortably on the forehead supported by the floor. The other members of the ensemble realized that their hero had passed out. Four of them hurriedly lifted his spreadeagled form which looked like a large tropical bird that had been shot and carried it away from the bright lights. We heard afterwards that on the advice of his wife they had placed the shot bird under a water tap briefly just as it was and that he had made a splendid recovery within two hours.

Meanwhile, the crackling and strident public address system made many nervous attempts to soothe the public. While a nondescript local tabla player filled in, there were repeated assurances that Panditji was only temporarily indisposed and would soon be back to lift our spirits to celestial regions. At long last he was sighted again, dried, combed, and changed, but slightly wary. There was no euphoria in his demeanour this time as he took his place on the stage. To our enormous surprise, he immediately broke into a rhythmic Marathi abhang, the kind of light and short piece he usually reserved for the tail end of a very long recital as a sort of inconsequential dessert. He did a competent, business-like job of it and after exactly ten minutes rose, folded his hands in a namaste and walked off the stage. People rushed towards him as he was coming down the ramp and begged him to favour them with the full exposition of any raga of his choice because this is what they had travelled hundreds of miles to hear and what they had been waiting for since the start of the festival. The abhang, in their humble opinion, could always have come at the end.

'What? Do you mean to tell me that you people did not hear the raga Malkaus which I sang for two hours before I came to the abhang? Where were you?' Panditji countered.

There is no doubt in my mind that he was absolutely sincere when he said that, and that he truly believed he had given a fullfledged conventional concert that night.

So far as my own performance was concerned, I knew I would have to tell them sooner or later when I would like it to be. I felt as though I had the freedom to decide the time of my own execution. I chose early morning the next day in the hope that the audience would be manageably thin after the previous night's exertions. Furthermore, no celebrities were likely to appear at the site until later in the day so I would be spared the feeling of inadequacy and presumptuousness that assailed me when I compared myself to some of them. I also felt safer with the devotional flavour of the morning ragas because, like eggs, it is a dish one cannot easily ruin, however nervous one might be.

I had carefully prepared myself for the kind of audience I would have to face. But when the big moment arrived, the sheer size of the stage and the vastness of the numbers paralysed me. I wasn't sure I could produce any sound at all. I took a deep breath as I had been taught and brought it out in a single note like a sleepwalker. The primitive loudspeakers boomed and crackled, and I began to listen as though it was someone else who was trying to sing. The raw response of the people to the simple but powerful lines of Bhairav came at me like a moving truck and ran over me. I felt as though I was one of the listeners, one to whom something was happening rather than the one who was producing the sound. At first the singing did not seem to have much life. But slowly the tentative, rather feeble pulse of the music became stronger. It would survive, I thought passively, but with relief. My love for the music was willed out of me by something outside myself—the place, the people, the force of their expectation, their faith. What I experienced was not the usual performer-audience chemistry that one often encounters in this business but a kind of revelation that is impossible to describe. When it ended, I realized that I had been on the stage for more than an hour and they had not booed me off. This alone meant that I had been a success. I was in the seventh heaven when I collected my things and retired to the tuning tent. It was the happiest moment of my life.

Before I left the stage, I had noticed a massive matriarch dressed in the local salwar kameez and dupatta looking intently at me and knitting furiously at the same time. She was surrounded by six younger women who were obviously her satellites. Two of them carried bundles wrapped in thick woollen blankets. These turned out to be either comatose or extremely undemanding babies. When the music stopped, a third one began to dispense rolled up parathas from an enormous tiffin carrier to those around her. My sarangi accompanist Sabri Khan, an old habitue who knew Harballabh like the back of his hand, told me that these were family members of Gurdial Singh, proprietor of Vinko

Rubber and Steel Industries, a pillar of the festival who had been donating generously for years. He pointed out that all the men of the family, young and old, worked selflessly as volunteers behind the scenes day and night and were therefore never to be found enjoying the music among the audience. He made them sound like war heroes, which was quite appropriate as I discovered later.

I was warming my hands over a charcoal bukhari and generally unwinding in the tent which served as a green room when the matriarch sailed up to me like an ocean liner and said in broad, idiomatic Punjabi, in a startlingly unmodulated country accent, 'We want to congratulate you.' She was flanked by several other women who beamed silently at me, nodding their heads in support of what their leader was saying. These must be the simple but discerning listeners I had heard so much about, I thought to myself. It was my ardent hope that they had sought me out because they appreciated my unusual approach to Bhairav. I waited modestly for the praise that I was sure would follow her opening words. But nothing came except more beaming smiles and a long though easy silence.

'It is very kind of you to come to me. I am glad you enjoyed the singing', I said.

'I don't know much about that. It must have been very good. But I was telling my daughters-in-law here that I was very happy to see you on the stage. You looked very nice.'

The daughters-in-law nodded eagerly in unison. But I was taken aback at the statement because of all the things that could happen to me, looking nice on the stage was the least likely. For one thing, I was now grossly overweight. My excuse was that for nearly a year I had just been sitting in one place with my instrument, or so I liked to think. For another, good looks had never been my strong suit even at the best of times, that is, even when I was young and slim. In this city of plain speaking I didn't quite know how to take what these women were telling me.

'Oh, no, no!' I protested. 'I'm not . . .'

'Absolutely!' the ocean liner asserted encouragingly. 'I was telling my daughters-in-law how good you looked in your red sari.'

She stepped up and thumped me solidly on the back to reinforce her compliment. There was still no word about the singing, I noted with a sinking heart. Sensing my discomfiture she said reassuringly, 'When you got up on the stage, you looked so solid! One felt that a real person was on the stage. Someone who has eaten and drunk well! Not a waif who can be wafted off the stage by the wind, like the lady yesterday! That one I could blow away like a feather with just one breath!'

She blew softly on the palm of her hand to demonstrate how easily she could achieve this. I realized with alarm that she was referring to the slight build of the great Gangubai Hangal who had been my idol since my childhood and who had given an electrifying performance that everyone was talking about on the opening day. It dawned on me that this group of discriminating listeners, at least, hadn't the faintest notion of the significance of Gangubai even though she weighed only seventy-five pounds or of the distance between her and the likes of me. Fortunately no one else could overhear her compliments to me, otherwise I would have died of shame. I wondered wistfully whether I would have the courage to share this anticlimax with anyone, friend or foe. I had been applauded after the most important concert of my life only for my hefty proportions and well-fed look!

My supporter was still waxing, although her theme seemed to have changed from how substantial I looked on the stage to 'us women'.

'I was telling my elder daughter-in-law that it was a matter of great pride that our ladies too could get up there right next to the professional Khan Sahibs and do exactly what the most classical of them did, and do it just as well. I told her that your singing was as pukka as anyone's. So high class and difficult that no ordinary people can understand it. Just imagine! No, it seems we ladies are not behind in anything any more. I was telling her . . .'

My attention wandered away from what she had told her daughter-in-law and I felt a serious loss of focus. Now I really did not know what to make of Harballabh. It had been a long day and I was exhausted in every sense. I asked to be dropped to my digs in Kamalaji's house where a late dinner seemed about to begin. Six or seven people were hovering around the food on the table but not eating because they were waiting for someone to ask them to start. They seemed to be new guests whom I did not know at all. It emerged that they were a group of vegetarian accompanists who had just arrived from Bombay, extremely agitated because the house where they had been put up had served them lamb biryani by mistake. As usual, Kamalaji had leapt to the rescue although she herself could not be there at the time. She had telephoned instructions to her household that a blameless meal, without even onions or garlic, should be cooked very quickly and served. The first part had been done but not the second. Balam Singh, the cook, had put the food down on the table and vanished without trace. My seniority as a guest exceeded their's by a few hours, so I took the liberty of acting as hostess and asked them to drop their shyness and help themselves. They fell on the food and I went looking for the cook. I finally tracked him down in the back storeroom, peering through a small hole in the wall which the house shared with a commercial cinema house located in the same building. I could tell from the worn, black hand marks on the wall that he had been watching movies through this hole for years. He looked a little sheepish when I came upon him. I persuaded him to abandon his viewing for a little while because I didn't know where the glasses were in case the guests wanted to drink water after their meal. He did comply but with ill grace; grumbling under his breath that because of this wretched festival he still didn't know what happened to the heroine after the train blew up. Every time the film got to that point, some great musician wanted lunch, tea, or dinner!

It struck me with the force of a revolutionary new idea that Harballabh meant different things to different people. It was certainly not a place of pilgrimage for everybody as I had grown up to think. For instance, it seemed to be no more than an exciting new kind of cocktail party to Rehana. To Rais Khan it was an adventurous flight into the unknown on the alluring wings of romance. The knitting matriarch and her galaxy of daughters-in-law obviously regarded their attendance at the festival compulsory since it reflected the growing affluence and social standing of the family of Gurdial Singh of Vinko Rubber and Steel. To Kamalaji and thousands of other religious-minded citizens of Jullundur it was a delicious and enjoyable way to serve the goddess Saraswati and earn merit. To Bhimsen Joshi's wife Harballabh was undoubtedly a trial and a threat because she was on alien territory and not in as effective control of the situation as she might be where she understood the local language and idiom. To Balam Singh, the cook, it was just a nuisance that came in the way of his well-worked-out entertainment routine.

But what had it meant to Kesar Bai who had started it all in my mind twenty-five years earlier? On my way back in the special train, I realized that just one exposure had changed the picture of Harballabh which I had carried in my heart for so long. It was no longer the beauteous, inscrutable face of a god perfect in all respects, but that of a world-weary sage who was also part clown. Surely Kesar Bai had seen that too. I wondered what made her abandon, year after year—and that too during the height of the music season—the comfortable concert circuits of Bombay, Poona, Kolhapur, Delhi and Calcutta where she was without question the crowned queen. Why had she preferred a difficult train journey of more than a thousand miles to the rough and cold arena of Harballabh where she had to wage war anew each time before she could claim victory over its earthy listeners? Something told me that at heart she must have been a warrior who could not resist the lure of conquest. Suddenly my whole being brimmed over with warmth and respect for her. I wished devoutly that all those years ago I had not gone to see *Snow White and the Seven Dwarfs* in defiance of her. Instead, I wished I had gone down on my knees before her and at least thanked her from the bottom of my heart for offering to teach me 'one or two things'.

TEN

Mrs Henderson from Ohio

I had a wife-to-wife encounter with Mrs Henderson which I am sure left a permanent mark on us both though it was brief. Like me, she was the wife of an economist, a clear category that the academic world in the 'fifties readily recognized and made provision for in planning the activities of visitors. In those days there was heavy international traffic in economists and one of their favourite landing stations seemed to be the Delhi School of Economics, where my husband was employed, which is putting it mildly because he was obsessed with the School and its concerns. These were the early years of our marriage which I felt deserved a little more attention, occasionally. I can hardly remember a time when the School was not playing academic host to visiting luminaries who flew in from the United States, from Canada, from Cambridge and Oxford in England, from Australia and from Japan. This was all very new and exciting for those who were in a position to be intellectually stimulated, but there came a time when it began to present some difficulties to me personally.

Most of the eminent foreign visitors were men whose wives just came along for the ride. The tourist agenda for the 'wives' was expected to be set up and executed by the host 'wives'. While the men busily discussed economic matters at seminars, lectures, and official lunches, the wives had to be escorted to the Cottage Industries Emporium for ethnic shopping, shown the sights of Delhi, and exposed to various regional cuisines and customs. My husband had acquired the generous habit of offering my services for this role. The only problem was that I had no time and no resources to do justice to it. I was a junior Assistant Editor in the Publications Division of the Ministry of Information and had a regular nine to five job which really worked out to an eight to seven job because of press deadlines: I was also trying to become a professional classical singer and had to find at least three hours a day to practise. We had no car, no telephone, and no money for taxis. Despite this, I went along with my husband's wishes for three years, spending money we did not have, and donating many precious Sundays and holidays to planning and carrying out guided tours to the Red Fort, to Dariba—the silver bazaar in the old part of the city—and to the Qutub Minar monument, instead of tuning my tanpura and trying 'to find myself' as my music teacher had strongly suggested. I did try, but my contribution to the cause of the visiting wives was dismal on the whole.

I could not even organize average hospitality in our home at that time because I was a hopeless novice at housekeeping. Such cooking as went on was done by Bala Dutt, a domestic servant from the hills of Almora that my mother had arranged for me to have. We lived in one-third of a decrepit old bungalow allotted by the university to my husband. Basically it consisted of two dark rooms (most of the windows having fallen to the share of the family that had the central part) and a kitchen with a primitive choolah of brick and clay which Bala Dutt used to light with charcoal after much struggling. There was no point in inviting any formal visitors to share my hardships. One evening, after a particularly gruelling and lunchless day at the office, I tottered home to find Bala Dutt fiercely blowing into the erratic choolah to light it so that we could think about dinner. It was such a major operation that he had taken off his shirt and trousers and stood only in green striped underwear with the air of a mechanic who is about to crawl under a car to get to the bottom of the trouble. Suddenly life seemed unbearable and I burst into tears. Bala Dutt obviously had exactly the same thoughts because he left us for good the next morning.

His successor was Buddhi Ram, a khansamah of British Indian vintage, an old relic of the long since dismantled household of some impoverished Anglo-Indian Sahib. He had a kindly, weatherbeaten and lined face, magnificent flowing white moustaches and an impeccably polite manner. With his impressive personality to back me, I ventured to invite two 'visiting wives' to a dinner of roast lamb and potatoes, to be followed by a poisonous looking but fairly eatable yellow custard pudding. These dishes were in Buddhi Ram's repertoire, I knew, and they seemed a comparatively risk-free choice at the time. But we never got as far as the actual eating of the dinner. The main guests took ill suddenly and had to leave at once, without warning but with profuse apologies. I was mystified by the hurried departure, but a friend who was helping me host this dinner guessed what must have caused the exodus. Buddhi Ram's ingenious way of making the dinner plates gleam was to blow at the eating surface with his breath and then rub it vigorously with a rag, as though he was polishing some vast reading glasses. This activity had apparently been sighted clearly through the open door as he was laying the table and might have sent our guests scampering back to the more sanitary environment of the university guest house. To me this was the final statement on my bankruptcy in the matter of entertainment. This fiasco was crowned by a quarrel with my husband when he returned from a long and fruitful seminar, glowing with the intellectual stimulation he had received. I told him this was not fair. After an hour of near hysteria from me, he gave in and agreed. It was mutually decided that I would never again be called upon to lift a finger in the cause of the 'wives' unless I myself felt I was able to or wanted to. I was overwhelmed at such reasonableness.

This understanding lasted only two months. Then, one morning of a second Saturday of the month, which used to be a much cherished holiday for employees of the government, I found Mrs Henderson standing at my doorstep smiling expectantly while my husband explained to me somewhat sheepishly that this time I would not have to go out of my way at all to take care of her. 'Mrs Henderson is deeply interested in Indian music so she will just sit and listen while you practise', he said with an anxiously polite smile. 'I have to take Dr Henderson to a special lecture at the Delhi School. We will be back around six, to pick her up.' The men left in a cloud of animated conversation. Clearly my unscheduled guest was 'spending the day', I thought, dying a little. 'I am glad that you are interested in Indian music', I said, trying to break the ice. 'I was just about to start practising. Would you care to listen?' She took in the shabby surroundings with determined broad-mindedness—the dusty veranda with its floor of uneven bricks, the scruffy she-dog who had adopted us unilaterally and chosen a corner to litter in, the faint smell of bats that refused to go despite my best efforts, and my neutral, slightly less than welcoming expression. Both of us had to put the best face we could on the situation.

'Thank you. That is really kind of you. What kind of singing do you do, Missiza-a-a Daar?'

'North Indian, or Hindustani classical. What I am trying to specialize in is the khayal of the Kirana style.'

'Oh, but don't you do the Car-na-tick? That's the one I really wanna hear. That's the purest, isn't it? Because they didn't have all those invasions and things, like you had in the North. Least, that's what my book here tells me.' She guffawed as she fished out a copy of Fodor's *Guide to India* from her huge handbag and stroked it fondly.

As I was to notice later, this handbag carried other aids to life for her hazardous six days in India—a tube of mosquito repellent, sun glasses, moisturizer, hand cream, lip salve, thick black notebook, travel brochures, Hindi phrase book, Kleenex tissues, a miniature aerosol breath freshener, and many other amazingly thoughtful standbys for all eventualities. I was deeply impressed because I had never met such a high-class traveller. But I was also a bit crestfallen that she was only interested in Carnatak music. She obviously wanted to use her precious time in India to savour the real thing, the unadulterated, pre-invasion traditional music of the most ancient people of India. I could hardly plunge into my impure Hindustani classical practice in these circumstances. If it had been wrestling or boxing we were talking about, I suppose I could have been resolute enough to go ahead with my plans regardless of everything around me in the approved fashion of dedicated musicians. As it was, I was at my wits' end. And I was going to be alone with Mrs Henderson on this desert island for the whole day!

The campus offered no distractions other than the coffee house which was just a stone's throw from our house. Anything was better than mutually joyless small talk so I persuaded her to come and have a cup of coffee to start with. It would give her a chance to see some teachers and students and get the feel of the place, and me a chance to evolve a workable plan of action for the day. The sight of Professor Shadagopan, head of the newly started department of music, sitting at a corner table, hectoring two meek-looking disciples, lifted my spirits. I felt that help was at hand. He was free enough to while away his time in the coffee house in the middle of a working day because work had not really started in the music department. Its activities were still mostly on paper. There were no students, particularly in the Carnatak section, for which he was directly responsible. 'Yanybody may say yanything, yultimately God is Love', he declaimed for the benefit of his devoted audience of two as we entered. I knew that Professor Shadagopan had recently ordered a sizeable collection of recorded music for the library of his department and this gave me an idea. After all there was something that Mrs Henderson and I could do together fruitfully and that was to listen to this music. I excused myself, walked up to Professor Shadagopan and begged for his help. He was most responsive, almost relieved to have a project he could be involved in. 'No prablam. No prablam', he said reassuringly. 'You go to department. Take American lady. Krishnaswamy is there. Tell him I sent.' Wonderful, I thought. A ray of hope at last.

It was a five minute walk through the campus to the music department which was housed in an old army barracks. The newly painted signboard fixed over a doorless arch in the primitive structure mentioned the benefactor whose endowment had made the music department possible. The text, 'The Lala Sir Shankar Lal Department of Music, University of Delhi', was arranged in a decorative semicircle. The Carnatak section consisted of one room, a small storeroom with a wooden almirah that presumably held the treasured discs we were after, a tanpura, a mridangam, two musicians, a clerk, an old cotton durree contributed by the university, an armchair with only three legs intact, a tin trunk which was wedged under the chair in place of the fourth leg, a chaprassi called Lachman whose only task seemed to be to fetch tea from a wayside stall nearby and to dust everything in sight, and of course the Head, who during this phase of the department's life was visible mostly in the coffee house.

As we entered, we saw Krishnaswamy and Subramaniam sitting on the durree on the floor, each draped over his instrument, in a state between sleeping and waking. A large, glossy calendar depicting the Siva Nataraja hung on a crumbling yellow wall. The apparition of a foreign woman (who showed every sign of being a glamorous American tourist) looming in the doorway, escorted by a 'local Hindustani classical type' was the last thing they expected to see on this peaceful morning. I quickly explained that we had genuine business with the department and that we had ventured in with the permission and blessings of Professor Shadagopan. 'This is Mrs Henderson from Ohio in the USA. She is very keen to listen to some good Carnatak music. I believe you have a fine collection of records', I said.

'Ooh, yes, yes', said Krishnaswamy, shaking his head vigorously from side to side in a gesture which anywhere else in the world would be construed as a 'no'.

'Well, could we please listen to something now?'

'Oh no, not today.'

'Why not? Professor Shadagopan said . . .'

'The records they are in almirah and yit is lock-a-da.'

'And the key?'

'Yit is with Mr Sharma, clerk.'

'Isn't he here?'

'No. Sick. On leave. Who knows when he coming here again', said Krishnaswamy, rolling his eyes and rotating his wrists neatly in the classical gesture of helplessness.

The conversation was at a dead end again. Subramaniam was wide awake by now but preferred to listen passively to the exchange. However he expressed his presence by striking the heads of his drum from time to time, producing short flutters of papery, rhythmic sounds in preparation for whatever might be happening next. Mrs Henderson was still looking determined and still smiling warmly at these new characters who might unveil the mysteries of pure Carnatak music before her flight next Thursday. Clearly, there would be no record-playing session to save our lives. In desperation I thought of something else to fill the yawning hours ahead.

'Mr Krishnaswamy, would you please sing one small kriti for this lady who has come all this way from Ohio in the United States of America? Just to give her an idea. Please.'

This was like pressing a magic button. Mr Krishnaswamy's eyes began to flash and he started to clear his throat. My request, which might have been the only one he ever received in his life, delighted him. The alleged deep interest of the American lady added to the significance of the event. We were all very happy, suddenly.

Mrs Henderson was offered the three-legged chair supported by the tin trunk and I sat down on the durree with Subramaniam. She began to tap her high-heeled foot in anticipation of the music which was about to engulf us, gazing dotingly on the prospective performer. Krishnaswamy cleared his throat once more and without further warning let off a powerful volley of sound which seemed to emanate mostly from his nasal sinuses. His voice, after some initial buffeting, perched on the tonic of the upper octave and produced some really intense blasts. From the shocked look on Mrs Henderson's face I could believe that this was her first exposure to pure Indian music. The explanatory notes in Fodor's

Guide were not quite the same thing as the actual taste of the medicine. Only the circumstantial evidence told her that it must be music she was hearing. She forgot to tap with her foot and the amiable mask dropped from her face. Krishnaswamy was looking heavenwards and belting the song out with renewed vigour, quite oblivious of our guest's distress.

When the raucous strains died down at last, she bent towards me and whispered accusingly, 'I never, but never, heard anything like that in my whole life.'

In the true spirit of the American tourist who is never at a loss for words because there is always more information that can be asked for, she went on, speaking clearly and slowly so that we could all understand. 'Could you tell me what the song is about? What is he saying? What do the words mean?'

'I don't really know myself', I said. 'The song is in the Telugu language which I don't understand a word of, but I will ask Krishnaswamy to tell us.'

Krishnaswamy was nodding sympathetically at both of us in turn but he wasn't able to grasp Mrs Henderson's English because of her intonation and twangy manner of speaking. So I paraphrased her question for him. He was most receptive, even a little intoxicated at the thought that only he could shed light on these deep cultural, literary, and religious matters.

'This is kriti by the revered composer Saint Thyagaraja. It is in aanar of the Lard Rama in the yincarnation of Kodandarama, or Rama with the Bow. Wo Lard, Wo Lard, the devotee cries in this kriti, yagain and yagain. Yagain and yagain devotee yappeals to the Lard to come down to yerth to save him and . . . salvate him, I mean cause his yinstant salvation.'

This time Mrs Henderson was at sea. 'Could you please translate that in English for me', she bleated, fully convinced that Krishnaswamy was still speaking in Telugu, the language of the song. I repeated the information in my sort of Indian English in an accent which was mid-way between Mrs Henderson's and Krishnaswamy's. That way both could understand at least every alternate word, but by this time the educational and cultural strain had become too much for my guest and she was ready to throw in the towel.

'I don't know who in hoot he's calling or what he's saying but I've a pretty good idea of why whoever it is ain't coming!' she said decisively, rising from her extraordinary seat. She looked exhausted but Krishnaswamy was glowing with pride and happiness. He looked as though he could guide generations of ignoramuses to the heart of traditional musical culture. As we prepared to leave, Mrs Henderson's hawk-like eye fell on the calendar. She smelt a deity. With luck it might even be the 'Lard' of Krishnaswamy's song and that would surely be an interesting coincidence.

'Who is that?' she asked boldly, now quite at home. 'Is it the same god you were singing about?'

'No, no, that is the Lard Siva in the Tandava posa. Yit is most primordial posa which you can see on all our ancient temple walls. Lard Siva in the Tandava dance shows the three aspects he is responsible for. Not wonly creation, not wonly destruction, but also maintenance.'

By now Mrs Henderson had tuned into the local intonation and could catch the general drift. 'I understand all that, but why is he standing on one leg? That's what I'd like to know.'

This time Krishnaswamy also got the question without my intervention. The communication was getting really good by now, with Subramaniam shaking his head by way of moral support to all. The only problem was that Mrs Henderson and Krishnaswamy were not thinking of the same leg.

'Modom, yif he lifts the other leg also, he will fall', Krishnaswamy said, as though he was explaining something obvious to a retarded child.

Mrs Henderson and I walked back to my place in absolute silence. There were still a good four hours to kill. In desperation I brought out the food that had been cooked for our dinner by a part-time helper who would not be back until the next day. I had learnt from my single experience with international airlines that serving meals was an effective way of compressing inordinately long time periods into manageable slots. I tried to fill the gaping hours with the business of heating and serving such food as there was in the house to Mrs Henderson for lunch. My small talk about recipes and the cuisine of northern India didn't sound convincing even to me. Suddenly the food we used to eat quite happily every day began to look yellowish brown, greasy, cold and unappetizing. She was willing to try everything once but clearly the fare in front of us, even if edible, was not worth learning about. So the whole exercise, followed by a short rest on our two easy chairs, accounted for another hour and a half at most.

There was still lots of time left. Both she and I were destined to suffer. I had no option but to carry her chair to the edge of my musical corner in the bedroom. I spread out my little rug on the floor, sat down, carefully tuned my instrument and started to sing. At first it was difficult to block out her earlier observation that my music was the outcome of 'invasions and things' but in the end I did manage to treat her to a leisurely display of how an aspiring Hindustani classical khayal singer of the Kirana gharana exercises her voice.

Her handy little black notebook could not possibly have described this day as exhilarating. At any rate it was far too long for us both. When Dr Henderson was driven up to our doorstep to take her away at last, the sun was already setting. Needless to say, the communication between my husband and me suffered a serious dip after this betrayal. His protestations of innocence and good intentions which all began 'But I thought . . .' maddened me even more. The fact that there was hardly any food left for dinner didn't help matters. On the contrary it gave him an excuse to work up a bad mood of his own. We spent a dismal evening and went to bed exhausted and feeling sorry for ourselves.

The news of my inept handling of Mrs Henderson's Saturday spread like wild fire on the campus. There were many households which would have been able to offer better entertainment and hospitality to the wife of such an eminent guest and would have been glad of the chance to do so. They were indignant to hear that all I had done for her was to drag her across the campus through the coffee house to the decrepit barracks that housed the embryonic Carnatak Music Department and then walked her back to my own house to kill time until the day was over. Mrs Chatterji, a professor's wife, was specially concerned that a valuable opportunity for cultural orientation had been lost and that the foreign guest had been left with the wrong impression that the academic community of Delhi University had nothing of value to offer. She considered her family a fountainhead of the generous culture of Bengal and regretted that she had not been called upon to contribute these riches for the general good. It was appalling for her to hear that Mrs Henderson's now famous visit to the Music Department had not included even a cup of tea. Being positive and liberal, she decided to do something to correct this state of affairs. The very next day she arranged a dinner in honour of the Hendersons to which we, the chief defaulters, were also invited.

If my house was a desert, Mrs Chatterji's bungalow on the main university road was a lush garden in comparison. Everything from the ornate hat-stand in the veranda to the delicate line-drawings on the furthest wall of the house spoke of grace and leisure. As we entered, we took in the easy chairs of colonial design with hand-embroidered cushions in the living room, the terra-cotta horses from Bankura on the old-fashioned mantelpiece, the Nandalal Bose original in the place of honour above it, and the strong smell of fish and mustard wafting in from the kitchen. This last was enticing to most of the guests, but I could tell that it made the Hendersons slightly apprehensive of what the evening held in store.

Our hostess was gracious and welcomed us with warmth and poise. I was lost in admiration because I could never have undertaken a venture of this sort without being in a flap. She was not only cool and smiling as though she had everything under control but also seemed to be enjoying the prospect of leadership in the matter of presenting a new and improved version of campus life to the visitors.

I was relieved that she was trying to undo some of the damage I had inadvertently done to the fair name of the community. I also genuinely respected, and even envied, Mrs Chatterji's total identification with and faith in a single, well-integrated way of life, She had a distinctive cultural turf to be on and belonged to a generation that was not torn by doubts about how to behave with foreigners. In comparison I felt that I was culturally confused and rootless, given to looking at everything from too many points of view, always uncertain what was expected of me and tending too often to explain myself as I went along. Moving too quickly from my Anglicized Mathur background to an American university and a marriage framed in orthodox Kashmiri culture simultaneously had robbed me of my spontaneous idiom. To me there were always many possible ways of expressing a particular thing: say, kindness, depending on the person concerned and the circumstances. I would not have been able to take for granted that pressing mustard fish upon Mrs Henderson was an act of kindness or hospitality. I would have been compelled to tune in to her psyche before deciding what being nice to her consisted in. In sharp contrast to my rather wishy-washy state of mind in such matters, Mrs Chatterji's confident, well-rounded attitude of generously offering a share in her good life to the guest stood out admirably.

I had put on my best cotton handloom sari from Bengal for the occasion and sported a large red bindi on my forehead in an unconscious effort to look like a member of the host family. They had come to the aid of the party as it were and I felt like making a gesture of solidarity with Mrs Chatterji. Besides, I really thought the Bengali look most becoming.

'Oooh, Meeshees Dhor, you look so nice! Jhaast like a Bangali lady! Pharst I thought you were Bangali Dhor, baat they tale me you are Kaasmiri Dhor! Caam and mit the gaystes. Haindersohns are already here.'

I marvelled at how every part of India could make English their own regional language, so much so that it was sometimes indistinguishable from the vernacular for all practical purposes. Mrs Chatterji was unbelievably sweet. The gentle, swaying walk, the soft brown eyes, the melodious speech and the faint odour of lavender in the freshly dusted talcum powder on her throat together seemed to imply that there were no problems in the world. At any rate there was nothing which her soothing, singsong, reassuring, 'there, there' kind of voice couldn't put right again. Mrs Henderson seemed to have recovered from her ordeal of yesterday and was beaming expectantly at all those present. Krishnaswamy's kritis had been a dead loss for her but she was an optimist. Something better was bound to happen, specially since her hosts this evening were so much more gentle, so much more sensitive to her needs than Krishnaswamy and I had been.

Dinner was served soon after every smiling member of the family had been introduced, specially the 'saan-in-low' who was 'bhery artistic' and sang 'bhery wail'. The dishes that had been cooked that evening were also introduced with the same affection and pride. 'The feeesh with hayd', 'danla' and 'shondesh' were brought into the conversation as though they were children of the house who were required to be nice to the guests.

Mrs Henderson was trying hard to soak in the ambience with the single-mindedness of purpose that had intimidated me the first time I met her. Someone was explaining to her with a laugh what the discriminating gourmet was supposed to do with the fine bones of the rohu fish. Finally, the dessert was served. It was received with welcoming cries and eaten to the accompaniment of many hymns of praise because it was indeed a masterpiece. At last it was time for the real treat of the evening which it turned out was a music recital by Mrs Chatterji's 'saan-in-low' and 'doter' because 'Meeshees Haindersohn like shongs.'

Her response to the announcement was to beam encouragingly at the prospective performers and to keep her high-heeled foot in readiness to tap out the rhythm of the music. The singing couple sat primly on a long cane sofa side by side, and quickly rearranged the expression on their faces from happy (at eating sandesh) to sadly sentimental as befitted the text of the ditties they were about to embark on.

They half closed their eyes and fixed their collective gaze soulfully at a fixed point in the middle distance which in the present case happened to be a light fitting. Amazingly, they looked more like twins at that moment than husband and wife. It was clear that they both felt very deeply the poetry of the song they were rendering. The music curled out from the depths of their being in very slow tempo and soon everyone in the room was swaying, as though in a trance. One sinuous melodic line followed another in poignant undulations. No beat was recognizable to the uninitiated ear. I noticed that Mrs Henderson's high-heeled shoe was suspended in mid air She had been forced to abandon her plan of participating by beating time to the music with her foot. Even the determined smile was fading. Perhaps Indian music was not her thing after all, but she was not going to give up without adding some information to her black notebook.

When the throbbing strains died down, there was a funereal silence because the audience was overcome with feeling. Mrs Henderson seemed to have a workable formula for such a situation. She had found from her experience in the Carnatak music department that the asking of inconsequential questions diffused tension and carried the social communication forward swimmingly.

'Now, that was quite different from what I heard the other day. Can you tell me something about the song? What do the words mean?' she said in a shrill, nasal voice, shattering the silence.

An uncle of the young performer took it upon himself to lead her through this cultural maze.

'Thees ees a phamous shong oph Gurudeb', he began in grave, worshipful accents. 'Actually, eet ees a bhery phierce shong.' He opened his eyes wide and shook his head from side to side to denote the fierceness of the Tagore poem. 'There ees descreeftion of the lashing and the dashing of the bhaves of the oshaan on the rocks in a storm!' he finished, pronouncing each word menacingly to bring home the raw power of the poem.

Mrs Henderson turned to me in disbelief, now seeing me in the role of an ally, and dropped her voice to a shocked whisper. 'Gracious, I couldn't feel the rocks or the storm! The whole song was liquid, if you know what I mean. No beat. And not a single bone in it. No sirree. To me it sounded like the progress of an earthworm!'

In fairness to her, it had to be admitted that the sweet and gentle cadences of the music seemed to most of us to be as far from the stormy intention of the song as anything could be. Mrs Henderson didn't want to be left high and dry. This was her last cultural evening in India and it was not going too well. She could not even beat time to the music! But she was not going to give up without trying at least once more.

'Don't you have anything more cheerful?' she asked brightly after an awkward pause.

'Ooh, yase. We hab so many modaarn compoger like Sholil Choudhry', said Mrs Chatterji glowing with satisfaction at the richness of the regional repertoire. After some nostalgic consultations amongst themselves, they chose a song. I still remember that the opening words were *'Dhitaang dhitaang bolley'*; or at any rate the way they were sung gave me the impression that this was a marching song. Compared to the earlier number, it sounded like a burst of artillery fire. The singers trilled and clapped and rocked and swayed with enthusiasm. 'That's more like it!' Mrs Henderson exclaimed excitedly as though she was egging on a race horse. She was back on firm land, at last in a position to beat time with her foot. After several renewed spurts of energy the song ended amid cries of joy from all concerned.

'And now, would you please tell me what the words mean?'

Here it was. The dreaded but inevitable question from Mrs Henderson.

Poetic translation was the forté of the uncle who had led us through the finer points of the Tagore song earlier. Mrs Chatterji signalled him with a smile and he started to explain passionately for our benefit.

'Thees shong ees laifteest in porport. Eet ees about the fermers in their filds. They are ripping the hervest of the crops on the land. They are girding their prodaacts, dancing round and round the ripped hervest, and also more or lace jubilating!'

This unscheduled raising of the radical red flag of leftist land workers in the middle of an innocent musical evening confused Mrs Henderson somewhat. These were the worst days of McCarthyism in America and she had clearly not been briefed for such a contingency. The best thing to do was to wear an amiable smile and steer the conversation away to something safer, which she soon did.

'I find the poetry in these songs very different from any folk music I've ever come across. It is most interesting', she said after a pause.

Mrs Chatterji found this opening irresistible. 'You maast also gait an idea of our poetry. Eet ees fool of filling. Badol will be happy to recite for you. He does Gurudeb's Shah Jehan whanderphully wail. Come, Badol, don't be shy!' she said patting her nephew on the back.

Badol obliged readily and the performance was really rivetting. Each sonorous line came spiralling out of a deep, primeval, reverberating ocean of sound. The voice of the reciter throbbed with controlled emotion as it scaled the octave, and finally burst into luminous rays like a Roman candle in the sky as the line ended on a high, trembling note. It was very moving though the only word I understood was the name of the tragic Mughal emperor Shah Jehan, which figured at the end of every stanza, and was pronounced each time with a different but very powerful evocation. Even as one poetic line was climaxing in the starry skies, the stirrings and rumblings of the following one taking birth at the bottom of the universe could be felt rather than heard deep in the throat of Badol. I was struck by the hypnotic ebb and flow of sound and meaning he was able to set up. I wished fervently that I could understand this magical language. The cadences, the rhythms and the whole feeling of the poem is with me to this day though all I can reproduce are mock sounds. 'Bhom bha bho bhoy, bhom bha bho bhoy, bhom bha bho bhoy, Shah Jehan!' I often intone it to myself and the nonsensical recollection can still bring tears to my eyes, though that evening there was much to smile about also.

As we said our final goodbyes on Mrs Chatterji's doorstep, I knew that Mrs Henderson would now be able to board her flight with a light heart. At least some of her time in Delhi had been fruitfully spent. She might even make some interesting entries in her notorious black notebook.

ELEVEN

The 'Cent per Cent' Gandhian

At the time when Mohan Rao was first inducted into the Publications Division as the deputy chief of production, the head of the office was Dr Sinha, a refined Westernized gentleman from Sylhet in East Bengal. He had been to both Santiniketan and England, culturally speaking. He was extremely well read and was equally at home with Shakespeare and Bengali classical literature. He liked opera but could also sing Tagore. He was a bald, rotund little man dressed in immaculate three-piece suits and shod in neat, well-polished Oxfords. He was married to a French woman and ate his lunch, even if it was just a boiled carrot, with knife and fork. Though he was a kindly man, the chaprassis and other staff were slightly intimidated by him because he smelt expensive and was clearly a more superior variety of sahib than anyone they had come across so far.

Dr Sinha was finicky about detail in all matters and not so concerned with the larger picture. Every manuscript that he came across claimed his personal attention. He couldn't help involving himself with delicate editorial nuances and spent hours improving the style of even publicity pamphlets. In his view, none of the editors on the staff could rise to the level of his over-cultivated literary sensibilities. He therefore ended up slaving over the manuscripts himself, at very heavy cost to the office because he had no time to fulfil the functions of the Director. Planning, administration, discipline and coordination had all been neglected until Mohan Rao joined as Deputy Director, Production.

Mohan Rao took in the set-up with deep disapproval and resolved to do what he could about it. Although it was not his area, he immediately came up with a large number of irresistible and necessary book titles which the government should, in his opinion, have undertaken to publish long ago: the collected speeches and writings of Gandhi, Nehru and other luminaries, biographies of the builders of modern India, basic books on India and being Indian for children and lots more. This sort of publishing proposal should properly speaking have emanated from the head of the office in consultation with the editorial section, not from someone in charge of production. But Mohan Rao brushed aside the conventional office procedures and managed to impose his programmes on the entire establishment by brow-beating and steamrollering everyone and everything that stood in his way. No one had the stamina to withstand him. Dr Sinha secretly resented Mohan Rao's interference and abhorred his aggressive and noisy style. Mohan Rao on the other hand did nothing secretly. For him there was no distinction between public and private and even though Dr Sinha could not decipher the text of Mohan Rao's daily verbal rockets, he understood perfectly that rebellion was afoot in his empire.

'I say, train will leave while you are putting in *chota chota* commas. Not fair to nation! Certainly not fair to nation!' he used to exclaim to his boss without the slightest hesitation and very inappropriately, in front of other colleagues. But his criticism had no trace of malice, and sooner or later everyone he came in contact with learnt to discount his rough, straight shooting manner. Everyone, except Dr Sinha, who could not deal with him at all. Once it became clear to him that the induction of Mohan Rao was a well-considered move on the part of the government to inject fresh blood and a new kind of life into the mouldering, bureaucratic leviathan that the Publications Division had become, he mentally started to pack his belongings and lost all further interest. For him there was no alternative but to withdraw. This process took almost a year in which Dr Sinha became listless and cynical.

Mohan Rao on the other hand went from strength to strength, spreading his wings over every section of the office, imposing his views freely on the administration, business, editorial, production and art sections. The problem was that for the first few months no one could understand a word of what he was saying. It was usual for everyone in the office to ask the person nearest them, 'What was that he said?'

This was because he really did not use language to communicate, at least not in the conventional sense. He had worked in Bombay with a nationalistic publishing house for many years and had a smattering of Marathi. He was born and bred in the town of Udipi in Mangalore and formally speaking his mother tongue was Tulu. He was also familiar with Kannada, and of course English. But none of these languages, either singly or jointly, could adequately convey his meaning in any given situation. And yet he was a great communicator and made strong and immediate contact with each of the hundreds of people he worked with. His main tools of expression were grunts, grimaces, unrecognizable monosyllables, hand gestures, and his severely abbreviated vocabulary which, in time, we all learnt to decode.

Even when he was saying nothing, one felt that he was bursting with reactions, opinions, and points of view. There was a constant emanation of energy which seemed to be addressing and enveloping everybody around him. The muscles of his face, his eyes and hands were always working, as though his entire being stood on tiptoe, spurting itself out under great pressure from within.

Finally the day arrived when Dr Sinha left for Europe. The wheels of government moved invisibly and Mohan Rao took over as Director of the Publications Division. Most people concerned were sure that there had been a terrible mistake somewhere. How could such a seemingly uneducated, rough-mannered, and inarticulate person be appointed to a position of such power and importance in the biggest publishing house of the country? What could he possibly know about books, they thought. But within a year almost everyone was convinced that Mohan Rao was the best thing that had ever happened to the Publications Division.

For most people this was difficult to believe because his many idiosyncrasies at first hid his personal and professional worth from view. He was a pleasant-looking person of about fifty years, neither tall nor short, neither fat nor thin. Sharp features, bright, alert eyes and bushy grey and black eyebrows gave him the air of an eagle, but his coppery complexion, silver hair, and noble facial expression somehow suggested saintliness. He always dressed in khadi bush-shirt and trousers, wore Kolhapuri chappals and constantly smoked bidis. He prided himself on these symbols of simplicity and patriotism. He had no polish of speech or manner and often managed to ruffle the feathers of the people he dealt with, but his good intentions and kindly nature always prevailed in the end.

Apart from his unorthodox vocabulary, he had a highly personalized, off-the-cuff system of assessment by which he would award marks out of ten to the subject under scrutiny. Although this was reminiscent of primary school methods, it had the merit of cutting through a lot of unnecessary verbiage which had been the bane of earlier staff meetings. Anything under the sun could be judged on a zero to ten scale. It could be a personality, a recipe, a place, a piece of music, a movie, just as well as a manuscript. For instance the character of Sardar Patel, his own aunt's coconut chutney, the Vrindavan Gardens in Mysore, Abdul Karim Khan's rendering of Raga Jhinjhoti, the Indian film classic *Dr Kotnis ki Amar Kahani*, and Bhabani Bhattacharya's first novel were all 'eight marks items' to Mohan Rao.

He had an uncanny feel for books though he was far from being literary himself. The entire editorial staff used to marvel at his sixth sense. We felt that he had only to sniff the pages of a manuscript and its entire future life as a book leapt out at him. On one occasion, he bounced a thick sheaf of papers that had been received in the office in his hands, put it down on the desk briefly, turned a few pages and began to thump the table excitedly. '*Lagao*', he shouted. 'Demy octavo, ten point roman, five thousand, fifteen. Next item'. This meant 'let us go ahead and accept it.' The specifications for the format, the weight and size of the paper, the size and style of the typeface, the print order and the selling price followed in the same instant, as part of his spontaneous formula which nearly always worked. 'Next item' meant 'let's not waste time going on churning out words and arguments when I know exactly what this manuscript needs.' He had an instinctive feel for the market, for what the public response would be, and for what was in the national interest. Sometimes the intrinsic worth or merit of a manuscript did not enter into his calculations at all. He was quite capable of saying of a manuscript, 'This is eight marks, but *chalega nahin*', which meant 'It is good, but it won't work.' He seldom had any explanation or argument to support his view, but from experience everybody in the trade knew that his judgement was infallible. 'I know what I am doing. You see, I am of the soil', was another frequent declaration. As all his associates learnt in time, the latter part of the statement meant that he was uncorrupted by any kind of sophistication, said exactly what he thought, and had no complexes.

According to him, the greatest man produced by modern India was Gandhi. He once expressed his admiration by saying ecstatically, 'Nine and a half? I tell you! What a man! Absolutely nine and a half marks man!'

One of the more literal-minded editors asked, 'Why have you taken away half a mark from this perfect man?' Mohan Rao was unfazed and answered in a matter of fact tone:

'Oh, I kept half mark back because that is reserved for neatness.'

He loved to share his enthusiasm and insights with anyone who cared to listen, specially with those he categorized as 'good' people. As employees, we didn't have much choice.

'I say, do you know what is the most sacred place in India?' His rhetorical questions always silenced one. One was not really expected to answer them.

'Why are you blinking? Of course it is Raj Ghat. Ask me why?'

'Why, Sir?'

'Thousands of people coming there. Not to say give my son-in-law promotion, make me well, give me grandchild. They do that in Tirupathi and other places. Here nathink like that. They want nathink. Wonly coming to say, my dear Sir, thank you very much. Hats off to you! Zimblee! No give and take! That what makes it the most sacred!'

There was nothing for it but to agree entirely.

'You know, my wife is like a flower', he once confided. 'Do you know why?'

'No, Sir.'

'It is because of me. *Am isko khoosh karta.* I am cutting vegetables for her yeveriday. I am sometimes plucking jasmine buds with my own hands and giving her for *veni.* Does your husband do that?'

'No Sir.'

'Rascal. Many like him here. Selfish. My wife, I call her the one and only Mrs Rao. Wherever I go I am bringing one sari. Makes her happy inside. So she looks like a flower, you will see, and sings like a bird.'

Once he came to the office in a new khadi-silk outfit, a bush-shirt and matching trousers. 'Not bad, what do you say?' he said to no one in particular peering at himself in the small mirror over the washstand in the corner of his office room. 'Distinguished', he added with conviction. 'I mean face shining, hair like silver. Quite O.K. I like it.'

The small group of assistants waiting in his office were being invited to share this view, in the same matter-of-fact way as one might say, 'It is a nice day, isn't it ?' At first we were all a little shocked at such vanity and immodesty, but even a short association with him convinced us that for him there was nothing personal in such personal observations and that he was being merely factual and objective when he said things in praise of himself.

He could also say extremely embarrassing things to other people without feeling the slightest embarrassment himself. He did not think much of Delhi, or of Delhi culture, having lived many years of his working life in a 'real' city like Bombay, and of course being 'of the soil' himself. Once at the early stages of our acquaintance while having tea at my house with his wife he remarked to her loudly in the hearing of my whole family. 'See, Delhi people how they invite. Just send mundoo to market quickly to bring ready-made snacks, samosa or some other rubbish. No work. Just show!'

I was indignant at his rudeness but when I saw that his face was glowing with pleasure and innocence, I knew that some other norms applied here. Again he was simply making a factual observation. Turning to me he said, 'See, my dear lady, when we invite to our house in our native place, we are taking lot of trouble. Lot of grinding. Ladies do themselves. Lot of work. Very tasty. Not like here. This is just daphrao. You must come to our place. You will see. We do with bhakti, not like this.'

'Daphrao' was a favourite word with him, probably picked up from local Bombay slang. I had never heard it before but learnt from his frequent use of it that it meant 'not genuine', phoney, or fraudulent. I had to admit the essential truth of what he was saying though it sank in slowly.

'Your Delhi is just make-up. Nothing real. See the ladies here. Just artificial silk and horrid, dark red lipstick. I tell you, sometimes when I am going in scooter, I have actually to cover my eyes with my hand. Chee, Chee, Chee!'

This last was a deprecating sound he often used to make. It did not come from any of the languages he spoke, but was his own original, extremely expressive invention to express disgust.

Mohan Rao had no qualms about making personal remarks and could say anything to anybody without a moment's hesitation. He had no idea that his remarks could cause acute discomfiture even in those he loved and liked. 'I say, Juneja, what are you wearing today? It really looks very funny,' he once shouted across the corridor to a young editor in the hearing of a dozen other people, referring to a new suit, which the man had probably got after months of saving and planning. 'You are a good lady. But why so fat?' he was once heard to say to a shy Hindi editor.

Mohan Rao had no status consciousness whatsoever and felt free to walk into the cubicles of any of his staff members at any time. Many of us wished he would keep out of our way at lunch time, but that was precisely when he was most active and mobile. He could not stand the peace that descended over the office for an hour. He would quickly finish his own vada and bananas in his rather grand office, light his bidi, and start on his feverish rounds, bursting with new ideas and shooting down everyone he could with them. Writers, translators, artists, production assistants, magazine editors, book designers, all gradually learnt to brace themselves for this unwelcome visitation during the sleepiest time of the working day.

I was once on a diet and had brought a boiled mutton chop to the office for lunch. As luck would have it, Mohan Rao burst into my cubicle just when I had finished eating and was hungrily chewing the bone. Being a very strict vegetarian himself, he had probably never seen such a barbarous sight.

'My dear lady, what are you doing? What are you putting in your mouth? Is it some dead animal?' he asked with the utmost candour and concern.

He was well disposed towards me and would have liked to save my soul. He also told me emphatically, while I was trying to dispose of the bone, that bananas were the ideal food and one need not eat animals.

'Chee, chee, chee! I can't believe! Such a nice lady!' he muttered, shaking his head sadly from side to side.

Within the first few meetings with him, everybody knew that Mohan Rao liked Gandhi, the Buddha, Ramakrishna

Paramahansa, cricket, the raga Puriya, arvikapatta, mango pickle from Mangalore, Lal Bahadur Shastri, the flavour of fresh ginger and green chillies, the singer Madurai Mani Iyer and the flute-playing of T.R. Mahalingam. He was suspicious of everyone who spoke English with a British accent, hated sophistication of any sort, and really believed that work was worship.

'*Arrey Mai, amko straight bolo*. Why go round and round? What is there?' he would say to anyone who explained too much, or went into too much detail.

This led to frequent skirmishes with the editors, who were obviously more interested in self-expression than in decisions and action. The usual officialese of government files, with its regular diet of 'On the one hand . . . and on the other hand' used to drive him wild. He showed his displeasure with malingerers and insincere workers by not giving them anything to do. The people whose work and style of work he liked were rewarded with too much responsibility and too many things to do. There were protests and minor battles but he was invariably the winner because his favourites did not have the stamina to fight his genuine trust and faith in their abilities.

It was a strong conviction with him that an honest man must come to his own conclusions, not take anybody else's word for anything, and resist being influenced by big names. He thought this to be a tenet of the Gandhian way of life, and practised it in his official life with some unintended ostentation.

'What is greatness? Tell me, you literature-wallas! I know what it is. I don't need Shakespeare to tell me.' This was in the course of an informal meeting with a group of editors.

Mohan Rao's spirited expositions had a way of exhausting his helpless listeners when they were actually taking place. But these very listeners had to admit that after a time lag the validity and wisdom of his outwardly simple observations surfaced with a new lustre.

'I'll tell you what greatness is. Nine marks here, and nine marks here', he thundered, thumping his head and heart alternately.

'*Barrobar*. Together. Wonly then. See, nine marks brain like C. Rajagopalachari no use. Because he has wonly three and a half here', he finished, slapping his chest vigorously to indicate the region of shortage in this case.

'Look at me. I too have at least eight marks heart. But only three marks head! I know. I am frankly telling. Doesn't matter. This I can always buy', he said hitting his temple with his matchbox.

'This', he went on, slapping his chest, 'you can't buy. You have to be born. God has to give. Only then! Nehru too has eight marks heart. But so much fuss about that! Chacha Nehru, Chacha Nehru! He loves children, they say! So what? I too love children. You should see how I play with them at Diwali. They are not Nehru's grandfather's property. And then, he has only about six and a half up here.'

Some of his audience made feeble sounds of protest at this last award to Nehru's mind.

'All right, all right, seven lagao, not more. I think he just missed the bus of greatness. But, Gandhi, that is something! That is really something!' he cried passionately.

It would be accurate to say that the very mention of Gandhi made his heart sing. It was for this reason alone that he overcame his native nationalistic resistance to foreigners and took an extremely British personality like Richard Attenborough to his bosom when he first came to India in the early 1960s in pursuit of his film project.

The vast empire of the Publications Division included an establishment called the Collected Works of Mahatma Gandhi. This was headed by Professor K. Swaminathan, a very saintly and eminent Gandhian scholar. Among other things, Attenborough wanted the script he was working with to be checked by this expert organization that he had heard about. He also had other matters to settle with the Government of India and hoped to do some actual shooting on the trip as well. His delegation consisted of eight people, which included Motilal Kothari, a London-based Indian sponsor who was also a friend, a small camera crew including two women, and other technical assistants. The entire company was ensconced in the Ashoka Hotel. It emerged later that they had been over-optimistic in thinking that they could get on with whatever they had come to do as soon as they had made contact with the right authorities. The right authorities were extremely hard to get hold of because they were always in meetings, or on tour, or on holiday. Those who could be located always referred the group to some other official or ministry. After three weeks of shuttling back and forth and heavy hotel expenses, no headway had been made.

Attenborough was fairly desperate when he drove up to the Publications Division in two DLZ taxis with his whole group. Technically the office of the Collected Works of Mahatma Gandhi fell under the jurisdiction of Mohan Rao and the bureaucratic slot machine demanded the proper channel for all movement. All Attenborough wanted from Mohan Rao was an official entry into the domain of the Collected Works of Mahatma Gandhi and an introduction to Professor Swaminathan. But Mohan Rao was not willing to be a passive cog in this, or any affair.

Sharada Prasad and I were summoned as official aides to the Director when these unusual visitors were ushered in. When their leader stated the purpose of their visit in an aristocratic British accent, Mohan Rao drew himself up, all prepared to defend the dignity and solidarity of India against presumptuous foreigners.

'I'd be extremely grateful if you could put us in touch with the Chief Editor. There is a script that we would like him to go through', Attenborough said.

Mohan Rao had no idea who his visitor was as he had hardly any contact with the Western film world. He had decided that in the national interest he must demonstrate that Indians could no longer be intimidated by the British and would act as they themselves thought fit.

'You see, I have to see the script before I can say anything', he said somewhat frostily.

'You really need not take that trouble yourself. The Ministry of Information and Broadcasting has asked us to approach Professor Swaminathan, but only through the Publications Division.' Attenborough sounded exhausted.

'Excuse me, I am of the soil. I like to know what I am talking about. I must see the manuscript before further action.'

'It is a rather lengthy one, I'm afraid. You'd need several hours even to skim through it', Attenborough said, stalling.

'What does it matter? You can leave it with me. Come back tomorrow.'

It became clear that Mohan Rao was not going to budge from this position. Attenborough reluctantly surrendered a copy of the script and withdrew with his company. As the posh DLZ cars disappeared in clouds of dust, Mohan Rao beamed at us, his expression proclaiming that he had won a major victory over a national enemy. However, he took the bulky manuscript home that evening.

When I entered the office the next morning, Mohan Rao was excitedly pacing the corridor, waiting for somebody to share the emotional storm that was visibly raging within him.

'I say, come here, come here!', he shouted. 'What a script! What a beautiful thing! Hai, hai, hai! On our own Gandhi! My dear lady, you and Sharada should both drown with shame, in a handful of water. Ask me why?'

'Why Sir?'

'Because some white man has written like this on our Gandhi, and you idle people are just walking about shamelessly! But it is okay. So what if he is white. I am broadminded. I have no complex. At least someone has written. I am so happy.'

He was in ecstasy, and now waiting longingly for the DLZ cars whose occupants he had spurned the previous day.

'That Englishman. I didn't know he was such a gem. I will tell him straight. I have genuine respect for such people.'

And then, at last the small delegation drove up again. Everybody knew by now that the Director considered this visitor extremely important. This time there was a big commotion with chaprassis running about announcing the event to the whole office and shouting unnecessary instructions to one another.

Mohan Rao leapt out of his chair to greet Attenborough and his companions with glad cries of welcome. Sharada and I were in attendance as we had been the previous day, and ushered the visitors to the chairs surrounding the Director's massive table. As soon as everybody was seated, Mohan Rao started bellowing in his hoarse, high-pitched voice.

'My dear Sir! I am so happy, so happy to meet you! I was just telling these blue-eyed editors of ours. Gandhi is not just for India. He belongs to the whole world. What a nice man you are! What writing! Beautiful, beautiful!'

Attenborough tried many times in the course of this outburst to open his mouth to speak, but was drowned out by Mohan Rao's vocal flood each time.

'I am just now ringing up Professor Swaminathan. We must be together. All right thinking people. You must come to my house to eat. You really deserve it. I never invite unnecessarily. Bring all friends. We will have a good time talking about Gandhi. We will have delicious preparations from our parts. You will definitely relish. My wife makes herself. She too will be so happy. We have special dosa. Not like here. We use three-fourths urudu, only one-fourth moong.'

The telephone connection with Professor Swaminathan came through at this point.

'One minute, *han*?' he said affectionately to Attenborough, asking him to relax in his chair with a reassuring hand. 'Professor, something fantastic I must tell you. There is a nice young man sitting in front of me just now. You should see how nice he is. He has written a beautiful manuscript about Gandhi. You must meet him. Tomorrow. At my house, for lunch. Yes, he certainly deserves it. If you see him and see what he has written you will agree. We will all have a nice time remembering our Gandhi, what do you say? This young man, he is English, but that doesn't matter. We are broadminded. We have no complex. I have told him.'

Attenborough had not been allowed a single word yet. He had tried to speak many times but was so slow to start that he did not get beyond clearing his throat. He just managed to make some polite, guttural, embarrassed and very English sounds in preparation for an important statement of some sort when Mohan Rao cut him off with yet another excited outcry.

'Just a minute. Let me not forget. I must tell Srinivas and

Nanjanath to come for lunch too. Good people. Let them enjoy also', he screamed, like someone cheering a winning hockey team.

The bell was rung, chaprassis rushed in, everybody he could think of was summoned and personally invited to the lunch. Attenborough was trapped in his chair, patiently waiting for Mohan Rao to finish organizing this event in his honour since he did not have enough stamina to stop him. After all the chosen ones had been invited singly and insistently and in the same impassioned words, there was a momentary lull.

Attenborough again cleared his throat and tried to say something in his soft, genteel manner but in the circumstances the only thing that might have worked was the blaring of several trumpets. Mohan Rao interrupted him once again.

'Oh, I almost forgot my editors. Shaila Dar, you too must come for lunch.'

Turning to Attenborough and pointing an accusing finger at me, he said, 'When she first came here she was nothing, I tell you. No thoughts. No values. Just blank. She belonged to what you call butterfly class. But I have injected her and injected her and now she can write well. Get your chapter on Gandhi from the children's book and show him.'

I just sat where I was, paralysed. Sharada was next.

'And this one. Fantastic editor. He too must come for lunch, of course. He is like an ass . . .' This introduction trailed off. Mohan Rao never finished his patent compliment to Sharada which we had heard many times before. He used to say: 'If errors are blades of grass, Sharada is like an ass, who will find and eat up each one of them.' But he had said it so many times that he took it for granted that everybody understood exactly what he meant when he compared him to an ass.

Attenborough and his companions were trying their best to focus, to get some sense of what was going on, but from their expressions it was clear that they were at sea, although they guessed that this man who pulled all the strings meant well.

My husband had once described Mohan Rao as a one-man mob. This morning I saw clearly what he meant.

At last everybody understood that Mohan Rao was anxious to host a lunch in honour of the visitors so that they could finally meet Professor Swaminathan. Attenborough was visibly relieved but like the upright English gentleman he was he did not want to benefit from the hospitality of a simple man under false pretences.

'Could I, could I please say something? I have been trying to tell you for the last half an hour that I have not written this script. I am Richard Attenborough, a film producer. I admire Gandhi and want very much to make a film about him, but the script is not mine at all. It is the work of an American writer who is not here with us today.'

Attenborough had speeded up his accustomed drawl considerably and spoken much louder than he normally did because he could no longer risk being shouted out. He was desperate to set the record straight.

The disclosure, clearly spelt out this time, fell like a bolt of lightning. Suddenly all the bustle died down and there was a hush in the room. Mohan Rao looked stricken. For a brief moment, words failed him. He narrowed his eyes and scrutinized his guest afresh, wishing fervently that the horrible thing he had heard was not true. He had become attached to his version of things and would have much preferred the author he admired so much to be sitting across the table from him, not invisibly ensconced in remote, inaccessible places.

'Oh!', he said and there was another long silence in which all the ten people in the room tried to smile politely at one another.

A few more minutes of this and Mohan Rao rallied, presumably with Gandhian endurance.

'Well, Mr Atten, you can still come for lunch', he said wearily. 'You are welcome, with your friends. After all, you are thinking nicely about our Gandhi.'

Apart from husband and wife, the Mohan Rao household consisted of their six teenaged children, five boys and a girl, four devoted nephews, and one more young person, a sort of cousin who helped in the kitchen by day and learnt typing and shorthand at night. The nephews were all studying for competitive exams of various kinds and looking for jobs. Mohan Rao considered it his duty to sponsor as many youngsters from his home town as possible and help them to stand on their own feet in the big city of opportunity. He made no distinction between these inmates and his own children. Everyone, including Mrs Rao, was expected to work hard, cheerfully, and be of service at all times. This was the rule of the household and Mohan not only enforced it but practised it himself. I discovered that his boast about slicing vegetables with his own hands after office was the literal truth. There were at least twelve bodies to be fed at every meal, but the cooking, serving, and cleaning was painless because the people in Mohan Rao's home, old and young, worked like elves in the fairy tale, each one anxious to take on as many chores and as much responsibility as possible.

We all felt rather spoilt and corrupt when we encountered this sort of domestic culture. It was true that Mrs Rao sang like a bird as she cooked, and looked like a fresh flower, with the jasmine veni in her glossy, neat hair. She was free to call upon any one of the young people the household was supporting for help. 'Will you stir this?', 'I need some ginger from the market', 'The thalis have to be washed', 'Can you make tea?' were usual things for her to say. Most of the time the devoted elves anticipated her needs and willingly did whatever was required. She was studying privately for a BA when I met her. She had got herself to this stage on her own, with encouragement from her husband of course, but without the benefit of school or college.

In many ways she was the best-educated person in the house. She had several Hindi-English dictionaries and was never too lazy to look up a word. Mohan Rao propped her up on principle and made much of her qualities, so she presided over the establishment like a little goddess. This was in accordance with Mohan Rao's personal definition of a domestic paradise, of which simple living and high thinking were also an inalienable part.

The government accommodation which had been allotted to Mohan Rao was not exactly a house but five rooms in a row, like cabins on a ship, in a hutment on Ferozeshah Road. Each room was accessible through a narrow veranda that ran the entire length of the house. When at home, Mohan Rao was most likely to be pacing up and down this veranda, interacting loudly with whatever was going on in the other rooms. He was the sun and every other member of the family a willing satellite. The first room was used as the kitchen. There was a kerosene stove on the cement floor, and a number of rough wooden shelves against the wall where a stack of spotless thalis and cooking pots were kept. Canisters of oil, sugar, rice, and flour were neatly placed on the floor next to the stove. A rickety kitchen table and four chairs stood in another corner. This is where the vegetables were peeled and cut. There was a low water tap in a corner of the room where all the washing of foodstuffs and pots was done. The preparation of the meals was a community activity in which whoever was available at the time participated. But eating was an ad hoc affair. The members of the household appeared in twos or threes according to their convenience, helped themselves from the pots that stood waiting, sat on the floor on small chatais to eat, cleaned up after themselves and went about their business.

It was to this set-up that Attenborough was invited, along with at least a dozen other guests. I was among the friends who were mobilized to help with arrangements for the event. Mohan Rao had decided that these people were exceptional and that he would make some special arrangements for them. Accordingly, Mrs Rao undertook a shopping expedition to Karol Bagh on a three-wheeler and returned home with teacups, china dinner plates, two dozen teaspoons, and small decorated glass bowls with stems. This was the first time that such things had been seen in that household. Except for some string cots, there was not much in the house by way of furniture. It was easy to clear one of the rooms and place twenty chairs in a circle for the guests to assemble. Only a few of these belonged to the house. The rest were borrowed or hired. Nephews shot off in different directions to bring the raw materials for the special meal that was being prepared for the 'Gandhi people' as we had begun to think of them. The cooking started a day earlier.

I was also expected to help the hosts in taking care of the foreign guests, specially Attenborough. When they arrived, I was already in position, hovering solicitously, ready with polite conversation. Mohan Rao was most excited at the prospect of treating these wonderful people to the fabulous dishes from his 'parts', and welcomed everybody with hearty shouts of glee. As soon as they were all seated in the circle of chairs, Mrs Rao appeared with a tray bearing the dozen new cups, smiling demurely and looking fresh as a flower. She offered the first cup to Attenborough, leaning attentively over him as he took it, peering suspiciously at the thin liquid which seemed alive with organisms. There were wisps of blood red tomato peel, filed black cumin seeds, and some moss green matter floating in a yellow-brown liquid.

'This is rasam. Please drink. It is like soup', she said sweetly. Attenborough obediently took an experimental sip.

'We use black pepper in this recipe', Mrs Rao continued in dulcet tones. Even as she spoke, the above-mentioned spice announced its presence to poor Attenborough's blameless throat.

'I know, I know', he spluttered, choking and gasping, looking even hotter and redder in his grey suit than he did when he first entered. Kothari took the teacup from him unobtrusively and substituted it with a cup of water from a furtive thermos they carried.

Now a nephew carried a large, steaming thali into the room and stood it on a table. Another brought a stack of wet, freshly washed china plates and distributed them among the guests. Mohan Rao appeared from the direction of the kitchen with a dozen teaspoons arranged like a Japanese fan in the breast pocket of his bushshirt. He surveyed the unfamiliar members of Attenborough's crew with a hawk's eye and started to pluck the teaspoons out, one at a time, handing them to everyone who was not Indian, and deliberately withholding them from those who were and should therefore be able to eat with their fingers perfectly well. I was firmly ignored. He didn't even look at me as he whizzed past. Attenborough got a spoon. So did the blonde girls of the camera crew and Kothari, as a special case. And of course the technical assistants qualified for the teaspoons too.

Not knowing what to do with their teaspoon, each foreign recipient held it aloft like a small flag at a convention. It became a token of special entitlement for the afternoon, a sort of medal.

'We have prepared a special dish today. It is famous where I come from. Its name is bisibeleholianna', Mohan Rao announced happily, pointing to the steaming thali. The guest of honour was served first. He couldn't tell from the faded mauvish brown colour of the dish which had the consistency of a thickish porridge what exactly had been cooked. His throat was still raw from the black pepper rasam. This was probably the first time he had strayed so far from roast beef and boiled brussel sprouts. He looked apprehensively at the helping Mohan Rao had piled on his plate.

'This looks interesting. What is it?' he said, trying to smile politely though his throat was still raw.

Mohan Rao passed on the job of serving the others to his son and stationed himself in front of Attenborough's chair, determined to educate him in the finer points of Udipi cuisine.

'You see, we first take this . . . um . . . *vangun*.' He couldn't immediately get the English equivalent, so he shouted to his wife through the door to the next room where she was busy spooning out the payasam into the newly bought glass bowls, asking her in Kannada what vangun was in English.

'Eggplant!' she sang back, at once.

'Yes, yeggplant', Mohan Rao repeated. 'We cut into small pieces. Then we soak the rice and dal. Then we grind the spices. Lot of spices. Lot of grinding. We put in this . . . what you call it . . . *dhania* . . .'

He again appealed to his wife for the English equivalent.

'Coriander', she called back with an indulgent laugh.

This exchange between husband and wife went on for quite some time, while Attenborough sat mesmerized. Mohan Rao would throw his vernacular term loudly at the open door as though he was serving a tennis ball and it would come back unfailingly translated as asafoetida, fenugreek, mace, nutmeg, clove, cinnamon, and so on. He loomed over his guest, bellowing the entire recipe at him, including all the elaborate stages of soaking overnight, drying in the sun and frying each ingredient separately in jhinjli oil.

'Yeat, yeat! Don't be ashamed. Take the spoon', he urged when he saw that Attenborough had made no move.

While the description of the recipe was still in progress, Attenborough placed a cautious spoonful in his mouth, as he had clearly run out of alternatives. As soon as he did that, the colour of his face began to change from lobster pink to greenish yellow, but he could neither swallow nor spit as Mohan Rao was still in full cry.

'And then we mix the vangun . . . yegg plant pieces nicely with the prepared rice and the dal . . . and stir on a low fire until it looks like this.'

Attenborough could not hold out any longer. He moved the contents of his mouth to one side, raised his eyes pathetically and uttered a single anguished word.

'Why?' he said.

His friend Kothari noticed his predicament at this point and came rushing to his side. He put a hand on his shoulder and asked with concern. 'Are you all right, Dickie?'

'I'll survive', Attenborough drawled, his mouth still full, 'but how do you chaps manage to eat this stuff? To me it tastes like stewed armpits!'

No business actually took place between Attenborough and Professor Swaminathan over this lunch. They met, of course, but agreed that it would be much better to discuss the script in the office another day. But no one present at the lunch, in whatever capacity, could ever forget the event.

Attenborough stayed on for about a month after this and met Mohan Rao several times. His arrangements for shooting the Gandhi film were not going too well at this time.

One day he said to me, 'Sometimes I wonder whether I shouldn't forget the old man and do a jolly little film on Mohan Rao instead.'

I still haven't been able to decide whether he was serious.

TWELVE

Cat Among the Bureaucrats

Every time a new minister was sworn in, there would be a flurry of pompous circulars proclaiming the government's intention to overhaul and streamline the Publications Division. The professed aim was to turn it from the sleepy old octopus it was into an efficient, profitable, modern and socially aware publishing house which could compare favourably with the best examples in the private sector. The main drawback in the realization of this aim was that each of the many limbs of this giant octopus was a law unto itself. The Editorial, Production, Business and Administration sections were not really in touch with one another. They communicated only in writing and in the old bureaucratic style.

The Business Manager neither knew nor cared to know anything about what he was required to market. The Chief Editor whimsically drew up lists of book titles to be produced without regard to public demand or any other consideration. The Production Section had no feeling for the contents of a book and was therefore quite capable of making a publication on ancient art look like a publicity pamphlet on rural development schemes, or vice versa. The General Wing which was supposed to keep house and provide transportation, stationery, and other essential services to the technical staff had an independent rhythm of its own and could collapse on a critical day simply because some clerk was on sick leave or because there was an important cricket match. There was no trace of the kind of coordination that must surely have been the basis of such an organization once.

Of course, nothing ever interfered with the regular disbursement of staff salaries. Nobody's future depended on excellence or even success. Promotions, increments, deputations, tours, and special assignments continued unabated while the financial viability of the organization sagged lower and lower. This dismal picture used to cause concern every ten years or so when there was a change of government or some other kind of spring cleaning. But then, after a short period of fuss and general turmoil, the Publications Division would settle back into its accustomed groove and plod on as before.

It so happened that a comparatively energetic and modern-minded minister took charge soon after a gigantic project of publishing the Collected Works of Mahatma Gandhi in English, Hindi, and Gujarati had been completed by the Publications Division. He was appalled to discover that huge stocks of unsold and undistributed volumes were gathering dust in expensive godowns. The editorial people, of whom I was one, had finished their job. The production people had finished theirs. Nobody had educated or motivated the business section to do their bit so they were treating the whole thing as a routine affair.

'This way the stock will never move, not in a hundred years', sighed the minister. 'We must change the existing specifications for the post of Business Manager. That is the root of the trouble', he declared. 'Being the graduate of a recognized university with five years' experience in a reputed publishing firm is obviously not enough. New requirements must be drawn up. The incumbent must prove that he is dynamic and motivated. Furthermore, he should be kept on probation for a year. His permanency in the post as well as his future prospects should be related to actual performance.' This last was a specially revolutionary concept for any government office, so when the new advertisement for the post appeared in accordance with the minister's wishes, it was considered a bit flamboyant, specially by the old, deeply entrenched crocodiles of the Information Service.

Anyhow, at the end of the ministerial exercise, the Publications Division acquired an unusual specimen called Oswal by way of a Business Manager. He looked startled all the time and walked the corridors of the office as though he was stalking a wild animal that only he could see. He embarked on his probation period with frightening intensity. Every moment he spent in the office was dedicated to proving that he was dynamic and motivated and because his career depended on his performance he was particular that every detail of this proof should be preserved in writing. It was he who made many of us really understand how a government file is conceived and born, how it grows and fattens, and how it never dies, at least not naturally.

Oswal had an unnerving way of breathing hard and putting on the face of a martyr. Most of the time he could be seen glued to his desk, unsmiling and inscrutable behind his tinted glasses, writing memo after memo to exhort the rest of the office to share some of the responsibilities that were weighing him down. He once asked the Librarian, in writing, to prepare a comprehensive list of educational institutions and libraries that would be interested in acquiring the Collected Works of Mahatma Gandhi. This mundane request was marked not only to the library 'for necessary action at the earliest' but also to ten other officers above

Oswal in rank 'for information only, please'. The main targets of Oswal's energetic missiles were DPD (Director, Publications Division), DDP (Deputy Director, Production), DDE (Deputy Director, Editorial), HPS (Head of the Photo Section), DDA (Deputy Director, Administration), and CECWMG (Chief Editor, the Collected Works of Mahatma Gandhi). The idea seemed to be to give the entire organization the opportunity to applaud his efforts in the service of the nation. Of course this resulted in the immediate birth of an official file because every word written on official stationery constituted a nearly sacred record which had to be 'processed'.

The contribution of the General Branch which acted as midwife for every file born was to add a sheet of their own to shed further light on the matter in hand and to identify the action to be taken. Oswal's note to the library was reinforced by them in the following words: 'Placed below is a note from BM (Business Manager) which is self-explanatory. The officers to whom it is marked may kindly do the needful.' This was followed by the clerk's illegible signature. Nobody ever understood the point of this totally redundant exercise. It just seemed to be a compulsory ritual known as 'putting up the file'.

The dozen other notes started by Oswal were still floating about in the office in different places, like spirits waiting to be claimed by the body to which they belonged. But ultimately they were destined to find their permanent home, along with his first note to the Librarian, in a file the General Branch called 'The dead stock of volume fifteen of the Hindi edition of the Collected Works of Mahatma Gandhi'. No one could have foreseen from its slim beginnings how fast this file would become fat. Oswal followed up his maiden note with another one in his usual style. This is what the official aquamarine sheet of paper looked like:

Page 2

I have taken physical inventory of the dead stock of the above title in order to keep myself abreast of the situation so that I can discharge my duties well and faithfully. From a total of 15,000 copies delivered to the godowns by the press in January 1971 the figure has gone down to 14,743 by today's date, i.e. April 4, 1971.

I have further ascertained that the shortage of 257 copies cannot be accounted for by sale, distribution, oversight or theft. I have investigated the matter thoroughly and have physical proof in my possession that the depletion in the dead stock has been caused by rodent menace. General Branch is therefore requested to supply the following items at the earliest:

1. One dozen (12) wooden rat traps, medium size
2. Eight (8) wire traps
3. Five hundred (500) grams of rat poison of reliable and tested make.

P.K. Oswal
Business Manager

DPD	
DDP	
DDE	May kindly see for information only please.
CECWMG	
HPS	
DDA	May kindly issue the necessary orders to General Branch to supply the above items at the earliest.
General Branch	For necessary action.
Business Manager	For further necessary action if any.

It took nearly a month before page 2 of the noting portion returned to Oswal's hands after its odyssey and another week before it could reunite officially with page 1 which was the opening note to the Librarian about mailing addresses. Dozens of uniformed peons had first to carry page 2 to dozens of PAs who in turn had to 'put up' the paper to dozens of officers who had to find the time in between meetings and closed holidays to affix their signatures to the note against their respective designations after the words 'seen, thanks' before the paper could trickle down, after the necessary orders of course, to the General Branch which was the one required to take action, as the case may be. When the file returned to Oswal for his information, there was fresh noting on page 3, as follows:

> This has reference to BM's note on page 2, wherein he has made a requisition for certain items required in the dead stock room of volume fifteen of the Hindi edition of the Collected Works of Mahatma Gandhi. The relevant portion has been sidelined A in blue pencil for ready reference. However, at this stage the General Branch is not in a position to do the needful for the reason given below:
>
> The said items 1, 2 and 3, sidelined in blue pencil and marked A on page 2 of the noting portion, are not in stock.
>
> Hari Ram
> In-charge, Store
> General Branch

Hari Ram's disclosure also followed a similar circuitous route up and around the administrative ladder, aiming to inform dozens of officers before wending its way back to Oswal's desk through many in-trays and out-trays. This journey took another month.

Altogether it was two months since Oswal had announced his startling discovery of the rodent menace and had asked for official pest control measures. Many of us wondered why he couldn't have crossed the corridor to the store and asked Hari Ram, Incharge, Store, with whom he had tea every day, to do something about rat traps. But we were firmly told that all official communication had to be in writing and 'through proper channel'. We also learnt that the only way to ensure long-term blamelessness, the most sought after ideal of the service official, was to follow the prescribed procedure and involve as many people as possible in every decision, big or small.

In these two months of fruitless noting, Oswal was not waiting passively. He had no intention of letting official inertia frustrate his display of dynamism during the critical period of his probation. A chaser missile followed his first one long before the earlier one had a chance to return from its journey. The text went something like this:

Page 4

> I had brought to the notice of the authorities on April 16, 1971, that 257 copies of volume fifteen of the Hindi edition of the Collected Works of Mahatma Gandhi had been consumed by the rodent menace. I had asked assistance of General Branch in fighting said menace. No action has been taken by them so far. It is already eleven days since they were apprised of the situation. At the latest counting of the stock which I conducted in national interest and on my own initiative yesterday, it has been found that the number of copies stands further depleted at 14,563. This means that the rate at which rodent menace is destroying Government property is about 16.3 books per day. Unless General Branch takes

immediate action, financial implications of this are likely to run into thousands of rupees per month.

P.K. Oswal
Business Manager

This and many subsequent notes of similar construction and design were launched at regular intervals by Oswal in the next few months. Each followed the same complicated route. The content of the communication became more and more ominous and the figures of the dead stock of volume fifteen continued to fall alarmingly with each memo. The administration did not budge from their position of being unable to supply the pest control items asked for. Apparently their stocks could not be replenished without a fresh budgetary sanction which in turn could only be given after the annual meeting of the finance committee. They dilated freely on their innocence and their difficulties in the noting portion of the file, which had now become at least thirty pages thick, not counting the missiles which were still on their way.

Oswal's notes steadily grew more irate and aggressive. He could afford to withdraw his earlier humility because now there was overwhelming written evidence of his concern for the public and for the nation and his confirmation was definitely in the bag. When he had only four more months to go before his probation ended, he initiated an unusual note:

Page 34

It is established that despite my best and single-handed efforts the General Branch has been unable to help me to curb the rodent menace in godowns. As a result, more than one thousand copies of volume fifteen of the Hindi edition of the Collected Works of Mahatma Gandhi have been consumed by the rats. The figure as of today is 13,869 copies as against 15,000 which were originally delivered to godowns eight months earlier.

My public conscience does not allow me to accept so much loss to nation. Therefore, out of my own resources and acting purely in national interest as a dedicated civil servant, I have taken the liberty of introducing into the dead stock room a domestic feline. It is a matter of common sense and there are instances where such remedies have been successfully tried.

This is for the information of all officers of the Division.

P.K. Oswal
Business Manager

This was followed by the usual ten-inch-long list of abbreviated designations of officers to whom the note was to be circulated, presumably so that they could marvel at the spirit and enterprise of the Business Manager and make sure that an asset like him stayed with the division permanently. After the entry of the cat in official business, Oswal's memos became much more frequent and self-satisfied than before. He recounted the past history of the ill-fated volume fifteen in each, and patted himself on the back for the brilliant and timely act of inducting the cat into the dead stock room. He was at pains to show that the figure which had been falling so alarmingly all these months was now steady as a rock. The number of books had remained unchanged at 13,869 for more than three months, an extraordinary feat made possible only because of his dedication.

By the time all these memos and notes had finished their wanderings and come home to the Administration Section to be processed, punched, tagged and sidelined in red or blue pencil in the Administrative Section, the now frayed and ragged file in which they were to be laid to rest along with all the comments and suggestions they had elicited in the course of their journeys was already 150 pages thick! Not only that. The year of Oswal's probation had also been simultaneously completed. It was too exhausting to do anything but confirm him. There really was no choice. Once this was done, and the necessary announcement circulated, Oswal threw away his 'servant of the people' mask and showed his real face with defiance.

The next note he sent out sang a different tune altogether:

> As DPD, DDP and DDA are aware, I was instrumental in arresting the destruction of above title from rodent menace through the introduction of a cat into the godown. I did this on my own initiative and with my own meagre personal resources. Furthermore, I have been sustaining the said feline by arranging for 250 mls of milk daily, including Sundays and holidays to make sure that the cat, which can now be regarded as a Government servant, remained in good condition to serve public interest satisfactorily. It is now time that the Publications Division took this responsibility from my frail shoulders and reimbursed me for the expenditure which I have already incurred on its behalf. The milk bill for last 96 days comes to Rs 67.75 and is placed below for DDA's perusal. I request that the Accounts Section be given necessary orders to process said bill and compensate me expeditiously for what I have already spent in public interest.
>
> P.K. Oswal
> Business Manager

This too was marked to the powers that be, but nothing like this could go past the all-too-solid Accounts Officer Krishna Iyer. His crisp rejoinder based on his Bible, the Government of India Rules of 1935, said clearly that it was not possible for the government to entertain a proposal such as the Business Manager had made because there was no precedent to go by. Moreover the rules were silent on whether an animal could arbitrarily be appointed as a government servant and deemed to be on official duty. He went on to say that as far as he could see, BM was not in any case invested with the powers to take any such decision.

This kind of response incensed Oswal who started frothing at the mouth and muttering obscenities to himself. He sent a bunch of flaming, threatening notes to everyone he could think of. Needless to say each one of these was paginated, punched, tagged and processed in readiness for its destined union with 'the main file'. His hysterical rages left Krishna Iyer unmoved and even more phlegmatic than before. There was an impasse which had to be sorted out because Oswal's rantings distracted the whole office so much that all work was in danger of coming to a stop. Mohan Rao, who was the Director at this time, begged the parties concerned to stop writing notes forthwith and to come to his room where they could all sit together and settle matters in an amicable way.

'Be reasonable, Krishna Iyer. If the fellow has really spent money on trying to save the books from the rats, there must be some rule that will allow you to compensate him. Why don't you try to be helpful!'

Oswal was staring at Iyer with undisguised hatred and it was clear that Krishna Iyer had taken a strong dislike to Oswal. It didn't look hopeful at all.

'Sir, I would find a rule if there was the slightest justification. But I can't do anything against my conscience. You know, sir, I am a God-fearing man. The whole basis of BM's case is that cat is eating rat. My problem is simple. I ask you, if cat is eating rat, who is drinking milk?' He opened his eyes wide, and blinked suggestively several times as he said this, trying not to look at Oswal. Oswal stormed out in a rage, ignoring Mohan Rao's conciliatory exclamations of '*Arrey bhai, tum kyaa karta hai*! Come back!'

The problem of Oswal's reimbursement was never solved. He spitefully but quite understandably withdrew the cat's daily milk. I stopped following the case in detail but heard from other people that soon afterwards the cat died and that the number of copies of volume fifteen again started to plummet rapidly.

Oswal's last note on the file, a sort of epitaph, said that the cat had passed away owing to the callousness of the Accounts Section and the general indifference of the administration. It said further that according to his family priest this was a very bad omen. The only way to neutralize its dire consequences was to offer a gold/silver image of a cat to a temple of Hanuman. The minimum cost of such an image would be Rs 750, considerably more than what the government would have had to expend on life-saving milk if they had come to their senses earlier. He asked the administration to hand over this amount to him in cash forthwith and went on to say, mincing no words, that if anything untoward happened to him or to any member of his family he would hold the government responsible and seek whatever redress he could.

I don't know how Krishna Iyer who was both religious and superstitious dealt with this. He was most uncommunicative and I lost touch. About five years later I had occasion to tell this story to Mrs G. When she quipped that the file, printed just as it was, would probably make much more interesting reading than some of the government's planned books, I made an attempt to go back and trace it, but without success. I had left it too late. Apparently the file listed as 'Volume Fifteen of the Hindi edition of the Collected Works of Mahatma Gandhi' in the records of the Publications Division had been subjected to a five-yearly government ritual known as 'weeding out'. Like the cat, the file had shuffled off its mortal coil, taking with it the manuscript of a wonderful story.

THIRTEEN

Mrs G and the Queen of Tonga

My husband's induction into the Prime Minister's Secretariat occasioned our first encounter with the lifestyle of the upper government circles in New Delhi. He had never been anything but an academic before this and the focus of our social life had always been the university campus. My own job as an editor in the Publications Division for more than twenty years had taught me something about how government business was conducted on files but had offered no lessons on the effects of status on behaviour. I was therefore unprepared to hear the wife of a Secretary to the government talk of 'our last posting', 'our junior', 'our lower staff', and 'our term of office' to the wives of other officials at a social gathering. She also referred to a couple who had 'worked under us for years'. This sort of terminology didn't seem strange to anybody else. On the contrary it was understood and accepted by all as part of a highly evolved common language. At official dinners, which insidiously became a regular feature of our lives, I picked up and learnt to interpret other interesting nuances that could throw light on the state of play in the status game.

For instance, when the wives of two officials met and greeted each other, I was usually able to tell whose husband held the higher position by the inflections of the two voices and some other not very subtle signals. If a Joint Secretary's wife said 'How are you?' to a Deputy Secretary's wife, only the first word 'How' was audible, while the 'are you' had to be inferred from the somewhat grudging lip movements. The one-syllable greeting, consisting mainly of the word 'How', was delivered in a low-pitched nasal drawl and accompanied by a too casual folding of the hands in which the fingers untidily jutted out at hip level. Other symptoms of officially derived superiority in feminine spouses were a tight smile and the deliberate erasing of all expression from the face for the duration of the exchange of civilities. If on the other hand it was a Deputy Secretary's wife who was greeting the wife of an officer senior to her husband, she would almost sing out the 'How are you?' Each word would be clearly pronounced and the 'are' stressed and prolonged to signify how important the well being of the recipient was. The face would wear an expectant but wary smile, the chin would be slightly raised to signify attention and deference, and the hands would be stiffly joined in a namaste and held respectfully at chest level this time.

I indulged in guessing games of my own to relieve the tedium of official dinner parties and was right nine times out of ten about the comparative official position of the husbands of any two interacting women guests. It was demeaning I thought that the women did not feel free to talk amongst themselves unless they knew exactly who the husbands in the case were and how much leverage they exercised. Only then could they drop their guard and say the right things in the right tone of voice. There didn't seem to be any simple way of protesting unless one was prepared to stand on a soap box and preach, which I wasn't. In any case it was I who was the newcomer, the oddity. It was not my place to offer alternative social strategies.

Once Mrs G, as we affectionately called the Prime Minister, invited us to dinner to her house so that my husband could meet informally some key people in the government that he would be dealing with in his capacity as her adviser. Such semi-official dinner parties were quite usual in her style of functioning and achieved more in the way of communication between those present than the stiff state banquets held in Rashtrapati Bhavan or Hyderabad House.

She entered the drawing room punctually at eight and greeted everyone present with a smile and a namaste. But the social context proved evanescent because some government business was on her mind and she started talking about it to a Secretary, one of the guests. The other men including my husband joined the group in a corner of the room. The women formed a knot at the opposite end. There had been no introductions so far but they all seemed to know one another. I was still an unlabelled object and being eyed as such. I was just on the point of introducing myself when the initiative was taken by the most elegantly turned out wife of the seniormost officer who finally deigned to address me and find out for herself where I fitted.

This lady had a well-groomed head of silvery hair with a stylish bluish tinge obviously acquired in a salon. She was draped in an exquisite handloom sari of khadi silk. A string of unobtrusive pearls, little diamond ear tops, and ethnic leather sandals with gold accents, completed the ensemble. Her appearance proclaimed that she combined in herself the best of East and West, and that she was the personification of enlightened Indianness, the ultimate repository of good taste. It was obvious to me that role models such as Mrs G and her aunt Vijayalakshmi Pandit had inspired the look. I envied her poise and her perfect toenails. I caught myself involuntarily pulling my sari down to hide my worn chappals and long neglected feet and defensively trying to smooth my suddenly untidy hair with my hands. The lady who had undertaken to find out exactly what weightage I should be given was really overwhelmingly presentable. I felt like a dish rag in comparison and I am sure looked like one as well. Judging from the dismissive glances of the other female dignitaries, I didn't seem to be anybody special, but in that case what was I doing in Mrs G's house? This was the tricky question. What if I turned out to be an important Member of Parliament or something unforeseen like that? They would have to tread carefully.

I felt all this on my skin as the elegant lady asked me sweetly, politely, and in simple Hindi, in case I didn't understand English, 'Which Ministry are you?' That is exactly how the question was worded. There was no mention of a husband, no mention of possible connections, just '*Aap kaun si Ministry hain*?', as though each woman present was the insignia of something impossibly important. In my case this important realm had to be identified and a single word was all that was required. Theoretically I was expected to respond with something like 'Defence', 'External Affairs' or 'Finance' and her question would have been answered. It was taken for granted that only people in the top positions could be present at this dinner so the exact designation was irrelevant.

As things were I could not have satisfied the lady who had asked me the question without a detailed preamble which would have gone something like this: 'We are new here though our hostess knows us both: me because of her interest in Bal Bhavan with which I have been connected and him because of his involvement with Kashmir, among other things. Recently, he has joined the Prime Minister's Secretariat as her Adviser. Therefore he cannot be said to be connected with any single ministry. In some sense he is concerned with all the ministries.' When I look back this would have keen a fairly simple thing to say. But at the time I felt quite unable to embark on any explanation of this type. Not only did I feel a resistance on principle but I also could not bear to wait for her verdict on my status while I finished saying my non-standard piece. So I decided in a flash that I would opt out of her game. I could only do this by playing one of my own.

All through my school and college days I had had a genuine interest in the theatre. I had also acted in juvenile plays and had the reputation of being promising in that area. However this promise had never had the opportunity of being seriously tested because I had given all my energy to the pursuit of music. In a split second I decided to test myself in this real-life situation by playing a role as faithfully as I could. A character whom everyone used to refer to as Bhaggo Dada ki Bahu, or the wife of Bhaggo Dada, in my childhood floated through my mind as a possible cover and even as the lady was waiting for my answer I asked myself what this character would have said if she were in my situation. What a perfect way out of my predicament! I would from this moment on until the end of the evening just be Bhaggo Dada ki Bahu and nobody else. I would think, talk, walk, and look like her. She was a real person who had as much right to exist as I. She had not been to school or college, could not understand English, and never went out to parties. She was simple and kindly, and devotedly kept house for a joint family of nearly fifty people. Her main interest was the kitchen and other household matters that would make her loved ones more comfortable. Everything else was the domain of the menfolk. There was no question of her preening or taking any interest in how her comfortable frame was clothed. I tried to sharpen my memory of her guileless face, her innocent, uncomprehending but well-meaning smile, and her lumbering, rather clumsy movements. Her eager and friendly spirit used to express itself through speech in the manner of a babbling brook. Reassuring but meaningless words would pour out, somehow upholding the Mathur Kayastha ideals of fellow feeling, self satisfaction, and well being. I remembered how she used to make instant contact by uttering harmless inanities like '*haan, yeh to hai hi. Bohat achhi baat hai. Maen to yeh hi kehna chah rahi thi*', and so on ('Yes, of course that is so. Its a very good thing too. This is exactly what I wanted to say.') Her unmodulated and broad speech seemed always to promise that some happy meaning was just round the corner and would soon catch up with the words that had already flown out of her like impatient heralds. It took me just a few seconds to recollect the entire person and slide into the role. The polite, enquiring face of the elegant senior official's wife was still waiting for my answer.

'Which Ministry are you?', she repeated.

'Oh, me? I don't really know what to say. I am just a housewife who attends to work at home. So I suppose you could say that I am the Home Ministry', I said, laughing comfortably at my own too obvious and not particularly funny joke.

As soon as the words 'Home Ministry' escaped my lips, another lady who had her ears cocked pounced on me, exclaiming, 'So you are Mrs Govind Narain!'

I realized that this was the name of the current Home Secretary. I tried to imagine the mortification and indignation Bhaggo Dada ki Bahu would feel if she was called the wife of someone who was not her husband.

'God forbid, God forbid', I said, holding the lobes of my ears in the standard gesture of outrage.

'Oh, I'm sorry. Well, what is your husband's name?'

'You know, in our community we never speak the husband's name', I said coyly, covering my head with the pallu of my sari. 'It is not considered proper. Our sisters-in-law are entitled to take our rings away if they catch us calling the husband by name. I just call him "Listen", but he isn't going to hear me here, is he?'

The ladies seemed to give up but not for long. Soon they were at it again, this time using another route to get the essential data. The questions were in a mixture of convent English and anglicized Hindi and my replies were in the broad Mathur dialect of the old city.

'Are you living in New Delhi?'

'Nai Dilli? Yes, yes, we just moved here. We actually belong to Old Delhi, but we had to move because of His work . . .', I trailed off.

'I see. But where are you staying now?'

A straight answer to this would have brought their research to an abrupt end. It is well known that in the official culture of New Delhi, the address of the allotted residence faithfully reflects status, seniority, importance, and closeness to the seat of power. If I had said we were in Race Course Road, the game would have been up and I would immediately have become the recipient of undeserved and unearned respect despite my slatternly appearance. On the other hand if I had said we were in Ramakrishnapuram's D Type Flats, I would have been rejected with a disdain I didn't deserve either. I couldn't afford to reveal our rather grand address if I really wanted to be judged for myself.

'You know, these long, English-sounding names of the roads in Nai Dilli are very confusing for me. I can never remember them. Every time, I have to ask Him, and even when He tells me the name of the road we live on, I can't really say it properly. I am used to places like Neel-ka Katra, Dariba, Daryaganj and Khari Baoli. Not to whats-its-name Dupply Road or Kichaner Road. See, even now I know I've got these names wrong. As I told you, I'll have to ask Him, but He is standing so far away. It won't look nice if I call Him too loudly.'

Bhaggo Dada ki Bahu could have clucked on in this strain indefinitely without being discouraged by any waning of interest in her audience. I tried to be faithful to her image, but the small audience I was catering to had by now physically moved out of earshot, probably in disgust. I considered this a small victory and turned off my waterfall of words with relief.

Soon we were all seated at the dinner table. The fourth lady to whom I had not yet been exposed happened to be sitting next to me. Usually men were seated on either side of women but tonight there seemed to be more women than men, counting Mrs G, her daughter-in-law Sonia (the son was away) and Padmaja Naidu who had just dropped in. Mercifully we were tucked away unobtrusively at the far end of the table. When the fourth lady smiled at me, I knew instinctively that she was feeling protective towards me. This was obviously because she did not entirely approve of the tenacious campaign undertaken by her colleagues to bare my identity at any cost. She was kindly, and had charming manners. I could see that the etiquette she had been brought up on included trying to put everyone at their ease in any social situation, specially someone who seemed out of their depth, as I certainly did.

She took an elegant little Japanese fan out of her small satin evening bag and started to fan herself, nodding politely to the guest to her left and the guest to her right. But she was specially concerned about me. She wanted to be friendly and give me some respite from the scrutiny she knew I had been subjected to before dinner. She turned her gallant attention on me and remarked with a beaming smile, 'Rather hot, isn't it?'

I was very touched by her attitude. It occurred to me that I had found all the Parsi women I had ever met to be generous and upright like my fourth lady. But I didn't dare to respond as I would personally have liked to, because the other three were watching and listening like hawks. I would have to play my role to the hilt.

'Yes, it has become hot now', I said in the most rustic accent I could produce, blowing air out of my cheeks, shaking my head from side to side and wiping my face with the end of my cotton sari. 'I don't speak English but I understand what you say. I have to hear it so much that I have got used to it. Anyhow, some nice things can also happen when the hot weather begins. As soon as it warms up, I start preparing my summer pickles. Even today I finished making a jar of lasora and another of small mangoes.' I went on prattling like this, trying to eat the small roast potatoes and peas on my plate with a dessert spoon, not hesitating to use a furtive finger to push the food back into the spoon if it slipped off.

'Which pickles have you made this year?' I asked my new supporter innocently.

'Oh, I don't really bother with all this at home. Fern's pickles from the market are quite good enough for us. In any case we don't use them very much.'

I could feel her enthusiasm waning. She did want to make me feel better but it was proving to be uphill all the way. She was compelled to give up after a while. As for me, I was able to carry my project through because the only person who could know for a fact that I was acting was Mrs G and she was sitting too far away to be able to see what I was up to.

At last the dinner was over. I had managed to remain a question mark all through the evening. Even Mrs G's mentioning my name along with that of many others when the goodbyes were being said didn't enlighten the curious ladies because they had not yet been briefed about my husband's credentials. I was elated and considered the evening a tremendous victory.

When I excitedly told my husband in the car what had happened and what I had done he was most unhappy.

'Why, why?' I asked him, feeling most frustrated at his reaction. 'What would you have liked me to do?'

'I hate it when people feel sorry for me. The picture you have painted of my wife will certainly make everyone feel sorry for me. That is something I cannot bear.'

The rest of the short drive to our new home on Race Course Road was a silent one. We both felt depressed and wronged that night. But some time later I discovered that at least one good thing had come of the experience. There were no attempts to enrol me in the community of official wives. My debut had been a flop and in the space of one short evening I had earned the reputation of being an oddity it was best to avoid. At any rate this is what I wanted to believe.

But this is not the way things ultimately turned out. There was no way in which I could escape the official social scene. After a rocky start I even began to enjoy the experience. All of it was not as drab and boring as my first exposure to the mindless snobbery of the official culture. In the nine years of my husband's close association with Mrs G, I also met many attractive and interesting people whom I still value greatly. I discovered that I was not the only one who found the stuffiness of the 'wives' ridiculous. Another person who felt the same way was Aziza Imam, a Member of Parliament from Bihar whom I first met at a formal dinner for Brezhnev, head of the Communist Party of the Soviet Union. She stood out for her naturalness, ready laughter and sensitivity and I wanted to know her better. I was charmed by the fact that she really enjoyed the glittering colonial splendour of the banquet hall of Rashtrapati Bhavan where the dinner was taking place and the impressive spectacle of the turbaned waiters and their scarlet and gold costumes. She applauded all this loudly, without any self-consciousness, like a child at a magic show, repeatedly saying '*wah wah*!' from the bottom of her heart. Most of the others, in sharp contrast, wore studied expressions suggesting that such grandeur was no novelty for them. She exclaimed in surprise when she discovered official interpreters lurking darkly behind every alternate dining chair. We together marvelled at their postures which could not be described as either standing or sitting but as something in between. She turned to the Russian dignitary sitting next to her with the hospitable intention of being friendly. 'This is indeed a happy occasion', she said in ringing tones, with a radiant smile. The dignitary carefully wiped his face clean of all expression and waited for the interpreter crouching behind him to translate for him before he could react. This was a slow and cumbersome affair and took about three minutes. We all waited tensely until the interpreter got his act together. After some awkward shuffling, he finally said something in Russian, presumably his rendering of 'This is indeed a happy occasion'. Only after this signal did the dignitary feel free to smile back at Aziza Imam in response to her greeting. Propriety demanded that he reciprocate with a fitting sentiment of his own on behalf of the nation he was representing. He composed a suitable statement in Russian which was delivered in English by the interpreter in due course and was something to the effect that the delegation was gratified to have a chance to visit India and hoped that more steps would be taken to strengthen the ties of friendship between the two countries. This exchange of two simple sentences was accomplished in fifteen minutes. The soup had been served and eaten and the dishes cleared by the time two more remarks were added to the conversation. It was as though we were watching ourselves in slow motion, like sleep-walkers floating under water.

The conversation seemed more animated towards the middle of the table though we could not actually hear anything. I remember that the President made a joke that he and all the neighbouring Indians at the table laughed heartily at. The Russians sat stiff and white faced while the Indians finished guffawing. Then the interpreters went into action. There was silence while their wheels turned to produce a translation of the presidential joke. It was a good five minutes before the Russian laughter could be released and made a part of the official record. Aziza and I felt as though we were in a badly directed play where the timing was the worst feature. But in a sense we intensely enjoyed being there. Aziza had the gift of life and could make the starchiest, most formal occasion glow with interest. Every person, place, or thing turned into an engrossing and amusing phenomenon as soon as it passed through the filter of her mind. Under her wing, I made another entry into the social life of official New Delhi, this time without pain or anxiety but with actual relish.

I took to seeking her out at all official gatherings and gravitating towards her. Her simple, naturally elegant style of dressing, her soft, well-intentioned chuckle, and her unselfconscious paan-chewing habit distinguished her from the rest. As soon as we met, she would entertain me and herself with her most recent experience, enjoying it as though she was also hearing it for the first time. She used to tell me hilarious stories about some members of parliament and politicians she had to deal with. She was a wonderful mimic and could reproduce the accents of rural Bihar to perfection. These accents figured in her story of a politician who was invited to a five-star hotel along with the French Ambassador and his wife and persistently misunderstood every single thing that happened that evening, including a European lady's gracious offer to dance with him. The efforts of the diplomatic corps stationed in the capital to cultivate this person, who was very important even though he had never heard of ballroom dancing, were a fiasco. He unfailingly suspected that his virtue was being attacked in some underhand fashion. According to Aziza, he was not too attached to his virtue but he was a patriot and was therefore particular that only bonafide Indians should be allowed to jeopardize it.

I knew that Aziza was trying to enrich the cultural life of her fellow members of parliament in various ways. She used to take the initiative in organizing Urdu poetry readings and classical music recitals to 'tame' some of her more rustic colleagues. One day she was very crestfallen because the same politician misunderstood her totally when she said she was arranging a wonderful musical evening so that they could all relax after a tense working day in Parliament. 'Ajija jee, make sure she is young and beautiful!' he is reported to have leered confidentially and gratefully. Aziza couldn't believe her ears and decided then and there to abandon her naive project. When she told me this, she laughed uproariously. It was clear that she considered it a story about her own foolishness and not about the failings of her colleague. I found this most endearing.

Playing the role of Bhaggo Dada ki Bahu at Mrs G's dinner party had been a successful experiment from my point of view. There were many occasions when that disguise would have stood me in good stead but instead of repeating the performance I exhorted myself to be innovative. Each time I tried to think up a new character which I would then try to portray faithfully. In the nine years that I remained in this situation, I created at least a dozen shadowy personalities to stand proxy for me while I watched from a distance. Political firebrand, aspiring author of cookbooks, dedicated social worker, dreamy music lover, lesser-known Hindi poetess, passionate supporter of the Montessori system of education, amateur astrologer, and part-time insurance agent were some of the people I became from time to time. I am now sure this had something to do with my secret longing to be an actress and my untried talent in this area. I enjoyed the opportunity enormously particularly because I was free to fail and start all over again without loss of face. There were minor problems if someone happened to remember me and my inconsequential conversation on a previous occasion, but these were not serious and could be handled. If that happened, people either squinted at me wondering whether they could be mistaken, or else decided that there was something very odd about me. Sometimes I talked my way out of things by explaining that my area of interest had undergone a change.

Mrs G's antennae were extremely sensitive. When she entered a room, she knew exactly what was going on in it. She once told me that she reacted to people with her skin, almost like an animal, and always knew what each one was thinking, or at any rate how each one was disposed towards her. If they felt intimidated, threatened, warm, wary, suspicious, or genuinely worshipful she could easily tell. If not, a little waiting and watching gave her

her answers. She also had an uncanny sense of hearing, I discovered. We were once having a desultory discussion about the connection between the words 'cha' and 'tea' at the tail end of a very long dining table at Rashtrapati Bhavan. She was seated in the centre, busy talking to the visiting dignitary in whose honour the banquet was being held. She suddenly turned towards us and said, loudly for her, 'They are two forms of the same Chinese word.' At first G. Parthasarathy and T.N. Kaul who had started the discussion didn't realize she was addressing them. When she repeated her remark with the additional information that one term was from northern China and the other from southern China, and a smile directed at them, they were stunned into silence. It was unnerving to know that she could sense and hear everything that was said, or left unsaid, even at that distance. After this the conversation at our end of the table dwindled into nervous whispers and then died altogether.

That evening I became certain that she must already know about my experiments in amateur acting. I felt awed and apologetic in retrospect and deeply appreciated the fact that she had never said anything to suggest that she was on to me. In several conversations I had with her in connection with a foreword she was writing for a children's book I had written to celebrate the twenty-fifth anniversary of the Indian republic, I discovered that she had a puckish sense of humour which her own life wasn't very hospitable to. I was emboldened to tell her what I thought were funny stories about the bureaucratic hang-ups of the Publications Division where I worked, and she was vastly amused. I remember one particularly relaxed evening in honour of Clovis Maqsood when she told many funny and uninhibited stories about her young days in England. There was definitely a sporting and fun-loving person in her that did not often get a chance to emerge. I saw many glimpses of that person and was both charmed and moved.

A state banquet in honour of the King and Queen of Tonga was an extraordinary event for me. I remember it specially because this time the dignitaries had no starch whatsoever. Their vast, innocent Polynesian faces were so different from anything I had seen in the gilded halls of Rashtrapati Bhavan, so totally disarming, that I simply forgot to play any role. It was quite a relief to be myself and be able to experience this rare encounter without the strain of having to act. The King first came up to the reception hall in a special lift all by himself because no escorts could fit into it with him. Once he arrived, he was heavily attended by his own aides and by Indian officials. He was going to be followed by the Queen who was also expected to be brought up singly in the lift. While we were waiting for her, the wives of the Indian officials drifted together and formed noisy little clusters of their own, ignoring the other guests, specially the ladies of the diplomatic corps. Mrs G was mortified by this and said in Hindi, in a tight voice: 'Someone should talk to our guests too.' The message went through the hum of small talk about servants and prices like a bolt of lightning and many of the wives sprang into action, extremely anxious to erase the bad impression they had created in the Prime Minister about their lack of etiquette.

The most energetic of these was a beaky, intense looking woman called Mrs Mongia. She was the wife of a Member of Parliament who, it was rumoured, was hoping to become a Cabinet Minister or an Ambassador at the very least. This was her chance to show Mrs G what she was capable of. Quite a lot might depend on how well she did tonight. She fixed one eye on Mrs G and the other on the Queen who presently entered the hall with a gait that can best be described as rolling. She had a smooth and bronzed baby face and wore her hair in two tight plaits that rested symmetrically on her shoulders. Despite her schoolgirlish appearance, she had an imperious manner but without the slightest trace of hauteur. The protocol people ushered her towards a large sofa and she sat down in the middle of it as though it were a throne while a dozen or so other ladies stood around her waiting for a chance to show courtesy in accordance with Mrs G's understated wishes. She spread herself out comfortably and made no move to accommodate any of them on either side of her though there was plenty of room on the sofa. There was something so artless about her queenly air that it reminded me of a child trying gravely to play the role of a royal personage in a kindergarten play.

Mrs Mongia dragged a chair forward with alacrity and stationed herself to the south-west of the Queen while everyone else was still shuffling around uncertainly. She was a purposeful woman and had armed herself with the relevant information before appearing at this event. She cast a final furtive look at Mrs G to make sure she was within earshot so that none of the gems she was about to scatter were wasted.

'Madam, I believe your country comprises more than hundred and fifty islands east of Fiji and south of Samoa in the Pacific Ocean and that climate is pleasant and subtropical . . .', she began.

The Queen realized in mid-sentence that it was she herself who was being addressed though she was not at all sure what was being said. She responded to Mrs Mongia's social advances with two kinds of sounds which were more like grunts than anything else. The first was a guttural 'hunh?' with an interrogative inflection in which the pitch travelled from low to high in expectation of some further clarification. The second was the same sound but with the pitch going from high to low to express some sort of finality or acknowledgement of meaning.

'I have heard that some islands in your country are of volcanic origin and some are of coral limestone formation . . .'

'Hunh?' and then after a pause, 'Hmm!'

'It is interesting to us in India that in your country it is hottest from January to March and coolest from July to September . . .'

'Hunh? Hmm!'

'Can you enlighten us about the activities of the ladies in your country? In India, you will find, Madam, that our ladies are in all walks. They are scientists, judges, doctors and business executives. And as you can see, our beloved Prime Minister is herself a lady of this country. Like that can you tell us about the ladies in Tonga?'

Mrs Mongia looked obliquely at Mrs G and raised her voice so that her signal contribution to India's prestige and her tribute to Mrs G herself had a better chance of being heard.

'Hunh? Hmm!'

Mrs Mongia was now well launched into her solo project and was not allowing any of the others to get a word in.

'Madam, what about your hobbies?' she said with an almost conspiratorial air. Now that she had broken the ice single-handed she felt entitled to ask personal questions.

'Hunh?'

'I mean, Madam, what do you like to do in your spare time?'

'Hunh?'

'When you are not busy with inaugurations and other state functions, Madam, what do you do?'

At last the Queen understood and spoke her first words since her entry into the reception hall. 'I just bees', she said simply, but with all the force of royal authority. She reinforced the pronouncement with a ringing 'Hmm!'

I was swept away with the wisdom and charm of a philosophy in which the savouring of one's existence could be an important and worthwhile preoccupation in itself. It seemed from the way she spoke that 'just being' was not only an honourable national obligation that she fulfilled but also a pastime that gave her immense pleasure.

It crossed my mind that Mrs Mongia probably never switched off her busy engines in order to 'just be'. The Queen's final response to her tenacious queries had foxed her somewhat. It had brought one line of questioning to an unceremonious end but we could all see that she had no intention of retreating. She had only allowed herself a little breathing space for refuelling before coming back with another equally impressive display of recently acquired information and diplomatic acumen.

'Madam, you must have heard of Holi and Diwali, two big festivals we have in our country. On Holi day, we throw colours on one another and on Diwali we light lamps. What are the big festivals your people celebrate?'

'Hunh? Hmm!'

'Is Tongatapu a big city? What is the approximate . . .'

Mrs Mongia's hope that Mrs G was listening to every word she said was probably well founded. Her uncanny sense of hearing was common knowledge in these circles. But she provided yet another proof of it by crossing the room briskly to come to the aid of her beleaguered guest of honour who was now beginning to look a bit fed up. She stood in front of Mrs Mongia's chair and smiled reassuringly at the Queen without saying anything, as though she wanted to give her some respite from the trying time she had been having.

She did direct a word of censure in the direction of the other ladies who had watched helplessly while Mrs Mongia exhibited her capabilities. 'You all should have looked after our guest', she said in Hindi as we went in to dinner, knitting her brow and frowning momentarily.

The conversation livened up at the dinner table but the women were unusually quiet throughout the evening. None of them seemed to be able to think of anything to say, which was not necessarily a bad thing, I thought. It allowed the Queen to just be.

PART II

The Cooking of Music and Other Essays

Publisher's Note

Sheila Dhar died on 26 July 2001, soon after finalizing the typescript of this book [i.e. *The Cooking of Music and Other Essays*]. Some of the essays that follow are new versions of earlier ones and will sound familiar to those who know her work. The majority, however, were written for this volume, after some careful cannibalizations from the author's own earlier writings.

Partho Datta refused to let us put his name on the cover as 'Editor', but that is what he has been.

The Afterword [in Part III] provides biographical information on Sheila Dhar, and appreciation of her artistic skills.

FOURTEEN

Sound and Hindustani Music

Reverence for sound is basic to Indian philosophy. Some schools, specially the Yoga and the Tantra, equate Nada Brahman, the primordial sound, with the Absolute, the Creator, the cause of the phenomenal world. While Nada is the sound of the Universe, the subtlest of all elements, Brahman is existence, blissful awareness, the taintless, imperishable supreme deity. It is significant that shakti, the energy of the creative power of Brahman, is also called nada (sound) or sabda (word). In the Hindu scheme of things, sound is of two kinds. The first, anahata nada, or unstruck sound, is not a matter of sense perception but a mystic experience in which sound and light are fused within a direct perception of the Absolute. It is the very hum of creation. The second, which concerns us here, is ahata nada, or created sound, which in its very distinction from the first implies an awareness of it.

The origins of the music of India are thus deeply spiritual and devotional. Symbolically, most gods and goddesses of the pantheon are associated with music and rhythm. The creative energy of Brahma is deified as Saraswati who is inseparable from the vina or lute, Siva dances to the beat of the damaru drums, and Krishna enchants his devotees with the strains of the bamboo flute. All manifestations of godhood are traditionally propitiated with song and dance. The beginnings of Indian music can be traced back to the chanting of the Sama Veda nearly four thousand years ago. The primacy of the voice and the association of musical sound with prayer were established early in the history of Indian music and remain essentially unchanged.

Music has been a cultivated art in India for at least three thousand years. Classical music today is a direct descendant of the ancient tradition, preserved, elaborated, and developed by hereditary musicians through the ages and passed on orally from master to disciple. This music is as true and real a part of life as it ever was, bringing to the present generation the still vibrant awareness of times long past and a range of emotional experiences that the modern world cannot provide.

The ancient music of India had been nourished from earliest times by diverse streams including the religious, the folk, the tribal, and the courtly. An example of the first is the prabandha, a poetic arrangement sung in a preset melody to a fixed rhythmic cycle. The outstanding Sanskrit opera, *Gita Govinda*, by the twelfth-century poet Jayadeva, was composed in this style and became a landmark in the history of Indian music. The theme of Jayadeva's work was the divine love of Radha and Krishna. The exceptional literary and musical merit of Jayadeva's work continued to inspire followers and imitators of the devotional genre for nearly four hundred years after him. The prabandha no longer forms a part of the repertoire of classical musicians today, and the original music of *Gita Govinda* is lost to us. However, the lilting lines of Jayadeva are still sung to tunes set locally in various parts of India, and improvised upon by dancers.

Around the twelfth century the northern part of the country began to receive a fresh infusion—melodic and Sufic influences from Persia. The contributions of Amir Khusrau, a poet and musician at the court of the Pathan ruler Alauddin Khilji, had a decisive hand in giving a new orientation to music. After the thirteenth century the music of India branched into two systems—the Hindustani or northern which is discussed here, and the Carnatak or southern. Although both follow the same basic principles, they differ sharply in musical intention and ethos.

The prabandha mentioned earlier was the precursor of the dhruva-pada or dhrupad which reached its full flowering in north India in the fifteenth and sixteenth centuries. This was an age of revival and exuberance, and under the patronage of enlightened rulers like Raja Man Singh Tomar of Gwalior and the Mughal emperor Akbar the dhrupad form flourished and reached its peak.

The dhrupad is a stately, formal, closely structured composition in which the text, usually in the Braja dialect of Hindi, consists mainly of hymns of praise in honour of gods and goddesses, and of heroes. Dhrupad singing always starts with alaap or free elaboration of the raga or melody in slow, medium, and fast tempos. The syllables used in this part, which precedes the text, are said to be taken from the various names of God and the atmosphere sought to be created is one of selfless devotion and serenity. The text of the composition follows in rhythm cycles of great grandeur and gravity which are articulated by a two-headed drum. The melodic movement uses pure notes and broad glissandos. No embellishments or tonal graces are allowed to interfere with the clear enunciation of the words. A dhrupad performance is a vigorous act of devotion to both the subject of the hymn and to the raga or melody in which it is rendered. This form survives to this day and is highly treasured by the connoisseur. A variation within this genre is the dhamar which is somewhat less austere in intent since it usually describes the youthful Krishna and his playful amours during Holi. The dhrupad and dhamar are a continuation of ancient classical textual forms enriched and modified by contemporary folk traditions and as such are the precursors of all later musical models.

A parallel development with the dhrupad and one which gave another powerful impetus to music in north India was the revival of the bhakti cult under Chaitanya in the later part of the fifteenth century. For nearly two hundred years there was a great upsurge of devotional music that spread to most parts of the country. The large number of saint-composers who wrote and sang simple, moving songs of extraordinary beauty during this period did much to make the world of music accessible to all, and to attune the Indian ear to receive the sophistication and refinement of later musical developments.

The most widely practised classical form of the Hindustani system today is the khayal, a Persian term loosely meaning 'idea' or 'flight of the imagination'. The khayal had first appeared soon after dhrupad, but came into its own in the early decades of the eighteenth century. As the designation of this form suggests, it allows the personality of the musician greater scope for expression and personal feeling than the dhrupad. It represents in many ways a subtle shift in musical values. The ideal of the structured awe-inspiring ritual of devotion seems to make room for the individual musician's aspiration. The presentation of a khayal is not the rendering of a song, for here it is not the words that are set to music but almost a reverse process.

This is not the case in thumri, a light classical manifestation which was developed in the middle of the nineteenth century by Wajid Ali Shah, the Nawab of Awadh. In this genre the stress is on the text of the lyric, which always has a romantic theme of love and longing, in the poetic folk language of the region where

Krishna is believed to have spent his childhood and youth. Thumri singing is the art of conveying the meaning of the words through acute suggestion. A skilful performer can give the same line of a lyric a hundred clearly different meanings through musical manipulation alone.

Although thumri is based on classical ragas, it is far less demanding in the matter of purity. Tradition allows the performer almost unlimited freedom to indulge himself. He may not only mix ragas but also insert textual material such as couplets in Urdu, Hindi, or Brajbhasha to make his rendering more poignant and instantly appealing. Current forms such as dadra, bhajan, kajri, chaiti, jhoola, and even ghazal are other manifestations in the same genre which accommodate a spontaneity unthinkable in dhrupad or khayal.

FIFTEEN

The Raga: An Inward Journey

The preoccupation of the traditional Hindustani musician is predominantly spiritual in the sense that he must first find and activate the inner source, the centre of his being, the bindu or core within himself where he rings most true and then draw it out with his life-breath, prana, and proffer it as sound. Tradition exhorts the musician to plumb the depths within him rather than seek range and variety. The shadaja, the tonic note, is the musical bindu which symbolizes eternal being. The term shadaja literally means 'born of the six (notes)'. It is the key which admits the listening ear to the meaning of the music. The tanpura or stringed drone which invariably accompanies Indian music continuously offers the reposeful sound of the shadaja. The musical utterance, whether vocal or instrumental, is the unbroken melodic line. These melodic lines are seen as an extension of the shadaja and draw their being and energy from it. The music unfolds when the reposeful but dominant tonic nucleus of the shadaja becomes charged through concentration and intensity and begins to emit musical rays, so to speak. These melodic rays and lines strain away from the shadaja and return to rest in it, thus creating pulsating patterns of tension and release.

Hindustani musicians undergo rigorous training and possess incredible skill and control. However, the central object of their labours is not the cultivation of a 'beautiful' tone but the development of an almost limitless capability in articulation. The physical sound of the music is, in ideal circumstances, only a medium and not the end product. To the connoisseur, a voice is only as beautiful as what it conveys. The physical body of the music is to the musician what a writing tool is to the poet. The listener is trained to tune in to the highly charged state of consciousness of the performer rather than to the physical condition of the sound that carries the music. Consequently, Indian ears are somewhat indifferent to the outer perfection of musical sound. Some of the most revered musicians have been and are people in their seventies. Their glory is in the truth of their experience and though their voices may have lost superficial lustre, the purity of their intention still shines through and is always the focus of attention for the initiated listener.

The human voice is considered the supreme instrument and the major musical tradition is embodied in a great variety of vocal styles and forms. Most stringed and wind instruments recall some quality or aspect of the voice. The singing voice in Indian music is the earthy unbeautified voice of everyday speech, not a musical escape from it.

Raga is a central concept in all Indian music. It is a Sanskrit term which literally means passion, colour, and attachment, something that has 'the effect of colouring the hearts of men'. There is an implied value here of an intensity, a singleness of colour—not a rainbow—that the performer must create anew in order to suffuse 'the hearts of men'. Most of the ragas which inhabit the world of musicians today are highly developed and schematic versions of the primitive melodies of the various tribal and folk cultures of the country. Each raga is an incipient melodic idea which uses at least five tones of the octave. Each has strict rules of ascent and descent, prescribed resting places, characteristic phrases, and a distinct ethos of its own. Each is assigned to a particular time of day or season and is invested with the power to evoke a state of feeling related to both the human condition and to nature. There are pre-dawn ragas like Lalit which are associated with the meeting of darkness and light. All major morning ragas such as Bhairav and Todi are sombre and devotional, for morning is a time for prayer and meditation. As the light gets stronger, more luminous ragas such as Jaunpuri and Bilawal enter the field. The Sarang family of ragas, performed in the early afternoon, are full of sunlight and emit a 'shimmering, leafy green colour'. The late afternoon ragas, like Multani and Patdeep, are restless, intense with heat, and seem to speak of a time when the day's activity is at its peak. As the sun sets, the sedate and tranquil evening ragas take over. Most members of the Kalyan family of ragas belong to this time of calm introspection and radiate a deep serenity. Between sunset and late night there are lyrical and romantic ragas such as Des, Tilang, and Khamaj. Ragas that are performed deep into the night, for example Darbari Kanhara and Malkaus, are profoundly searching creations, full of magic, mystery and depth. Additionally, there are ragas for the rainy season, for the spring-time, and for the harvest festival of Holi. Today, there are no more than a hundred ragas in the collective repertoire of the Hindustani musician. These are survivors from the thousands that were introduced at one stage or another through permissible choice and permutation of tones within the octave.

To the conditioned ear, each phrase of one of these ragas is like a limb that reveals the identity of the whole being and has the power to evoke in the listener its entire image. It is significant that the sequential order of tones in a melodic line does not mean anything by itself. Its expression and effect depend on its dynamics—on how it swerves towards or away from a tone or from silence; how it curves, dives, wafts, spirals, trails or plummets; on where it gathers its greatest weight and luminosity and on its grain and texture. Two entirely different ragas quite often have the same sequence of tones. It is the sculpting of the melodic line connecting the sequence that distinguishes one from the other, just as the usage of a word and the tone of voice in which it is spoken are what determine its exact meaning.

Hindustani music does not isolate individual notes of the scale but glides over the intervals that separate them. For this reason there is no exact universally accepted system of notation. For the same reason keyboard instruments are considered to be unsuitable. However, the melodic line does pass through tones, semi-tones, and quarter-tones, the frequencies of which are identified for purposes of clarity. There are twelve svaras or notes in the scale of Hindustani music, and ten shrutis or microtones. Literally, shruti means any sound which is capable of being heard and theoretically there could be numberless shrutis in the octave, but only ten are used in Hindustani music. The word svara means 'that which is luminous in itself'. To qualify as svara a note must shine like a gem in its setting of microtones.

In Hindustani music, a note is not thought of as a fixed point but, rather, an area through which a melodic line passes. The more developed a musician's sensibility and concentration, the more extensive this area becomes. It is these 'areas' that the musician shapes with delicate nuances and elaborate graces in the course of his extempore exploration of the raga. Obviously this kind of music cannot be captured in its entirety in a written score. The way to enter the music is by attentively following the moving melodic line whose many subtle and dynamic forms etch detailed and intricate shapes which are of great musical interest.

The musical vocabulary of intervals is a shared heritage familiar even to the uninitiated. Each note in the scale when heard along with the tonic yields, as a word does in language, a colour and emotional charge. For instance, one might say arbitrarily that the perfect fifth is red, positive, strong; that the third is sky blue, tranquil, lucid; and that the flat third or sixth is grey, introspective, plaintive; and so on. This sense of the inherent emotional content of intervals is a common language understood in general terms by all who share the regional culture of which this system of music is a product, just as those who are not themselves painters might still react to an array of primary colours. The skilled musician uses these colours, leading his audience into delicately shaded areas, carrying them all through the creative process, line by line, stroke by stroke, colour by colour—until he has infused into them the portrait of the raga as he conceives of it at the time. Dhrupad, khayal, and thumri compositions are not really compositions in the Western sense and allow far greater latitude to the performer, especially the last. If the musician were to sing or play the same 'composition' several times, each would be an irreproducible original, though each would be based on the musical concept of the piece that is being rendered.

Each composition or bandish is set in a known tala or rhythmic arrangement of beats in a cyclic manner. Each rhythmic cycle is divided into sections which may or may not be equal. It is complete in itself and continues to repeat itself faithfully throughout the performance of a particular piece. As the melodic lines strain away from the shadaja and return to it, so the beats of a tala emanate from the sam, the first beat of the cycle which carries the greatest emphasis, and travel in a descending arc to the khali (empty), at which point the rhythm gathers momentum again to ascend and culminate in the sam. The tala sets up an elaborate pulsating rhythmic pattern which the musician uses as a sort of frame on which to weave his melodic threads. The sam is both the beginning and the end of the cycle, and commands special attention, as the drum-stroke here coincides with a melodic climax in the composition, creating each time a burst of musical energy, a sense of arriving. This repetitive musical travelling and arriving generates a pattern of tension and release which is a special characteristic of Hindustani music.

In an actual performance, the singer first 'awakens' the shadaja, then in wordless syllables and in free rhythm draws some evocative melodic lines to usher in the raga in which the piece is set. This is the crucial alaap part, the foundation on which everything else will rest. He then begins the composition, guiding the drummer as to the intended tempo and indicating where he must come in with the first stroke or sam of the tala. After the first cue, the tabla player needs no further direction, only the most sensitive listening, so that the beat is in sympathy with the musical intention and provides an unobtrusive setting.

After the bandish has been outlined, the performer develops the raga in the manner of a pyramid, often using the suggestions implicit in the composition as a model for the proliferating lines. He explores and cultivates the lower regions of the scale in great depth in slow tempo and then rises in the scale of the raga, gradually increasing the tempo. The nature of this expression, which develops vertically as it were, is an intensification, a gradual accumulation of meaning, rather than an extended statement. However, it still demands to be heard as a totality, for a part of it would be as meaningless as a truncated sentence.

The first sounding of the upper tonic, the taar shadaja, is a climactic moment, for only at this point is the delineation of the raga completed.

The music is not 'prepared' beforehand and rigidly presented but is a live communication in which the listener contributes to the reality of each moment. The ideal of the singer is to share with the listener all phases of the creative process, much like an idea developed in extempore speech. The natural form of performance of this music is therefore the live chamber concert. The portrait of the raga, presented by the musician, is in a sense the product of the attention of all those present at its unfolding. This situation is quite different from that of the Western composer whose work is undertaken in relative isolation.

The musician envisions a heightened state of being through the portraiture of the lines of the raga. The lines, colours, and feelings offered by the raga create a field of awareness in which the listener can share in the intended evocation. What the listeners hear and acknowledge is the validation of what the singer is discovering in the moment. This live chemistry of participation is a vital factor in traditional performances where the performer is the leader and the listener the follower. Ideally, both experience the full portrait in sound simultaneously.

Of course, music can be and is presented at many levels. There is a greater demand for and therefore greater abundance of musical products with ready appeal. What makes such music unacceptable to the connoisseur is not its elementary character—for the greatest music can be extremely simple—but the fact that the musician is not seriously involved with a vision and is only making a studied effort to simulate it. What is significant here is that even in this simulation he acknowledges the essentially spiritual character of classical music by taking the trouble to imitate it.

As there can be many styles of calligraphy, so there are a number of styles in which the melodic line can be drawn on the canvas of silence. These styles of Hindustani classical music are called gharanas, and function like closed guilds. Gharana literally means 'family' in the sense of lineage. The personal style, musical attitudes, and predispositions of an acknowledged master are what give a gharana its distinctly recognizable melodic movement and dialect.

The transmission of traditional music from master to disciple is a very serious matter in India. *Seena ba seena*, from breast to breast, is a commonly used phrase in this context. What the ustad (master) passes on to the shagird (disciple) is the whole experience of his inner musical self, his entire 'quality'. Therefore nothing less than total commitment on the part of the pupil is acceptable. He has to be a vehicle that is fit to receive, cherish, and perpetuate the life and work of a great musical mind. The teaching is oral and very often secretive. The master teaches perhaps a son, or a nephew or son-in-law, or a deserving pupil who has proved himself trustworthy in every sense. For an 'outsider' to be accepted as a disciple is rare, an overwhelming and remarkable thing which happens only to the fortunate few. Reverence, humility, and the aspiration to merge with something bigger than oneself are such an integral part of the process that they almost enter the music as values, along with the values of purity and restraint. The highest compliment for an Indian musician is to be told that his work is reminiscent of the masters he admires and that he is a torch bearer. To most musicians this brings more satisfaction and fulfilment than being considered unique. Individual talent thus subserves and helps forge tradition in a sense very similar to that which T.S. Eliot and A.K. Ramanujan outlined for poetry in Europe and classical South India.

The characteristics of the dialect and style of each gharana originate in the personalities of the individuals who founded them. Even though the faithful preservation of these characteristics is applauded by purists today, with the greater access provided by electronic aids and increased physical mobility there is much more exchange and contact, acknowledged and unacknowledged, between the gharanas. Many examples of borrowing and mixing are audible on concert stages in India.

One of the remarkable things about traditional Hindustani music is the coexistence in its practice of the most rigorous discipline and a degree of freedom that is truly astonishing. The manifold disciplines are rigid and uncompromising: the rules of the raga, the time of the day, the intention of the composition, the confining frame of the tala, the prescribed form of presentation, faithfulness to the vani or style of utterance. These and many other considerations bind the musician, but at the same time tradition offers him extraordinary freedom to express his being. He is free to explore the areas in between the rigid 'notes' of the keyboard and free from objective time. The raga performance is an evocation that aspires to break free of time by itself becoming a kind of time, with a breadth and movement of its own. The unfolding of a raga is an act of persuasion and the time it takes is a purely subjective matter for both the musician and the listener. It is the attention of the listener, mobilized by an abundance of shared conditions, which can help this experience come to life.

SIXTEEN

Reflections on the Kirana Legacy

When we speak of the gharana of a traditional musician, we mean the family traits of the music he practises and owes allegiance to. The concept of musical gharanas is physically comparable to that of families or clans in general, but in reality it is far more extensive and complicated. It signifies not only the physical characteristics, temperamental leanings, and attitudes of the founder, in the same way as it would in the case of the ancestral line of a family, but much else that is contributed by all the talent that has come to drink at the fount of the master. This interaction and experience leaves an enduring imprint on the common pool of the gharana's wealth.

A musical gharana invariably grows around the genius of a creative master whose achievements automatically attract a collection of aspirants, admirers, and disciples. Traditionally, these masters command the kind of unqualified reverence that is associated with religious gurus. Their followers not only unquestioningly adhere to the musical principles laid down by them but also unconsciously imitate the physical characteristics of their role models. This small nucleus grows and widens as the style associated with the master gains prestige and acceptability among music lovers. Each gharana has a temperament since it reflects and carries within itself the seeds of the personality of the master with whom it originated. The outstanding khayal gharanas today are Gwalior, Agra, Kirana, Jaipur-Athrauli, and Patiala, each named after the original place of residence of the ustad or family of ustads around whom closely guarded musical guilds grew and flourished. It is fascinating to observe how the traits, aptitudes, and predilections of a master mould the musical approach and attitudes of a gharana.

Practitioners of the Gwalior gharana, the oldest of all khayal gharanas, clearly show their respect for both the vigour and the rigour of older religious forms such as dhrupad and give precedence to the demands of the bandish over that of their personal musical urges. Their aim is to adhere strictly to the structure and frame of the composition they are presenting even while improvising freely and spontaneously. This can be quite a feat of musicianship. Both the rhythmic and melodic aspects share the musician's attention equally. In a sense, the gayaki of the Gwalior gharana is the most disciplined and demanding because the practising musician cannot afford the luxury of specializing in any one aspect which pleases him most. He must master all the facets of music and a great variety of techniques if he is to be faithful to the original style.

Most other gharanas on the other hand display far more freedom and discrimination in deciding which aspects of music they would like to stress and make their speciality. These preferences of course reflect the personal musical affiliations of the masters they follow. For instance the Agra gharana is known for bold, staccato movements and full-throated evocations in which rhythmic interplay is used to enhance the persuasiveness of the music. The ideal that all singers of this gharana try to imitate is the overt and robust style of emoting that was characteristic of Ustad Fayyaz Khan, their idol.

The Kirana gharana traces delicate three-dimensional arcs, and draws from silence deeply searching spirals. The true Kirana musician believes that each jagah or 'place' in the scale of a raga is not a point but a musical area that must be explored anew each time and brought to life in the living moment. This introspective approach is also reflected in their style of raga development. The base of the edifice they build up, that is the 'sa' and the mandra saptak, claims the greatest attention. Once the foundation is laid, the angles of the rising structure are gently indicated while the apex is often left to the imagination of the listener, in deference to the underlying philosophy that a mere human does not have the ability to perfect or complete anything, including the portrait of a raga.

The Athrauli-Jaipur gayaki of which Ustad Alladiya Khan was the champion is known for its sharply etched and brilliant alankars or note patterns. The typical presentational model of this gharana is to outline the entire bandish in medium tempo at the outset and then to embellish and underline the structure with scintillating patterns of rhythm and melody. The strength of this music lies not in the nuance of expression or emotion but in the fluency and sparkling clarity and energy of the musical utterance which can be likened to a finely-cut diamond.

The Patiala gayaki stresses the presentational aspect and achieves its effect through an exuberance of spirit and a sense of abandon. The music often takes the form of a series of build-ups and climaxes, where the musicality of the moment takes precedence over sense of structure.

There are many other gharanas and styles in addition to these. The point here is to recognize that each is the embodiment of an outstanding musical personality and each has the potential of attracting to itself like-minded music lovers. The riches of the minds of the masters who have given rise to such a wealth of styles in India can be likened to the immoveable property of the members of the gharana which includes their disciples as well. Another kind of wealth which each gharana owns and which we can consider their moveable property is the repertoire of compositions and ragas they specially pride themselves on. This wealth is as jealously guarded by all members who identify themselves with the gharana as any other kind of riches and shared only with those who are admitted into the family by right of blood, marriage, or exemplary discipleship. By following both the manner and material of musical masters, their disciples give rise to a distinctive stream of musical practice.

The origins of the Kirana gharana go back a long way and include the contribution of luminaries like Bande Ali Khan, the legendary master of the *been*. Kirana is the name of a town near Saharanpur in Uttar Pradesh where the emperor Jahangir is said to have resettled many families of musicians after their homes were destroyed in a flood. Many sarangi and sitar players also trace their ancestry to this town. But the gayaki as we know it today is the product of two great musical minds—that of Abdul Karim Khan, and of his nephew Abdul Wahid Khan. Together they are considered the pillars of this musical legacy even though no two temperaments or personalities could be more different. While the uncle's forté was emotional appeal and delicate lyricism, the nephew's music was celebrated for its intellectual vigour, purity of raga, and relentless sense of structure. Abdul Karim Khan overwhelmed the listener with feeling, while Abdul Wahid Khan challenged his mind to its limits. Both are capable of miraculous musical feats in their separate ways. The manner of these two masters was followed by their respective disciples, thus giving rise to two distinct sub-streams of musical practice within the Kirana school.

The story goes that, at an informal family gathering, Abdul Karim Khan enchanted all those present with his rendering of the raga Mian-ki-Malhar. His concentration on tunefulness sometimes led him to take minor liberties with a raga. Only Abdul Wahid Khan's piercing mind detected that certain notes were being used in an unorthodox manner and that the purity of the raga as understood in the Kirana gharana was being compromised. He was severely critical at first but at the end of the concert, when he saw that the entire audience was spellbound, he remarked that Abdul Karim Khan's voice had indeed been blessed by divine grace and to find fault with his music was like challenging the Almighty.

The Two Streams of a River

Despite the seemingly wide differences in the musical manner of these two pillars of the Kirana gharana, their approach and concerns had much in common at a deeper level. What they shared distinguished them clearly from all other gharanas and was more vital and decisive than any physical dissimilarities could be. The common lineage that nurtured them had implanted in both their psyches an almost exclusive preoccupation with raga development. Both considered a sincere and penetrating search for swara more important than presentational aspects such as taal and ornamentation. Both chose depth over variety, suggestion over statement, quality over quantity, and the subtle and sophisticated over the overt and the obvious. Both shared the same concept of the unbroken melodic line which in the case of the Kirana gayaki arises from silence, stretches and gains body in an arc, and fades back into silence, without any abrupt breaks, angles, or jerks. For both the masters it is an article of faith that the exact place of a note in its surrounding aura has to be searched for and discovered anew every time a phrase is attempted. Its exact position cannot be taken for granted as though one had fixed it on the harmonium. Both masters are more attracted to the slow tempo than to the 'drut' since the leisurely pace affords the opportunity to explore the contours of the raga in greater detail. Both demonstrate in their practice that concentration on a small musical area, whether it is a single raga, or three notes in it, is more rewarding than restlessly moving from raga to raga, or indiscriminately adding to one's collection of compositions. In deference to this conviction, both prefer to present serious ragas that have a rich development potential and are not usually attracted to sweet-sounding or popular ragas that do not seriously challenge the mind. This tendency can be seen in all singers of the Kirana school who specialize in profound creations like Todi, Yaman, Shuddha Kalyan, Puriya, and Darbari and do not generally attempt easy-to-please ragas like Chayanat, Nand, Desh, and Khamaj. Not only that: they tend to treat even a light raga with so much depth that it acquires new characteristics. Abdul Karim Khan's Abhogi Kanhra is a case in point. The original Carnatak raga that was the inspiration for it is beautiful and lyrical, but nowhere as profound and majestic as the conception of the raga envisioned by singers of the Kirana gharana.

Abdul Wahid Khan was once asked why he limited himself to only two ragas, Todi and Darbari, which he practised day in and day out. His response was that he would have dropped the second one too if morning time could last forever. One lifetime, according to him, was not enough to do justice to any raga. He was forced to change from Todi to something else only because of the setting sun and the gathering darkness.

The musical values that these two great masters held dear to their hearts in their own individual ways were broadly the same. All musicians of the Kirana school are aware of the two main streams that they represent within the same value system and consciously adhere to one or the other, or a combination of the two, in a proportion which is congenial to their musical personalities. They are also aware that, despite superficial differences in manner, both streams address themselves to the same musical concerns. The similarities outweigh the differences and establish a common ancestry.

Supremacy of Swara

The Kirana gharana developed in response to a deep urge for personal self-expression. Masters like Abdul Karim Khan concentrated their entire attention on the poignance and nuance of the swara and did not make very active use of rhythm in creating the desired effect. The luminosity and exact placing of the swara in the raga became so important to the practitioners of this style that they laid themselves open to the charge by other gharanas of neglecting the tala and the bandish. In this sense the Kirana gharana was an unorthodox, even in some senses an erratic, development. In order to give the utmost latitude to the alaap element, which is the most evocative and emotive part of raga delineation, both Abdul Karim Khan and Abdul Wahid Khan reduced the tempo of the bada khayals to the slowest it had ever been in the history of the khayal. It was their conviction that the meditative, contemplative, and emotional aspects of music which attracted them most could not possibly be coaxed out of music at a brisk pace. This development resulted in impressive feats of musicality at a very high level, and began to be imitated by other gharanas as a necessary condition for evoking feeling from a raga. Many performers of the Jaipur gharana, for instance, have now begun to preface their recitals with slow alaap in the Kirana mode which would have been unthinkable for them fifty years earlier.

This is true of some other gharanas as well. In fact the walls of the gharanas have become more porous than they used to be and there is much unconscious borrowing and lending in a competitive spirit. With the greater access provided by electronic aids and increased physical mobility, there is much more exchange and contact, acknowledged and unacknowledged, between the gharanas and many examples of mixed gayakis are audible on concert stages today. The interesting fact is that today no singer or player of any school can resist the lure of the slow badhat which used to be the exclusive preserve of the Kirana school. Even those who point out that the emphasis given to this aspect is lopsided cannot but extend silent respect to the meditative vilambit and leisurely badhat of the Kirana style. The most conclusive and effective compliment to this speciality is that it is imitated across all frontiers of gharana or style and has gained not only acceptability but universal prestige. At the same time it must be admitted in fairness that some Kirana singers in their turn try to outdo the tayyari or fast singing, which is a speciality of other gharanas and not their own forté, in an effort to measure up and not be found wanting in any aspect. Even so, it is possible to distinguish the special traits that were originally contributed by the Kirana gharana.

The Melodic Line and Sense of Structure

One outstanding feature of the Kirana gayaki is the refined sculpting of the melodic line. The practitioners of the Kirana style tend to regard the entire scale as a continuous flow of musicality and not a series of separate notes. Conceptually, every phrase in a raga is represented by a flowing line which passes smoothly through all the gradations of the participating notes without revealing the joints. The extremely fine tuning of the intonation of the line conveys the emotional intention, subtly and enduringly, as though it were not a string of notes but a single musical sound with a distinct expression. In other words, the Kirana sensibility aspires to absorb the emotional ambience and aura of a particular limb of the raga instead of hearing a series of notes separately and literally. This gayaki abhors angles and abrupt breaks so that the continuity of the spirals that the voice traces is maintained. It is the unceasing effort of all practitioners to make this their second nature. Attention is given not only to where the melodic line originates and ends, but also to its thickness or thinness at any given point. This type of detailed and delicate calligraphy lends the music a third dimension of physical depth which is palpable to the ear.

Another speciality of the Kirana approach is that the raga is conquered not by treading relentlessly up and down its scale but by locating and controlling the crucial pressure points in its structure. For instance in most sampoorna ragas, an understanding of the function of the nishadh and the madhyam, or of rishabh and dhaivata, or of any two notes and their mutual relationship, holds the key that could open the doors to the raga's innermost recesses. These are not accessible by mere force of practice. As a corollary to this way of looking at the raga, the typical Kirana singer fashions even his fast taans from a structural rather than an ornamental point of view, that is to say he takes into cognizance the vital organs and anatomy of the raga with a view to capturing its distinctive flavour and essence. He is not content merely with weaving attractive note patterns that may be pleasant to the ear. The progress of the perfect Kirana taan thus satisfies the connoisseur's sense of structure as much as, and sometimes even more than, his melodic expectations.

Restraint as a Musical Value

Another area of subtlety is the use of silence and understatement as effective musical elements. The comparatively low-key sensibility of the Kirana singers is also expressed in their leisurely but meticulous attention to the mandra saptak. As we have already seen, the raga is developed note by note in the manner of a pyramid. The tempo of the music also rises as the structure progresses. When the apex of the pyramid, the taar shadaja, is reached, it is not punished overtly and repeatedly as in many other styles, but merely suggested, as though the music was being completed in the mind rather than physically. An example of this is found in the music of Amir Khan who adopted this attitude from the Kirana principles and carried it to an extreme because it admirably suited his introspective and meditative nature.

The cursory treatment of the antara in a bandish can be seen in the music of Abdul Wahid Khan. This indicates a preference for understatement and gesture over physical completeness. A mere pointer to the taar saptak which finally reveals the face of a raga can sometimes be more aesthetically satisfying to an evolved musical taste than an overt and detailed treatment of that area. Abdul Wahid Khan never repeated the antara on principle and preferred to position it in such a manner that it did not occupy the whole space of the vilambit taal cycle, usually the fourteen beat jhoomra, but accommodated itself within ten or eleven matras. It is well known that most traditional vilambit khayal compositions that have been handed down through this stream allow three or four beats to pass after the sam before the antara is taken up. The significance of this practice is only psychological in that it reflects a kind of restraint, and a faith that, musically, suggestion and delicacy are more appealing than outright statement and mechanical reiteration.

All singers of the Kirana gharana share this conviction in their different ways and to varying extents. And yet each has an emphatic individuality. In fact, the test of a genuine gharana is not only that at least three generations must have upheld the tradition but also that each single exponent should be able to express his individuality and leave his personal stamp on the music. If this condition is not met, then the teaching is open to the charge of being nothing more than an opportunity to imitate. The gurus of the Kirana gharana pride themselves on their ability to transmit the technique of the art so that their followers can distinguish their own musical urges from the mannerisms of their masters and still express them through the traditional idiom they have been taught. The success of their efforts is borne out by the fact that the music of each singer of the Kirana gharana reflects an original individual personality and not a stereotype.

Among the disciples Abdul Karim Khan groomed are Roshanara Begum, Ganesh Ramachandra Behere, Balakrishnabua Kapileshwari, Firoz Dastoor and Sawai Gandharva—who in turn trained Gangubai Hangal and Bhimsen Joshi. Each of these artistes has a distinct style even though they adhere to the same principles. This also applies to Abdul Wahid Khan's star pupil Hirabai Barodekar, a daughter of Abdul Karim Khan, who in her turn became the idol of singers like Manik Verma and Prabha Atre. In the course of his stay in Lahore, the master also taught Jeevan Lal Mattoo, his son Jawaharlal Mattoo, and his daughter-in-law Madhuri Mattoo. All three were lifelong practitioners. Another faithful pupil was Pran Nath who dedicated his entire life to upholding and popularizing the style and musical attitudes of his guru. In the USA, where he spent the latter part of his life, he continued to teach the music of the Kirana school according to his lights and built up an extensive archive of recordings of compositions bequeathed to him by his master.

In general it can be said that the sub-stream represented by Abdul Wahid Khan is drier and more austere than the evocative and poignant manner of Abdul Karim Khan, but from the technical standpoint the former is regarded more authoritative by most people. The attitudes of the two masters colour their musical expression also. The accents of Abdul Karim Khan are tender, full of love, and go straight to the heart. It is said that he was greatly influenced by the feeling that thumri singers like Moijuddin Khan were able to evoke in their music. On the other hand, the utterance of Abdul Wahid Khan, though equally persuasive, was somewhat intimidating by comparison.

Perceptions of the Present Generation

The foregoing observations provide only a bird's-eye view of the trends that have been followed in the Kirana gharana. However, in the present generation, those who like me have been fortunate enough to study with Ustad Fayyaz Ahmed and Ustad Niaz Ahmed of that gharana, have had the chance to look more closely at this legacy and all that it implies. One of the most impressive elements in it is the teaching techniques that have been developed and perfected by these ustads.

In musical matters, the two brothers seemed to have one soul, even though their bodies were separate. They communicated perfectly at many levels without having to use too many words.

Apart from the natural affinity between brothers who have grown up and received their musical education in the same environment, they had common musical values as a matter of personal preference. They were inheritors of the same traditions and reacted to musical questions in the same way. For these reasons they were able to evolve a highly efficient method of teaching in which the labour involved was intelligently shared between the two of them. Each took responsibility for a different requirement in the grooming of a pupil. Generally, Fayyaz Ahmed taught the nuances of the chalan of a raga and outlined the compositions while Niaz Ahmed ensured that the minutest details of each lesson penetrated deeply and became an inalienable part of the pupil's musical vocabulary. The elder brother enriched the teaching with extraordinary refinement of feeling, while the other brought to it an equally impressive discipline and devotion. But these roles could be interchanged if need be. However, for the most part the strong points of both were imaginatively made available to each student in the manner most advantageous to them.

The two ustads did not have a blanket prescription for all their students, but devised, most painstakingly, the best course of 'treatment' for every known musical 'malady'. Their diagnostic ability was also phenomenal. When I was first examined by them for possible discipleship, it took them no more than five minutes to discover that I had a tendency to be nasal, that my meendh was rough and jerky, that my pitches in the aarohi tended to be higher than in the avarohi, and that I lacked serenity. But they kept this bad report to themselves lest the disclosure shatter my self-confidence at the outset. Much later I was gently told about this only as a matter of interest, and only after these faults had been treated and corrected to the extent possible.

My lifelong experience with music teachers had led me to

believe that teaching simply meant the opportunity to imitate. I realized only through Niaz Ahmed and Fayyaz Ahmed that teaching music was a highly developed art, quite distinct from the art of creating music but every bit as challenging. My teachers prided themselves on the teaching skills they had learnt in addition to and as distinct from their musical training. Their sincerity and inventiveness in this area was remarkable. I remember many feats that are still talked about among their students. They once cured a disciple who was chronically kamsura by holding up three parallel fingers every time she touched the taar sa and telling her that her voice had reached only as high as the first finger whereas she actually needed to pitch her voice to the third one. They gradually guided her ear and her psychology until she got her bearings and readjusted her ear to the right pitch. Another instance that comes to mind is that, once, they succeeded in correcting the inflection and intonation of a typical phrase in the raga Mian-ki-Malhar by telling a student to actually sing the mandra saptak pa while keeping her mind firmly on the *sa*! This took several hours of trial and error since it was not an old and tried remedy but one invented on the spot to solve an unexpected problem that had arisen.

It had been ingrained in Niaz and Fayyaz Ahmed by their ustads and elders that the musical treasures they were in possession of were not their personal property but wealth which they held in trust and which it was their sacred duty to pass on to deserving aspirants. They did not merely pronounce this but actually lived it in their professional dealings. Their generosity in teaching was phenomenal. A lesson ended only when the pupil simply could not absorb any more.

The willingness to impart, which is in any case a rare quality in traditional circles, is not always matched by the ability to do so. In the case of this duo it was. Their teaching skills were of a very high order and were constantly fuelled by a bewildering variety of demands from their students. Each individual had a different problem for which corrective remedies had to be devised. Each had specific requirements and preferences so far as material was concerned. The two ustads who worked as a team saw to it that every student of theirs was satisfied and on the right track. They never gave up and never discouraged anybody lest it break their spirit. These human qualities and considerations were impressive considering that in matters of music the two brothers were absolutely uncompromising. Association with such teachers exposed their pupils not only to the finer points of music, but to an infectious value system that embraced both aesthetics and ethics.

Maulana and his Bhai Sahib

The clean, disciplined, and self-denying lifestyle of Niaz Ahmed Khan earned him the title of Maulana. Not only his extended family, but the entire music world knows him by that epithet. His dedication to the purity and practices of the Kirana gharana is a matter of faith with him. But there are lesser-known facets of his personality which occasionally surprise his devotees. His forté is a systematic and meticulous style of raga development, but he can on occasion render the most touching and emotional thumri in the vein of Abdul Karim Khan. He once ended a concert in Bombay with the famous jamuna ke teer in Bhairavi and there was hardly a dry eye in the hall when he finished. Some of us have even heard him sing a beautiful dhun he composed for a ghazal, in a rare light mood. He stopped in embarrassment when his elder brother happened to walk in accidentally, but everyone present, including his elder brother, was amazed at the range of his musical sensibility.

The performance mode of the two brothers was quite different from the teaching one. One might well ask how two separate people can possibly express their innermost musical urges together, and yet this is exactly what they succeeded in doing. In fact, as performers they achieved more in partnership than they would have as individuals. They used their separate strengths as an advantage to extend the reach of their music. Each in turn securely held the frame of the structure they built up, leaving the other free to explore the furthest limits of his imagination. Fayyaz Ahmed Khan skilfully and delicately filled in the colours of the raga, while Niaz Ahmed Khan animated it with brilliant embellishments and taan patterns. Neither would have been able to go as far as they did in their own preferred area of creativity but for the support and strength of the other. Fortunately for posterity, an example of their best work is available in a series of recordings by HMV. The Yaman recorded by the two brothers is a feat of musicianship which is universally acknowledged as the definitive interpretation of the raga and is still referred to and cited by aspiring singers.

There were some values which they stressed again and again and one of them was spontaneity. They seldom discussed or rehearsed what they were going to sing together. What they might thus have lost in physical slickness was more than made up for by the freshness and genuineness of their expression. '*Nit naya*' was a constant ideal they followed. For them, nothing could be less desirable than stale musical clichés. They never encouraged their students to pre-plan their recitals, but always urged them to be true to the moment and listen to what the tuned tanpura seemed to be suggesting before deciding what they felt like singing.

The sculpting of the melodic line and the meendh was a constant concern for them. Every student was required to understand and observe their very strict rules about the movement of the line. They tirelessly explained how to raise a note, how to stay on it, how to leave it and how to travel to the next note. There were also very detailed principles that governed where the voice should apply force and where it should be allowed to drop by itself. Their formulations were so strict that they used to remind us of the laws of gravity. The structural use of kana was another extremely important lesson that they tirelessly stressed and asked all their pupils to practise. They explained to us that the emotional expression of a musical phrase depended on the movement and conduct of a melodic line, including the *sut*, or fine thread of sound with which a musical phrase fades out, and so it was deserving of the most delicate attention. There were numerous such refinements in their teaching which they normally undertook separately, so that the pupil could concentrate better on the matter in hand. They were rarely present at a lesson together, unless there was a specific reason for it.

The compositions of Fayyaz Ahmed Khan, or Gunarang, are very special and bear his unmistakeable stamp. They have the aroma of the graceful khayals of a bygone age and carry within them all the sensitivity and depth required for a complete grasp of the intention of a raga. For many listeners, these khayals used to be an added attraction at any concert of the two brothers. Even after Fayyaz Ahmed's death in 1987, Niaz Ahmed Khan and some performing pupils continued to feature these compositions in their recitals as they are masterpieces in a distinctive style which one associates with the gayaki of the two brothers.

One quality which stands out in these compositions is that they do not lose their sense of repose, however accelerated the laya might be in the drut. Usually the exact pitches of the notes of a raga have to be sacrificed for the sake of speed and tayyari. Nor can the arches of the meendhs be faithfully traced in the fury of the increased tempo. This is not the case in the compositions of Maulana's beloved 'Bhai Sahib'. There are numerous examples. To pick some at random, his drut ektal compositions in Megh and Mian-ki-Malhar, or his taranas in Malkauns and Kausi Kanhra, are feats of musicianship as well as aesthetics which uphold the ancient values of purity and restraint. These compositions have been added to the repertoire of the common pool and are a living proof of the invaluable contribution of the two brothers to their inherited legacy.

It is rare indeed to find the highest standards of professional ability mingling so easily and comfortably with the broad sympathies and human qualities for which Niaz Ahmed Khan and Fayyaz Ahmed Khan are so widely known. In our own cynical times, where self-interest and self-propagation seem to be the only surviving values, this might well be their most enduring and far-reaching contribution.

SEVENTEEN

The Cooking of Music

Interestingly, the term for classical music in everyday speech is 'pakka gana', or music that has been subjected to the process of pakana, ripening or cooking. The Hindustani word pakka has a chequered history and has ended up in English dictionaries as 'pucka', meaning genuine, solidly built, of full weight, enduring, and therefore emphatically *not* ephemeral. In relation to music, the word is not just descriptive. It couches a thin layer of warning which seems to say this path is not for those looking for instant gratification. There is enough in the term and its associations to intimidate the prospective aspirant, however adventurous. The technical jargon used by professionals to fend off the casual and the merely curious is no help at all in making 'pakka gana' less forbidding to the outsider. 'Insiders' actually derive some satisfaction from the fact that common musical terms like gharana, meendh, gayaki, samvadi, and abhog are only their preserve and as unfamiliar as Greek to most other people. This esoteric aura coupled with the raucous, uninhibited singing voices of most ustads does not affect the listening pleasure of afficianados but jars on the ears of the uninitiated. I remember that as children (brats really) we used to take malicious pleasure in mimicking such voices as an act of heroic irreverence. But it was reassuring to be scolded for playing this insolent game because it confirmed that the seemingly harsh world of 'pakka gana', though not instantly enjoyable, must in some ultimate sense be good and valuable like religion and medicine.

A word that is commonly used in northern India in praise of music is mazaa, or enjoyment. This is a coarse version of the classical concept of rasa but its closest associations are with food, though it can be stretched to encompass other senses too. What the performing musician in the Indian classical tradition sets out to do is very similar to the aims of the chef. The dish must be prepared according to ancient recipes that have stood the test of time, it must be creative and carry the personal signature of the cook, it must preserve and serve the original flavours of the ingredients in all their freshness, it must ensure that all the spices and condiments come together in a single confection, and most importantly, the experience, the taste, the mazaa should live in the mind of the consumer, that it is pakka—which is the chosen antonym for kaccha—meaning uncooked, weak, breakable, and fragile.

The lore of classical music gladly, even boastfully, accepts that this does not always happen, that things do not necessarily come together simply because the right recipe has been faithfully followed. In fact there is a common saying with which frustrated pupils are often consoled. '*Raag, rasoi, pagree, kabhi kabhi ban jaye,*' that is to say, perfection in presenting a raga, creating a culinary dish, and tying the pagri cannot always be achieved. It is also well known that these are areas in which deliberate effort is likely to be counterproductive and that the crucial element in the success of such undertakings is an uncontrollable magic which works in mysterious ways.

The similarity between the two activities of producing music and producing food is quite compelling. Both rely more for their quality on spontaneity and the ruling instinct of the moment than on any rigid recipe. In both, the dish tastes different each time it is attempted and the sharing of its goodness is crucial to the endeavour in both cases.

However, there is a built-in technique in the classical tradition which ensures that the ineffable, delicate musical creation of the artist is not dependent on spontaneity alone. Conceptually, this technique owes quite a lot to the culinary field. The freshest green vegetable, if left in its pristine state indefinitely, loses its crispness, colour, and fragrance. After a time, it becomes stale and finally begins to rot and smell bad. The only thing that can save it is pickling in brine or vinegar. This preserves its essential nature and flavour, but at a price. The immediacy, the raw taste of the artist's personal feeling, which is his alone, has to be sacrificed in the interests of durability and wider comprehension. Expressed in the language of the raga, the musician's emotion undergoes a process of distancing and a virtual rebirth. It is poured into a traditional mould and ideally emerges as an expression which is recognizable and universal, even though the imprint it bears is that of the individual artist.

Very roughly speaking, the way it works is this. Let us say that the musician at the time of performance feels inspired to paint a portrait of his anguish. He will then choose an appropriate raga, one that bears in its prescribed and approved structure the seeds of the anguish that musicians before him have felt for hundreds of years. Of course, his personal anguish cannot ever be exactly the same as that of the collective entity of the musical past we are talking about, but if he renounces tradition and goes it alone, so to speak, two dangerous things are likely to happen.

One, that his original cry from the heart remains a cry in the wilderness and goes unheard because it does not use a language that anybody else can fully understand. Even if he manages to communicate the emotion he is experiencing, there is a second danger he faces. The emotion, since it has not been treated with any kind of preservatives, becomes stale and tiresome in the minds of his listeners after a while. Hundreds of examples of bad music come to mind where the main thing that has gone wrong is that powerful feelings have been directly aimed at the heartstrings without any distancing or 'cooking'. However beautiful or fragrant a musical idea may be at birth, it cannot retain its freshness and beauty unless it is treated in some fashion that guarantees long-term health. Leaning on the restraint and purity of the classical idiom usually achieves this end automatically.

What the performing musician does is to try and salvage the emotion he is experiencing from oblivion by translating it in the sturdy and weatherproof vocabulary of an ancient musical language that people trust, understand and love. To go back to the anguish the musician wishes to express, he has a wide choice of ragas he can use for the purpose. He will pick a suitable one much as one picks out the clothes one feels like wearing on a particularly sad day. Most ragas that use komal or flattened *re* and/or *dha* (for instance, the Todi family, or Bhairavi, or Asavari) would normally fit the bill.

The fact that the ragas as they exist at present relate to what someone else has felt at one time does not necessarily imply that today's performer must slavishly echo the feelings of masters who have gone before him. It only means that he is processing his creative urge and using the raga he has chosen as a blueprint to work on so that he can truly share the outcome which still remains his personal statement. There is an apocryphal but serviceable story that when Tansen died, his son Bilas Khan mourned him by singing a Todi which was a spontaneous variation of something his father had composed. This new raga, one of the most mournful of creations, was given the name Bilaskhani Todi and won a place of honour in the repertoire of Hindustani musicians. During the last three hundred years or so, it has been sung and played by every single master of every gharana and no two renditions are even faintly alike. Each is an original musical portrait, though it embodies a poignancy that someone else first felt and expressed many years ago. The model only provides a frame of reference, a sort of common musical language. It certainly does not dictate in a manner that might snuff out creativity.

My experience is limited to the luminaries and musical ustads of the north Indian heartland: I have never encountered one to whom the cooking and serving of good food was not extremely important. Granted that in India, as in most poor countries, feeding is the most obvious way of expressing love and concern. But in the lifestyles of the personalities I am thinking of, it has a slightly different cultural resonance. It is a symbol of the desire to create exquisiteness and to allow equally the more favoured and less privileged to bask in it. There is a faint suggestion of princely generosity, of *mahadaulat,* in most such gestures and they are so graceful that it is invariably a pleasure to be at the receiving end.

When Zia Moinuddin Dagar travelled to New York to stay with an ardent American disciple, the first thing he did was to take charge of the kitchen and start operations on the lamb korma so that it would be ready by the time the first day's music session ended. Only then did he settle down to tune his rudra veena. The lesson progressed while the dish slowly cooked. Throughout the day, he would periodically rise from his instrument to peer into the pot intently and stir it a bit. The ardent disciple ended up learning at least as much about Mughlai cooking as about raga and playing technique. Within twenty days the resident smells of Italian sausage, spaghetti sauce, and oregano in the old Manhattan apartment yielded unconditionally to the more authoritative odours of coriander, cumin, and garam masala. The ustad confirmed that the tone and pitch of the pupil had simultaneously become so much more satisfactory that it was time to have a combined food and music feast for all friends and acquaintances.

This is indicative of a way of life that was common to most musicians in northern India. Pandit Pran Nath used to say that real music was only for those who could replicate the aroma of kababs in every note. Bade Ghulam Ali Khan once announced to an inadequate host that he could hardly be expected to produce his kind of music if he was given grass to eat. '*Ai khana, te ai gana*?' he had exclaimed in shocked tones when he viewed the watery vegetables he had been served. Ustad Fayyaz Ahmed Khan's favourite topic, next to ragas, was the culinary creativity of his wife. He took every opportunity to display her many wondrous feats as often and to as many people as he could. Every disciple, colleague, and acquaintance waited eagerly for the next culinary celebration in his home. Himmat Nivas, Munnawar Ali Khan's mansion in Bombay, was also a legendary centre of hospitality and good eating. Siddheshwari Devi was an inspired cook and a compulsive feeder of all and sundry, just as she was in the way she served her music to her audience. So was Begum Akhtar, though she was somewhat more discriminating. Her invitation to me to visit her in her home in Lucknow was prefaced with a promise to treat me to special kababs for which the neighbouring village of Kakori was famous. Of her recollections, the most graphic were descriptions of the cuisine of the princely state of Rampur, specially the biryani and the badaam ki jaali. The kinship between food and music, at least in the nawabi tradition of northern India, is undeniable. I have heard it said many times by ustads, '*Ek hi baat hai*', meaning that both deal with regaling the senses with refinement, both endeavour to heighten the impact of taste, aroma, and ambience, and that both promise a feeling of repletion.

This leads to the very large and open question of taste, of what will satisfy whom. Some people prefer bhindi to karela. Some prefer sweet to sour. No value judgement is possible here, and nothing is better or worse than anything else. But while retaining one's individual taste, it is possible to aspire to higher levels of enjoyment. If one likes sweet things, sugar by itself is no treat. The sensation of sweetness has to be carried to its furthest possibilities for it to make an enduring impact on the sensibilities of the listener. Once one has tasted the delights of bitter chocolate, it is difficult to return to the uncomplicated pleasure of one's first rasagulla. There are many ragas which do not sound delicious at first hearing (for instance Pat Bihag, Shiv Kalyan, among many others), but the ear can be nurtured to a stage of sophistication where it acquires a taste for refinements like spices, black coffee, pickles, and caviar.

EIGHTEEN

Fear of Recording

The Non-Westernness of Hindustani Music

The Indian mind—and there is such a thing—has never taken kindly to the idea of formal records or, to stretch a point, to the activity of recording. It is well known that for this reason formal history was virtually unknown in the country until outsiders who had more faith in factual correctness than in philosophical generalizations took the matter in hand. The chronicles of ancient India were often just impressionistic and fanciful accounts that gave as much weight to myth, prophecy, hyperbole, and romance as to fact. But the total impression they conveyed was perhaps closer to the underlying reality than any listing of events. I cannot help feeling that there is an indigenous Indian way of looking at things, of stepping back, squinting at the view, and screwing up the eyes in an effort to spur the senses to inhale the essential truth of what is presented and to reject or discard the merely literal in the belief that it can veil or distort reality. Essence is a lazy and tricky word but it is useful in that it gives instinct time to stall until exactly the right note has been sounded and one's whole being can say yes, this is it. In many important matters, certainly in music, reality is seldom the sum of its parts. The blue colour of the sky is not the result of contributions by a number of elements. On the contrary. No single element that enters into the physics and chemistry of our perception of the sky's blueness is in itself blue. Something of this sort holds good even more strongly for Indian music in general. In any case, it is difficult to talk about music without resorting to analogies. There is no other way, for music is its own justification and can speak of nothing but itself.

Since Indian music focuses less on the physical perfection of sound than other systems of music do, it follows that the concept of recording music cannot have the same associations and purposes. Or the same import either. It is sometimes easier to arrive at an understanding of Indian classical music by starting at the wrong end and eliminating all the things that it is not meant to be. First, it does not aim to please the ear by falling pleasantly on it. It does not tell a story or describe changing moods. It is neither the innermost personal expression of an individual sensibility, nor just an effort to interpret an ancient and rigid tradition—though it undeniably includes elements of all these. However meticulous and faithful the recording of an artist, a single occasion in the studio cannot yield a fair example of his work, because this music comes alive only in the process of improvisation and is never pre-planned or scored. We can compare it to the dying art of conversation which would cease to be just that if it were carefully planned or written down beforehand. Electronic recording inevitably involves the sort of pre-planning that cannot help changing the nature and intent of Indian classical music. That is why the best recordings today generally represent the poorest material while the best music available is usually embedded in recordings of such indifferent quality that one can hardly decipher it.

In the case of a Western composer, a recording celebrates the perfection and completeness of a scored work. It is a single, clearly projected musical statement. The differences in the interpretation of different conductors and players on different occasions are a matter of detail and largely at the level of nuance. The recording stands for all time as a reference point, as a musical monument, an almost permanent structure through which the listener can always unfailingly gain access to the musical awareness of the composer at the time he created the piece. This is not true of Indian classical music where the most valuable element to be celebrated is the fluidity, and the genuinely unpremeditated nature of the musician's utterance. The difference between the two is of kind, not of worth. If one is a perfectly structured sonnet, the other is spontaneous conversation which has no predetermined aesthetic goal. The level of wizardry in the two examples could be the same but it would always be located in different areas.

Imagine the raga as an incense stick with a particular perfume. Every time the musician lights it, wisps of smoke arise from it in configurations that change continuously and cannot be foreseen even though they carry the recognizable perfume of the raga that is being presented. This spiral of melodic lines that emanates from the incense stick of the raga can never be the same on any two occasions. The designs formed by the rising spirals of smoke are part of the ambience and certainly engage the listener, but arbitrarily recording any one of these moving lines and treating it as though it represented the whole musical intention of the artist can be misleading.

Of course the listener responds to the specific piece that is being performed but that is by no means the only source of his pleasure during a recital. The connoisseur's ear is automatically trained on other attendant skills that the performer inevitably betrays without directly displaying. For instance, his skill in articulation and the quality of his ambassadorship of the musical lineage he represents: these are crucial to the enjoyment of Indian listeners. The particular piece that is being performed is not considered a finished work of art by either the musician or his listeners. It is only an occasion for the artist to take his audience on exciting musical journeys which are effortlessly different each time he performs, even if it is the same raga or the same composition. That being the situation, the recording of any given piece is like taking a still photograph of a moving, palpitating animal. It is useful and valuable undoubtedly, but a mere stance. That obviously cannot be a substitute for the real thing. At best a recording can only capture what is called the andaaz of an artist, which means the particular flavour of their personal manner. The music itself arbitrarily represents only one of countless possibilities. It is an indication of an artist's potential, not his total creation in the sense in which a fully notated and scored work is. Actually, the recording of a piece of Indian classical music says less than it leaves unsaid. And it is the unsaid that is more relevant to the pleasure of both listener and performer. By that I mean the bouquet, the flexibility implied in each musical statement, the luxurious sense that each such statement could be made in infinite ways, the thrilling and urgent awareness of the living moment in which music is made in the form of an intimate personal communication. I suppose elements in this category would be considered valuable in all music but in the case of Indian music, where skill in improvisation is the heart of the matter, they form at least three-fourths of the cake. As such, a recording is as satisfactory or unsatisfactory as a clue. It is no more than that.

What we hear in a perfect recording of Beethoven's Fifth

Symphony is certainly not just a clue to the genius of the composer. It is a creation which is complete in itself, a masterpiece which needs no additional exposure of any sort to make its full impact. The same is not true of say a recording of Raga Darbari by a maestro like Krishnarao Shankar Pandit. The recording of a single piece in his case would be no more than a sample of an extraordinary musical creativity. What the listener appreciates in these two specific cases is not comparable at all because the two are not immediately accessible to the same degree. The Indian example cannot be received by the listener with the same sense of completeness unless he first familiarizes himself with the work and the vocalization of Krishnarao Shankar over a period of time, the longer the better. Only then is there a chance that the listener can grasp the totality of the musical intent and accord to the Indian piece the level of admiration it is entitled to, a level which the Western piece, being complete in itself, commands without any annotation or footnotes. The achievement of the Indian piece is that it carries and imparts a sense of infinitude in the literal sense. Fluidity and freedom are inherent in any utterance in this tradition and there could be infinite possibilities of musical intention. That is what is valued most and for this reason it has to be accepted that any recording is bound to be a limiting thing since it arbitrarily captures only one facet of the artist's conception of what he is trying to portray and misses several important dimensions. What is more, it wrongly implies that the facet that has been captured is the whole being—as it indeed is in the case of the Fifth Symphony.

When the idea of recording first penetrated the Indian music world in the second decade of the twentieth century, it was regarded with the same mixture of distrust and fascination that any import from the West receives in our culture. Many of the pillars of the music world succumbed to the fascination and lure of immortality and there was a spate of 78 RPM discs which are invaluable today. But these examples, in which masters of the art have managed to condense two-hour performances into two and a half dazzling minutes, are like a collection of exquisite swatches of weaves presented in commercial houses to prospective buyers. One can revel in their beauty and marvel at the skill and resourcefulness which make such presentations possible, but there is no getting away from the fact that these recordings are not great feasts in themselves but only tasting opportunities, and in each case conclusive proof of the existence of wonderful cuisines.

Cultural collisions can produce anomalies of various kinds and the Indian attitude to recording, like the Indian attitude to American blue jeans, is one. I give this example because it is easy to understand. The young in India took to jeans like ducks to water, but they misunderstood or disregarded the underlying philosophy that went with the faded colours, torn edges and patches. For a good ten years jeans remained the preserve of the affluent and fashionable few. Young women were often seen alighting from expensive cars in high heels proudly sporting their ragged jeans, while deferential uniformed chauffeurs held the car door open for them. The mincing walk and the helpless manner of these women suggested that they regarded their attire as a status symbol, which is precisely what it was supposed to neutralize. The advent of the recording industry in India is a comparable phenomenon, in the sense that it gave rise to similar attitudinal confusions in the music community. Ripples of excitement at the novelty of the idea alternated with serious misgivings about the harmful effects of electrical gadgetry on the voice. It is widely known that many of the artistes who succumbed to the temptation of recording in the 1920s and early 1930s feared that at the very least their work could be stolen and passed off as someone else's. This is why many of the old 78s end with the artist shouting out his name urgently and somewhat nervously in the naïve belief that this would be a safeguard against plagiarism and pirating. Many of them were sure that even worse things could happen to them. For instance, the microphone if given a chance might secretly siphon off all the goodness and power in their voice, just as making soup out of meat and vegetables robs them of their nutrients.

It took more than a decade of exposure and gentle persuasion by knowledgeable and caring people for this resistance to be overcome. But then, gradually, the pendulum swung to the other extreme. Being recorded began to be considered the most prestigious thing that could happen to a performer. The more snobbish wives and mothers in families of musicians lost no opportunity to announce to less privileged rival groups that Khan Sahib was hardly ever at home these days because of the demands of 'rekartin'. By the 1940s and 1950s opportunities and openings to record for commercial companies and the radio were universally sought after, even though the format which recording studios demanded of musicians was strange and inhospitable. The physical placing of percussion and other accompaniment naturally gave precedence to the requirements of electronics rather than to the accustomed rapport between the musicians, which is the life of any performance. It was a daunting experience if not an ordeal for a singer to sit far away from his tabla and sarangi and still be able to warm up, as in a live concert. But this was one uncomfortable artistic situation most of them resigned themselves to in the hope of larger audiences and immortality. In any case, from being something new-fangled that was resisted on principle, recording became the new status symbol, like American blue jeans, and introduced a shift in the traditional attitudes to classical music.

Recording does play a crucial role in the Indian music world although it is a different kind of recording. Our music could not have evolved to the degree to which it has without preserving in some form the achievements of the past. An awareness of what has gone before or of what succeeding generations are building upon is crucial to the health of any tradition. It is a constant reference point which safely anchors the perception of both musician and listener in such a manner that further creative explorations and experiments can be based on it without endangering the entire structure. In fact recordings of all significant work done in the field are constantly in use, even though they are not electronic recordings but only recordings that exist in the mind. This is not surprising considering that we are talking about an oral tradition in which nothing is transmitted by any other means. It must be stressed that these 'mental recordings' of great masters form the heart of musical awareness in India and exercise a far greater influence on creative activity than any physical records could possibly do. That is not all. They are transferred to every succeeding generation of musicians and listeners, so that the process of evolution and enrichment remains continuous. The inheritors of the tradition not only reproduce it but recreate it anew each time, according to the demands of this art. The great advantage of this form of recording in musical lore and collective memory is that the present generation of performers can still be nourished and inspired by giants who were never recorded electronically. There are countless examples of this phenomenon.

There is hardly any passable recording of legendary names like Abdul Waheed Khan of the Kirana gharana, or Aman Ali Khan of the Bhendibazar gharana, or Rajab Ali Khan of the Gwalior gharana. But every serious music lover today is familiar with their style and accents because faithful imprints in the music of their devotees have been acclaimed by a core of older listeners who have heard the originals and shared their perceptions with the next generation. This happens on a very large scale and as a matter of course, much as the features and traits of a grandson can be likened to an ancestor whose spitting image he is reputed to be. I have never heard Aman Ali Khan but still have a pretty good idea of his style because all reliable ears in the music world recognize and point out that Shiv Kumar Shukla in his prime was a perfect clone. I am also familiar with the music of Abdul Waheed Khan and Abdul Karim Khan because of living musical contact with those who knew their music intimately. Admittedly this cannot be the same as actually having heard them but for the purposes of continuity and inspiration this kind of indirect transmission has proved to be immensely valuable. Today I can hear the three masters I have mentioned to my heart's content in the singing of a much-recorded artist like Amir Khan and, what is more, distinguish the individual contribution of each to his style. Amir Khan based his life work on these three models though he forged a perfectly integrated new style of his own which he called the Indore gharana. The well-known Kumar Gandharva was deeply affected by the music of Onkar Nath Thakur of his own Gwalior gharana and the emotive utterance of Abdul Karim Khan of the Kirana gharana. Onkar Nath in an earlier generation was clearly affected by Rahmat Khan of the Gwalior gharana whose accents and style are preserved in the collective unconscious and the lore of the music world. One can hear Vilayat Khan, the sitar maestro, in the Darbari rendering of the sarod player Amjad Ali Khan, and Amir Khan in his Bilaskhani Todi. It is quite common during a concert for the audience to enjoy and point out similarities with earlier masters and to give credit to absent donors. The manner of Roshanara Begum, Hirabai Barodekar, Akhtari Bai, and Siddheshwari Devi is still imitated indirectly by aspiring women singers. The imprint of the vocalization of Kumar Gandharva on the singing of Kishori Amonkar, Veena Sahasrabuddhe, and even Malini Rajurkar is unmistakeable, especially in the bhajans, though each achieves a creative transformation of her own. Despite the recreation which is an important part of this type of transmission, the sources of the streams are clearly recognized by all concerned. The other day a brilliant young vocalist, recording her first CD, honoured the master she admired most simply by singing in his special manner. Everyone present recognized the tribute without a word having been said. 'I just felt like writing a love letter today', she remarked later.

Almost each time Mallikarjun Mansur sang Raga Jaunpuri, he would interrupt himself to tell his listeners that he was singing the antara in the characteristic manner of Manji Khan, a guru whom he adored. After a few minutes of demonstrating this, he would stop again to add that Manji Khan in his turn had got it from Rahmat Khan, an old master of an earlier generation whom Mallikarjun himself had probably never heard. Sharing his pride and joy at this rich lineage with his audience was often the high point of the concert. In this tradition no great musician lives alone on the creative mountain top. That is not considered an ideal either. In a sense, all outstanding achievement in this field is collective, and there is a sense of participation by a warm, closely connected joint family which lives in the mind of the musician and provides him with all the earlier recordings he might wish to refer to. In fact a sense of identification with what has gone before is so much a part of the culture of this tradition that it almost enters the music as a value.

NINETEEN

Sunlight in the Raga

My friend Nalin had a dubious project he was very earnest in. Every Sunday morning, he would play selections from his favourite Indian classical music for the benefit of American acquaintances whom he hoped to convert. His much admired and very expensive sound system occupied most of his tiny mid-town Manhattan apartment. The handful of people he managed to lure to these sessions sat on floor cushions, eagerly awaiting enlightenment and spiritual enrichment. The staying power of the enthusiasts was erratic, so there was a new lot every week. Even so, the host was happy to guide the listening of those present, confident that he was opening for them doors to undreamed-of celestial spaces, spiriting them as far away as possible from the brutal Monday-to-Friday global investment business routine in New York City in which he himself was hopelessly enmeshed. He was convinced that the slow, meditative khayal was the surest remedy for the jangled nerves and fractured minds that led most of his American friends routinely to the couch of psychoanalysts.

Into this set-up entered Beatrice, a Wall Street colleague with whom Nalin was in the process of getting romantically involved.

He viewed her as a possible 'life partner' and for Nalin it was vital that a prospective spouse be as impressed with the greatness of Indian music as he himself was. He confided in me and asked me to help him in communicating with the Sunday group, with special attention to Beatrice. I was an old hand at all this, being a jaded veteran of wordy sessions called seminars by various arty outfits I was in touch with.

The first item on the agenda was the relationship between the North Indian ragas and the time of day when each could appropriately be heard. I droned on in a practised way about the relevance of both Nature and the human condition to the mood of the music. I had had to do this kind of thing countless times in my career. But today, as young Beatrice twinkled with interest and tossed her bright yellow curls excitedly, I felt rewarded. She was positively incredulous when I added that the physical quality of the musical sound was not as important as what the music said, and that our most famous singers could be, and often were, eighty-year-old asthmatics with a permanent wheeze. Twelve people were intrigued enough to promise to turn up at dawn the following Sunday in order to listen to morning ragas at the prescribed hour, starting with Lalit, the first raga in the diurnal cycle.

Five of the twelve actually arrived. To Nalin's relief, Beatrice was among them. We started with one of our most treasured archival recordings of an old master from the Gwalior school. I was so solicitous of Beatrice that almost immediately my own hearing broke into two distinct channels. The messages my brain was receiving through the left ear tallied with what I was used to, but the right ear seemed to be doing the listening on behalf of Beatrice. When I transferred the rough and weighty voice of the eighty-year-old master from my mind to where I imagined Beatrice to be, it became a hoarse echo coming from a dark, bottomless well where nothing much seemed to be happening. 'Wait! Be patient! It *will* happen, I promise you!' I screamed silently, but the fact that she was fidgety, and thrashing her jeans-clad legs around, confirmed that even with the best will in the world she could not receive the perceptions I thought I was trying so desperately to beam in her direction.

The recorded master took his time with the comprehensive alap, the composition in slow tempo, the jod section, the drut, the bol tan and the fast tan. As he warmed up, the raucous vocal flourishes (which were only the outer garb of the divine music, as I had ritually warned the assemblage earlier) became bolder and more frequent. Beatrice could not believe the sounds she was hearing and was soon totally at sea. The well-intentioned Nalin was clearly oblivious to the effect his idols were having on his friends. As the music finally died down a good forty-five minutes later, he took over the commentary and requested the listeners to notice that this raga did not use the pancham or the fifth because that note represented the sun, and in this particular raga of the dawn the sun had not yet risen. 'All sandhi-prakash ragas or ragas meant for the time when darkness meets light are sombre and mystical', he said, his eyes swimming with devotion. 'We will now go on to Todi, another meditative and serious raga of the morning. When the sun can be seen on the horizon, it is time for Todi and that is why this raga allows the pancham or perfect fifth in its scale.' 'Oh, no. Not another one!' the horrified Beatrice gasped. Nalin, engrossed in sliding an LP worshipfully out of its sheath, did not register her response.

Two of the five people in the group that morning hurriedly departed before the second item could unfold. I could see that Beatrice was tempted to join them, but steeled herself to stay on. She really liked Nalin. He was now putting on the music, eyes half closed in reverence. This time a master of the Agra gharana rendered all the labyrinthine stages of the raga, taking all of fifty minutes. I was full of admiration for the singing but half of me could not help listening as though I were Beatrice. The stentorian, rasping voice did really sound like furniture being shifted on a stone floor. Without the magic key which Beatrice did not yet have, the piece was a dull and claustrophobic exercise, a realistic representation of a slowly winding underground tunnel at the end of which there was only more darkness and confusion. When the Todi was over, Nalin sighed and nodded his head with deep satisfaction.

'This brings us to Jaunpuri, the third morning raga, which is performed when the sun is a little higher on the horizon, just beginning to light up the sky. But the feeling in the melody is still one of wistfulness and longing . . .', began Nalin, trying faithfully to track the musical day of traditional India living itself out according to the rules of the game. Beatrice could not contain herself any longer. 'Doesn't your day *ever* pick up?' she burst out, staring at her watch in disbelief. She collected her things hurriedly and rushed out, mumbling incoherent apologies. Nalin looked stricken and shocked at the same time. Naturally, the budding romance quickly withered after this episode.

Beatrice was borne away from both my life and Nalin's on a meditative Jaunpuri note, but the concept of the sun in the pancham stayed to haunt me periodically. It was not something that had newly occurred to me during Nalin's fateful listening session. None of the dozen teachers I had learnt from over the years had ever articulated it to me clearly as a theory, but it must have somehow seeped in through an unconscious channel and stayed with me like an item of incidental luggage. Now that Beatrice had taken away with her body the distracting first part of my double role of interpreter and connoisseur, it made even more sense. In Lalit, the raga of the dawn which we had played first, the pancham was conspicuously absent, like a strong opinion deliberately not stated. The raga released its expression only when the two madhyams below it and the delicate komal dhaivata above it wove elaborate tonal patterns around the area where the pancham, representative of the sun, would normally have been placed had it existed at all in the scale of Lalit. As it was, the entire raga seemed to be inspired by the night's longing for the morning, notwithstanding the urgently clanging fire engines and the gruff howls of the ambulances in the street below, competing for the listener's attention.

'It makes all the difference to the mood of a sandhi prakash raga whether it is darkness turning into light, or light fading into darkness', I remembered one of my teachers saying long ago when the statement had meant nothing to me. I had taken it as the deliberate mystification that pliers of the musical trade in India delight in intimidating their dependents with. Now, thirty-odd years later when I genuinely felt the freshness of the morning air in a sunless raga like Lalit, I was suddenly ashamed of my early scepticism. The late night raga Malkauns, which also omits the pancham, is every bit as dark as Lalit, but this darkness is quite different. For one thing it feels like an end rather than a beginning, an experience of depth that suggests magic and mystery, with no intimations of the coming day. Further the sense of the melody is, for want of a more accurate term, erotic. The rasa sought to be evoked is shringara, not philosophic devotion or bhakti as in Lalit, though the texts of some later compositions show a cavalier disregard for the natural bent of these ragas. Even marginal listeners are familiar with a well-worn Tulsidas bhajan in honour of Rama that has been beautifully and successfully set to the romantic Malkauns. Similarly, a description of cavorting maidens spraying colour and throwing flower garlands at besotted spectators is the subject of a much sung composition in the introspective strains of the ethereal Lalit! Incredible as it may seem, the results of such license can sometimes be so unexpected as to be truly wondrous, like a combination of colours that has never been seen.

Though Beatrice was long gone, the ear with which she had tried (and failed) to listen to Nalin's music stayed with me. I found myself scanning the diurnal arrangement of the ragas in Hindustani music like a tourist, pouncing gleefully on the slimmest evidence of a relationship between the strength of the pancham in a raga and the brightness of the sun in the sky at the corresponding hour. Bhairav was a perfect example. The fact that it was a morning raga was proclaimed by the fully manifested pancham, the risen sun, even though its positive rays in this raga seemed to be framed by the delicate greys of the komal hrishabh and the komal dhaivata in deference to the earliness of the hour. As the day progressed, these two notes in the raga clock tended to rise from their prostrate position to their full height as shuddha notes, either one at a time as the *re* alone in Jaunpuri, or together, as both the *re* and the *dha* in the fully lit Sarang family of ragas which unquestionably belongs to the noon. These were highly exciting observations for me, bringing back resonances of pedagogic voices I had never understood during my early training. Now a pattern seemed to be emerging. I actually experienced at first hand that the behaviour of the notes did have an organic connection with the time of day and the state of Nature. Although this had been instilled into me indirectly by a procession of teachers over the years, I had never really believed it until now.

However, there was still a problem. The more deeply I surveyed the scene, the more exceptions I found to my personal revelations about the time theory of ragas. This was unnerving. If the sages have a reason why the *re* and *dha* should be komal in morning ragas, why is this not so in Bilaval, I wondered. For each raga that fell neatly into place in the clock, there was at least one which suggested just the opposite, nipping all my enticing formulations in the bud. Still, the idea that the ragas in some way reflected the time of day was too alluring to abandon. I justified my position with the thought that most things Indian are made up of such widely varying strands that nothing one can say is wholly true or wholly false. Besides, the pristine state of Nature can hardly ever have been a realistic background for any listener, especially for today's listener. Could anyone, in natural circumstances, ever have heard the sombre morning ragas without having to block out the shrill cries of the kabariwala and the vegetable hawker who have equal rights on that time of day?

Such unwelcome thoughts had been indirectly bequeathed to me by the Beatrice phenomenon. However hard I tried, I could not erase the memory of her imperviousness to what was in a sense my religion. She appeared like a phantom whenever I tried to connect music with the time of day, inextricable as chewing gum in my hair. Jaunpuri, instead of evoking a late morning hour, conjured up for me images of Beatrice jogging in Central Park after fleeing Nalin's apartment. Busy and frenzied afternoon ragas like Multani and Patdeep became the backdrop for shopping at Bloomingdales. The time for the serene Kalyans of the evening was, I was sure, when she walked her dog. Durga was a short drink at a mid-town bar, and Bihag a leisurely dinner at an Italian restaurant in Soho. This was a hopeless state of affairs. I simply had to rid my mind of Beatrice so that I could get back my lost world of music.

To this end, I sought out Alaka, a nostalgic exile whose enthusiasm for Indian classical music bordered on insanity. I began to do all my listening in her company, in the hope that she would reinfect me back to my original state. She was a guaranteed antidote. In my more responsible moments, I suspected that the remedy was worse than the ailment, but on the whole I preferred it to the virus of scepticism. Needless to say Alaka was not a discriminating listener. She was just passionately in love with all ragas. Not only that. She indulged in deep affairs of the heart with individual notes. At this stage of our association, the object of her adoration happened to be madhyam, the fourth interval. 'It is velvety, dark blue, so rich, so mesmeric!', she breathed shyly, as though she was reluctantly sharing a secret about a lover. 'Let's listen to something that really celebrates its wonderful sound', she pleaded with a touch of possessiveness, as though the note was her personal discovery if not her own creation. So we selected a vintage Kedara. When the raga developed enough to reveal the madhyam and came to rest on it, we exchanged involuntary glances in recognition of her passion for the note. At this point she actually blushed like a self-conscious schoolgirl. Her obsessions were clearly even more arbitrary than mine. This was dangerous territory and all the road signs I could see were unreliable. There was nothing for it but to return to a solitary state of listening and come to my own conclusions which were probably located in the wide space between the positions of Beatrice and Alaka.

I reminded myself that my favourite note was *sa*, named shadaja because it gives birth to the other six notes in the heptad and notionally embodies them all. Every teacher had told me that the melodic line approaching the *sa* should be so accurately and sensitively drawn as to reveal the entire raga. This became my new guideline for assessing the musicians I heard, though I still tried to relate the ragas to the time of day. I had been saturated with morning ragas at Nalin's sessions, so I now turned my attention to the evening ragas. I saw that they trace their slow way from failing light to gradually deepening darkness, travelling in the opposite direction from the sandhi prakash ragas of the morning. When the day is done, it is once again time for reflection and meditation as in the morning. An evening raga like Puriya Dhanashri, for instance, evokes a similar mood. It is lit up with the glowing pancham of the setting sun, but the komal *re* and komal *dha* in combination tone down the brilliance in anticipation of the gathering darkness. The difference is the entry of the teevra madhyam, the sharp raised fourth note, just a little below the pancham. This note is sounded strongly, without any undulation, pulling keenly away from the pancham and thus introducing a kind of tension usually not encountered in morning ragas. The interplay between these two notes determines the mood and character of many ragas that suggest twilight. A specially interesting raga for the time when the sun dips below the horizon is Marwa. Here also the sun or pancham disappears, as in its morning counterpart Lalit. Both ragas are full of yearning and depend heavily for their effect on the physical silence of this note, which though never sounded in either raga is nonetheless overwhelmingly present as a concept in both. The omission or sparing use of a strong note which could serve as a resting place in the development of a raga is a technique which is sometimes used with telling effect. Marwa is an interesting instance of this. Here, the tonic *sa*, though not altogether absent like the *pa*, is nonetheless elusive in most of the raga's phrasing. Normally a primary resting place, the *sa* is held back by design in this twilight raga in order to express its restlessness and agony.

The Kalyan family of ragas enters the field when the day's activity has subsided. Here the pancham in consonance with the serene shuddha gandhar ushers in a characteristic tranquillity. In this group, pancham is no longer king, so to speak, and has to share its radiance with gandhar, which acts as a competing satellite. Gradually the darkness deepens, inviting elements like mystery, grandeur, and romance. Malkauns, the Kanhra family, Bihag and Bageshri are typical examples of late night ragas. In the first, the pancham is omitted altogether. In the others it abandons its literal role as the sun but contributes light with much greater delicacy and subtlety than in the morning ragas. And so it goes on through the night, until dawn breaks once more.

An awareness of the diurnal cycle has stayed with me in all my listening and performing, like a second skin. I still do not know whether it has any real basis or whether it is just an attractive notion I want to cling to. There can never be a final verdict on the time theory of ragas which I can accept without being plagued by the demons of doubt. To really know the truth, I need the visceral experience of listening in the company of an improved model of Beatrice, preferably in a new avatar.

TWENTY

Begum Akhtar

To my ears, the sound of the Urdu language and the ghazal were most enticing when I was in my teens even though I could not understand most of the words. I had no idea that the couplet had a form, and that it was necessary to tune in to the conventions of the ghazal to truly appreciate it. We studied Hindi and English in school and spoke a broad, not very elegant Hindustani at home. But despite my ignorance the recitation of a ghazal always transported me to a romantic world of make-believe which I preferred to all others. The heartbreak of unrequited love, the incredible selflessness of the lover who gloried in the pain that connected him to the beloved, the perfumed gardens where the rose and the bulbul conversed about life and the spinning planets of the universe—all merged into an illogical resplendence that was quite addictive. I could easily get my 'fix' by chanting some memorized lines and pronouncing the special q, z, gh and kh sounds of Urdu with dramatic exaggeration. Even though the meaning of what I recited was a mystery to me, I could summon up the atmosphere. My friends envied the access they thought I had to the glamorous world of Urdu poetry. Akhtari Bai Faizabadi as she was known then was the authentic symbol of this world and her voice was the most effective magic wand there could be for me.

Many genres of Indian singing entail softening or modulating the voice in an effort to create delicacy and beauty but this was not her way at all. She seemed to collect herself like an archer taking aim, and hit each note dead centre with great energy, allowing the surplus charge of sound to spill over naturally. She was genetically so tuneful, so sureela, that the directness and honesty of her voice-throw sometimes resulted in a characteristic break (or patti) in her voice which 'killed' connoisseurs and was hailed by listeners as an inimitable core of beauty in her music. Her audiences always waited for such euphoric moments in each recital and greeted them with sighs of rapture. She never tried to produce this effect. It happened spontaneously, almost absent-mindedly, but the effect was electrifying. The impact of her voice on the note produced sparks, as when flint stones are rubbed together. Her famous patti became the envy of all her contemporaries and as a ghazal singer she had no equal. Even her rivals had to concede this.

I loved her voice and needed no special education to react to it. But to understand the art of ghazal singing at its most evolved was another matter altogether. I never set out to learn the structure and dynamics of the couplet. But comprehension was forced upon me as a by-product of the simple and most enjoyable process of listening to Akhtari Bai with attention over a period of years. This also revealed to me some finer points of her craft, notably the skill with which she could combine and balance music, words, and meaning in a single creative impulse.

Purists have a point when they say that music is articulate only in its own language and in no other. Pure music is not concerned with the meaning of the words that accompany, embellish, or assist it in any fashion, however poetic or moving those words may be. And yet the harmonious coexistence of poetry and music runs through the fabric of the Indian tradition as exemplified by the bhakti saints, Sufis, and folk singers. In these cases, music can owe a good deal of its poignance to the words it clothes but that does not change the fact that words and meaning are extraneous to music. The ghazal too is a self-sufficient literary form with an integrity of its own. If it has vitality and enduring value it should need no aids or props from the world of music. The greatness of poets like Mir, Momin, and Ghalib owes nothing whatsoever to music. In fact originally the ghazal, which literally means 'addressing the beloved', was never meant to be sung or set to music. The practice of reciting in tarannum is still frowned upon by orthodox literary connoisseurs because the intrusion of melody, which sneaks in with a small demand of its own, blurs the word structure and disturbs the natural flow of the line. Akhtari Bai sang the ghazal with such insight and sensitivity that she created a new area where poetry and music were simultaneously enhanced.

Her first principle was to leave the greatest poetry alone, so that her music would not flounder under its heavy weight. This principle was obviously and sensibly borrowed from the thumri form where the poetry of the text is suggestive and ambivalent by design so that the interpreter can choose freely from a multiplicity of possible meanings. Guided by this experience, Akhtari Bai usually picked lightweight ghazals that could be easily moulded to a musical purpose without damage to either. Her most popular ghazals, *Ai muhabbat tere anjaam pe rona aya*, and an earlier hit, *Deewana banana hai to deewana bana de*, are examples. Even when she chose to render verses of indifferent literary value, they leapt to instant fame while the bulk of the output of their authors sank into oblivion. Aspiring poets vied with each other to get an entry into her repertoire because that was a guarantee of recognition.

Another principle she adopted was from the genre of the khayal where the words of the composition exist mainly as sounds and not much as meaning. In her singing, the long vowels became flowing, graceful melodic arches while the hard consonants formed the pillars that supported them. She used the vast range of sounds offered by language, the liquid sounds, the sharp sibilants, the harsh gutturals, the nasal, throaty, or breathy consonants as musical raw material, and she did this with such amazing skill that the stoniest lines became delicious to the ear, as in her rendering of Iqbal's *Kabhi ai haqeeqate muntazir nazar aa libaase majaaz men, Ke hazaaron sajde tadap rahe hain meri jabeene niyaaz men* . . . The remarkable thing was that her musicality never lost track of the meaning of the poetry and her command over both was absolute.

Listening to her showed me what the structure of a typical couplet or sher of a ghazal was. Each is a self-contained unit in which the first line makes a non-committal statement which is not poetic or philosophic in itself. It only serves as a sort of background to the rules, as it were. The actual game begins only with the second line which retrospectively illuminates the introductory line and reveals the hidden meaning in a powerful backlash. There is a point at which the second line turns and looks over its shoulder at what has been said in the first line, suddenly suffusing it with a significance that was not apparent before this point. For instance, *Yoon to har sham umeedon men guzar jati thi* is the innocuous first line of an unremarkable couplet. It is just a setting of expectancy meant to highlight the flash of comprehension located in the second hemistich, *Aaj kuch baat hai jo sham pe rona aayaa.* As I recognized this pattern in verse after verse, I realized that I had been led to this understanding only by the cadences of Akhtari Bai's music. The low-key statement of the first line was set to music that in a way matched an introductory alaap. The music rose to a climax at the precise point at which the couplet turned to look back and shed light on the meaning of the whole sher. There was such a close correspondence between the ebb and flow of the music and the dynamics of the couplet that an understanding was almost thrust on me. No other ghazal singer can dance so gracefully, so closely with the poet.

Indeed, she became better and better at her art as she matured. The last ten years of her life represented a pinnacle that her earliest work had promised. My first recollection of her is a high-pitched voice, urgently announcing her name at the end of a ghazal sung on a 78 rpm disc brought out by HMV. 'Mera naam Akhtari Bai Faizabadi', the voice proclaimed, abruptly cutting off the magic of the music and the glamour of the poetic Urdu words that had gone before. I was then not old enough to understand the relevance of this strange vocal signature. The grown-ups in my family who swooned over Akhtari Bai's music explained that many artistes who recorded in the decade between the 1920s and '30s followed this practice of shouting out their names at the end of each recorded item in the innocent belief that it would prevent their work from being plagiarized or pirated! I was as fascinated by this as by the music and played the discs again and again, fantasizing that this famous singer, who was a living legend even then, was personally telling me her name. I could never have imagined that one day, forty years later, this would really happen, that she would actually speak to me and that we would become friends.

Much happened in these forty years. The attitude to music and musicians among families like mine became much more tolerant and receptive. Listening to music and even learning it were no longer frowned upon by 'respectable' families. On the contrary I felt that my love for music and my hero worship of personalities like Akhtari Bai were things my family began to be proud of. To my delight, all my moves in this direction were applauded. In these forty years Akhtari Bai also went through a metamorphosis. She had always been an extremely competent professional performer but over the years she matured into a creative musician who lavished extraordinary riches on the music world and contributed to it an irresistible manner and style which sent her listeners into ecstasy. She flowered into almost a cult figure, an ideal personality invested with such charm and charisma that an entire generation of women passionately wished to emulate her.

The impact of Begum Akhtar's music and personality on our generation is in many ways an inexplicable phenomenon. Many of her contemporaries were as gifted, as well-trained, and as much in command of their audiences as she was. Some were decidedly more hard working and unlike her did not spare themselves in the matter of discipline and practice. Many had larger repertoires and more extensive vocal ranges. Their singing styles were more elaborate and complicated than hers, and their musical material far more sophisticated. Yet her voice had a magic that nothing can explain and this special something had very little to do with musical skill or training.

The single most important quality that characterized her was effortlessness. She sang like a carefree bird, with no sign of strain on her features, her beautiful hands flowing like water over the keys of the harmonium. She smiled more with her eyes than her lips and despite her mercurial temperament always carried herself with the utmost grace and dignity. Her contribution to our lives was a by-product of the full self-expression of an extraordinary personality, not something she consciously sought to achieve. One can say that she had no message to give but the way she lived, savouring to the fullest all that life had to offer, even if it was pain. She instinctively looked for beauty and refinement in all things and was truly upset each time they failed to appear. I remember an occasion when she was shocked by a music organizer of Delhi when he paid her her professional fee by thrusting a wad of notes into her hands, without even bothering to put it in an envelope.

She herself had so much polish in her manner that most things that happen in the music world seemed crude by comparison. '*Ishq se tabi-yat ne, zeest ka mazaa paaya; dard ki dava paayi, darde-la-dava paaya*' was one of her favourite couplets of Ghalib because she truly believed in the values set forth in it. The lines implied that the joy of living comes from the intensity of love, which is both an anodyne for pain and itself a pain without remedy. Akhtari Bai could not live without ishq, without being in love. If love did not happen, she had to invent it. And if the love she experienced was devoid of pain she had to invent the pain too. Only then could she feel alive. She lived each moment intensely, giving it all she could, but with great restraint and style. To my mind this temperament was responsible for her inimitable musical quality in which melancholy and sparkle were equal partners.

Akhtari Bai was born in 1914 to Mushtari Bai, a well-known professional singer of Faizabad. It was discovered quite early that this child had enough natural talent and charm to support herself if properly trained. Circumstances took her to Calcutta where her mother arranged for her to be trained in classical music by Ata Mohammad Khan of the Patiala gharana. She simply could not take the hard work that this rather dry style entailed and, after a break in which she sang not khayal but ghazal, thumri, and dadra, she tried again to learn the khayal gayaki from Ustad Abdul Waheed Khan, a pillar of the Kirana gharana. She was far too sensitive and intelligent not to have imbibed the basics of his invaluable training, but after a brief stint she discovered that khayal was not her forté. She never once sang khayal in public, though that was the only formal training she had received. She had grown up with the sound of music and the sweetness of Purabia, Avadhi, and Bhojpuri in her ears, so she evolved her own distinctive repertoire which captured the ethos and nostalgia of the culture of UP. To this fabric were added the rich nuances of Urdu poetry. Her music creates in the listener a yearning for a world of romance and dreams but at the same time imbues things of long ago and far away with the earthy flavour of the here and now. Her own personality underlines this synthesis, for she is both myth and fact. Hers is an utterance which is not only beautiful, but also faithful and true. It echoes the earthy sounds of the folk music of the Hindi belt as well as the sophistication of the princely courts which she frequented in the course of her career. The nawabs of Hyderabad, Bhopal, and Rampur and the maharaja of Kashmir employed her as a singer from time to time, and treated her with special respect because of her dignified ways and the rare charm of her personality. Though she lived the life of a courtesan in the earlier part of her life, her natural bearing compelled the awe and deference usually reserved for royalty.

Despite the countrywide adulation she received, something in her hankered after a more settled and 'respectable' lifestyle, possibly because of its novelty, possibly because she got tired of dressing up for a new part in a new setting every day.

With marriage as the goal, she set her sights on Ishtiaq Ahmad Abbasi, a talukdar of Kakori near Lucknow, and courted him in all seriousness. He was fond of music, like all affluent members of his class at the time, but the main attraction of Akhtari for him was the novelty of the relationship and the fun it promised. He was a barrister-at-law educated in London. He sported a bow tie and rode to court in an old Chevrolet, but his attention was not on being a successful lawyer. Nor could his sprawling household of relatives ever have run on his professional earnings. When they got married, he happily basked in her glory and treated her like a great artist because the world told him that is what she was. In a sense he was her ultimate patron. She got a thrill from being a begum, as distinct from a bai. She relished the role of a devoted wife and used to polish her husband's shoes herself, as a matter of principle. For a while she willingly donned the shackles of life behind the purdah, and stopped singing altogether. But this could not last because music really was her life. At last Abbasi Sahib permitted her to perform again, provided it was outside the city of Lucknow.

An outstanding feature of Begum Akhtar's life was that she straddled two different worlds and wrested her identity as a woman from both without abandoning either of them. As a member of a puritanical Muslim family, she was never ashamed of being the rasika that she was. To her, life was to be savoured and enjoyed, not just endured. She appreciated good taste and subtlety in all things—music, poetry, food, speech, dress—and was never ashamed of the little vanities that can bring pleasure to a woman's life. The poise and aplomb with which she lived her complicated life seem in the context of today the achievement of a pioneer and are bound to be valued by Indian women of our time who are asking penetrating questions about their entitlements.

Her evolution as a human being is all the more remarkable considering the class and background she came from and the fact that she had hardly any formal education to speak of.

Begum Akhtar's music stands apart for its spontaniety and its fidelity to the classical idiom. Nothing she sings is a recipe worked out beforehand. For her musical communication itself is a creative act wherein she remains true to the reality of each moment. Never is hers a passive, premeditated recital. I remember an occasion when she was invited by All India Radio to sing four selected ghazals of Ghalib to celebrate the centenary of the poet in front of a live audience. I dropped in to see her in her hotel room just before the concert. She said casually to the small group of close associates who had come to escort her to the concert hall that she had decided on the ragas that would be suitable for the mood of each of the ghazals—Chayanat, Kedar, Darbari, and Khammaj. There was a cry of approval from all present. However, when she began her recital only an hour later, her feeling had changed completely. She sang all four ghazals in Bhairavi, each different from the other and each outstanding! We were all dumbfounded. Her inexhaustible innovative skill could always be counted on to ensure that each musical moment was heartfelt and genuine. Her technique was also impressive. She leaned heavily on the khayal gayaki in which she had such excellent grounding and borrowed its stylized idiom and detachment even for light forms like thumri, dadra, kajri, and chaiti. This lifted her utterance far above the merely personal and imbued it with the enduring, universal quality one associates with classical music.

TWENTY-ONE

Go, Lady, Go

Lady Linlithgow and the Taming of Raga Adana

No one who had seen Vinayak Rao bustling about the grounds of the music college in khaki shorts, knee-length stockings, and solar topi could possibly have imagined that he was the doyen of Hindustani classical music, an old-fashioned pandit at heart, an upholder of the performing traditions of the Gwalior gharana, and a nationally acclaimed figure in the music world. In the 1940s, an obsequious colonial culture still ailed government-aided institutions and his unlikely outfit that evening was perhaps an unconscious tribute to the Vicereine of India, Lady Linlithgow, who was expected on the premises at any moment. She was the chief patroness of the institution that employed him as a teacher of the khayal style of singing. In this case it only meant that her name was embossed in gold on their official stationery, even though all she had ever done for the institution was to lend it her weighty name, a gesture which presumably guaranteed that her imperial good wishes would be with them in all their cultural endeavours.

But now, the last Viceroy of India was leaving the country for good. It was only proper that his gracious lady, who had adorned the letterhead of the college for so many years, should be given a proper farewell. Arrangements for this very special occasion were under way. The principal had mobilized the entire staff to put their best foot forward. Vinayak Rao was supervising the seating and other mundane details in his khaki shorts, but his most important contribution to the musical evening planned for the dignitary was a khayal he had specially composed in her honour. His colleagues were intrigued and excited to hear this. But when they pressed him for details, he coyly said he would make the necessary announcement at the right time, that is, just before his performance.

The chief guest arrived punctually, escorted by Sir Ramaswami Mudaliar, an eminent member of the Viceroy's Executive Council. They were trailed by an assortment of aides and ladies-in-waiting. There was a sudden hush in the hall as the imposing procession approached the special upholstered seats in the front row. The only sound to be heard above the cautious whispers of the assembled gentry was the whirring of ancient ceiling fans and the authoritative tap-tap-tap of the high heels of Lady Linlithgow's splendid white court shoes on the cement floor. She wore matching elbow-length white gloves, a wide-brimmed summer hat decorated with bunches of violets, and a muslin tea gown in a print of overblown yellow roses. Her escort was almost equally resplendent in his compactly-fashioned traditional turban of beige and gold cotton. He was on hand to receive and respond to any casual remark issuing from the lips of the honoured guest, and generally interpret the goings-on, which were still strange for her, despite her many years in India.

The proceedings began with orations and eulogies directed at 'our noble patroness' who had 'graced this occasion with her august presence'. Each member of the staff undertook this exercise in turn, displaying a wide variety of accents, styles, and tonal pitches. Lady Linlithgow smiled and nodded her head ever so slightly in gracious acknowledgement, dabbing her beaded upper lip with a lace handkerchief. Then it was the turn of the B list. All participants, including electricians, caterers, casual helpers, and guests were also thanked profusely for their various contributions in making the evening memorable. With all this out of the way, it was time for the *piece de resistance* to be unloosed on the audience.

Behind the curtain, Vinayak Rao was still in a dither, hissing last-minute instructions about the refreshments to be served during the interval while his pupils tuned the instruments. It had slipped his mind that he was still in the working outfit he had donned while supervising arrangements earlier in the day. A senior colleague pointed out that he could not go on stage like that since no Indian raga could possibly be evoked in a solar topi. Then it all came back to him. Of course he had brought along his regular concert clothes in a bundle in the morning! He flung the offending head-dress off and replaced it with a pugree. He covered his shirt with a long button-up coat of khadi silk. Half a dozen glittering medals awarded for extraordinary feats of musicianship at various times by various princely states were already affixed to the upper part of this garment as it was part of his special concert costume. A dhoti restored him to the image his audiences associated with him, but at the last minute he forgot to discard the thick sports stockings. A faithful pupil resourcefully flung a shawl over the master's feet as he settled down on the dais between two tanpuras.

It was clear that the music community was awaiting the promised announcement more eagerly than the chief guest who could have had no inkling of the trial in store for her. 'It is my proud privilege to present a khayal I have specially composed in honour of our gracious patroness', Vinayak Rao began in the approved eulogistic style of the day. 'It is in the festive and joyful Raga Adana. The song is set to teen-taal, a cycle of sixteen beats. The text celebrates the name of the noble Lady Linlithgow who reigns in our hearts this evening.'

In keeping with the prevailing custom, which had also been adopted by comperes of All India Radio, the eminent performer recited the opening words of the text of the khayal he proposed to sing. This practice normally served the double purpose of both setting the right mood for the impending recital and of identifying the opus for future reference if need be. However, in this case, the opening words were not exactly suggestive since they consisted only of the name of the distinguished personage sought to be honoured. 'The opening line of the khayal is Lay-dee Lin-litha-go', Vinayak Rao announced with folded hands. He then cleared his throat, nodded his approval of the tuning to the accompanists and started to sing.

The first word of the song was 'lady'. He pronounced it 'Lay Dee' and delivered it in two powerful notes, one for Lay and one for Dee, giving both syllables absolutely equal weight, as in a spondee, innocently defeating the word's original trochaic intent. A long and very pregnant pause separated the two syllables, presumably to heighten the dramatic effect of the climax of the sung line, or *sam*, when it occurred. This delectable moment at the end of each rhythm cycle is what lay listeners avidly wait for. The *sam* is as crucial as the punch line in a joke and has therefore to be tight and perfectly timed. In this recital, it coincided with the 'gow' of Linlithgow. The preceding syllables in the word, that is 'Linlith', had to function as a sort of musical run up to the *sam*, rather like the spurt of speed a bowler puts on before he actually pitches the ball at the wicket. With this kind of musical end in view, Vinayak Rao hurled the available syllables in the air, like a whiplash before it lands to punish the target. 'Lay-he-dee—li-hi-li-hi-tha—*go*', he sang in perfect rhythm to the beat of the tabla. The only trouble was that he had to drop the 'n' sound from the dignitary's name because it simply did not fit the metre. So the 'n' faded from the scene without so much as a murmur. Nor did the regular listeners miss it. Lady Linlithgow was obviously not one of them. In fact this was the first (and probably the last) time she had been subjected to such a performance. In any case, she had no idea that the singing had anything to do with her name. Any resemblance promised by the announcement had long since been obliterated by the energetic embellishments lavished on the music by Vinayak Rao.

'Lay-dee go, go *go*, lay-dee go, go, *go*, lay-dee go, go, *go*', went the passionate song. The singer intensified its burden by shifting the accent across the syllables in mind-boggling variations such as '*Lay*-di-go, lay-di-*go*, lay-*dee*-go, *lay*-dee-*go*, lay-dee *go*, go-o-o-o. . . .' All Lady Linlithgow could make of this was that some mysterious musical compulsion caused the artist to emit an ear-splitting 'go' at regular intervals. She was also convinced that the word 'go' was directed at her, because each time he sang it, he would open his eyes wide and stare at her meaningfully. This was supposed to be a farewell in her honour. In the circumstances, urging her to 'go' was hardly a civil way of expressing parting good wishes. She was genuinely puzzled, and wondered whether she should resort to the stiff upper lip or call for a clarification.

She opted for the latter. Turning to her escort she said with a characteristically British mixture of frost and wit, 'The gentleman seems overly insistent on our departure, considering that we are leaving shortleh, anyway.' It took Sir Ramaswami a while to get her drift, since he was not too familiar with the local cultural and musical idiom either. But he gallantly resolved to find out what had been troubling her. He summoned one of the students in attendance and confided to him in a stage whisper that the singer's repeated stress on the word 'go' had given the chief guest the impression that she was being urged to leave, which was not very polite, to say the least.

Of course, this was a disastrous development. Nothing could have been further from the intentions of the institution. The student was terribly flustered and rushed backstage with his explosive information, which was relayed in several stages and dialects to the innocent perpetrator. The singing stopped for a moment while a staunch supporter explained the nature of the misunderstanding in broken Marathi.

Vinayak Rao was unfazed. He had been nurtured by the sturdiest of classical traditions and had the resources to overcome any difficulty, musical or otherwise. 'I can settle this in no time, thanks to the training I have received from the gurus of the Gwalior gharana', he said confidently to the small group of devotees who had gathered on the stage around him in this hour of need. '*Bol baant* (word division and syllable-play) is a speciality of ours. You will all see for yourselves what I do now.'

The new motivation made the second phase of the concert more urgent and intense. As he had done the first time, Vinayak Rao threw the syllables Lay and Dee into the air, as an invocation to the guest of honour. This time, even she recognized the direct address. But then, he suddenly switched the position of the component syllables. What accosted the ear sounded like an entreaty constructed with spondees. 'Lay-dee, Dee-lay, Dee-lay,

Dee-lay, Lay-dee!' The surname was abandoned as a measure of caution, since it contained the explosive syllable 'go' and tended to spill out of the traditional beat. The revised version of the presentation repeatedly requested Lady Linlithgow to delay her departure. This was done in a dazzling display of metrical feet. '*Lay*-di, *Dee*-lay, *Lay*-di, *Dee*-lay, *Lay*-di, *Dee*-lay', he sang in perfect trochees, followed by iambs and spondees in a bewildering variety of permutations and combinations. Lay-*di*-di-*lay*, Lay-*di*-di-*lay*, Lay-*di*-di-*lay* formed an attractive triplet (*tihai)* which fitted neatly into the case provided by the versatile sixteen-beat cycle. Vinayak Rao's inventiveness was breathtaking. His consonants hopped, skipped, and collided as he subjected the words 'lady delay' to the full treatment, as though he had put the text in a food processor and was chopping it up into every possible shape and size.

The recital ended in triumph. With so much expenditure of energy, it could hardly have been otherwise. Lady Linlithgow may not have grasped the finer points of Vinayak Rao's singing style, but the message couched in his strenuous efforts was now crystal clear.

He did not really want her to go.

TWENTY-TWO

A Taste of British Guiana

Many years ago, my husband was posted to British Guiana. Abhinav, my four-year-old son, was quite lost in the strange new environment. He did not yet know a single word of English and I was his only connection with life. He followed me around all day, clinging to the palla of my sari, unable to make any sense of the sights and sounds of the world to which he had been exiled. He demanded that I distract, reassure, and comfort him all his waking hours, in addition to interpreting everything new he encountered. I could not free myself for the very urgent business of setting up house unless I deposited him in a school. My husband was certainly not going to share any babysitting with me. He was completely immersed in his UN assignment and quite understandably expected me to deal with everything else in our lives.

I heroically decided to deposit Abhinav in school and face the necessary traumas as they came up. The Convent of the Good Shepherd was recommended by casual neighbours. I immediately presented myself and my unwilling offspring to Mrs Ambler, an earnest British missionary who was the head of the nursery section there. I explained the situation and the language problem.

She was most helpful and admitted him right away. He was finally led away to his class kicking and screaming, unmoved by the soothing, cooing sounds Mrs Ambler directed at his reluctant ears. I left with a heavy heart but a feeling of freedom.

Abhinav had to be driven to his place of execution every day and abandoned for several hours before he was rescued. The first month of school was nerve-racking for all concerned. But what happened next can only be described as a gradual miracle. He began to speak the sing-song patois of the street with ease and increasing enthusiasm. The Hindi he knew disappeared without trace.

'Dat boy, he comin down the street an hittin me, maan. So I hittin he back,' he told me one day. The accent, intonation, and local liberties with grammar made this variety of English an intimate and warm tool of communication. The dramatic, all-pervasive present tense and the innocent linguistic economies charmed me. More than that, I was relieved that Abhinav would at last be able to crawl out of his isolation into a more normal life.

He grew more and more confident with his newfound language and began to use it even to communicate with me. 'My teacher, she stoo-paid!' he declared one day. I tried to hush him, lazily explaining that one did not say things like that about one's teachers. The remark popped up again a few days later. 'Miz Ambler, she stoopaid, I tellin yo, Ma.' When it became a regular refrain in the next few weeks, I decided to probe.

'Why do you think that?' I asked.

'Every day she aksin me hello whats yoh name an I tellin she my name be Abnow, but she still aksin and aksin hello whats yoh name!'

This was not enlightening. Nor did the song die down on its own as I had hoped. I was a neurotic mother trying to bring up my first-born according to Dr Spock's classic textbook and therefore morbidly believed that my son's unfamiliar name in this alien setting must have made him a butt of ridicule in school. Undoubtedly Dr Spock's view would be that an awareness of being somehow different from his peers would damage my child psychologically. The thought scared me. There was no choice but to call on the good Mrs Ambler with all the tact I was capable of. I dragged Abhinav along as a sort of key witness in the case.

Obviously I couldn't tell her exactly what my son had been saying again and again about her being stupid. But I produced an edited version which might serve the same purpose without being offensive.

'Abhinav feels you are having some difficulty with his name,' I stuttered. 'If that is so, we could simplify it. We sometimes call him Abe at home . . .'

She was frankly puzzled.

'Oh no, not at all. I know the name of each child in my class very well. I make it a point. There is no problem at all. Your son's name is A-B-H-I-N-A-V, is it not?' she said, slowly spelling it out for me, and pronouncing it with startling clarity.

She gazed expectantly at me. I had no idea what to say next. There was an uncomfortable lull in which I looked at the floor and Abhinav fidgeted maddeningly.

'What does the child actually say to you?' she asked in a clear voice, peering at us through gold-rimmed glasses.

'Well, he seems to think you say hello to him every day when you ask him his name . . .'

'Hello? That is extraordinary indeed! Umm. Let us see what this could possibly be.'

She turned the word around in her mind like a detective who

has scented a clue. After a moment, the penny dropped. She put her hand on her forehead and allowed herself a girlish titter.

'It's the Lord's Prayer he is talking about! Well, I never! You see the class is expected to repeat the prayer after me every morning. Each child is able to say Our Father Who Art in Heaven, Hallowed be Thy Name. Everyone except Abhinav to whom the words still mean nothing. So he just stands there. When I prompt him, the only response I get is "My name be Abno"!'

The mystery was cleared. Poor Abhinav's recent linguistic achievements could not possibly include words like 'Hallowed'. Both Mrs Ambler and I reconstructed the scene in our minds. During the scripture class, Mrs Ambler would fix her eye on him and say encouragingly 'Hallowed be Thy Name', trying to guide him to speak the line along with the others. What he got from this daily exercise was that Mrs Ambler had made a routine of saying 'Hello, what's your name', despite his telling her his name every day. And so he had come to his own conclusion about her mental capability.

Ours was the last house on Campbell Street in Georgetown. Beyond this freshly painted new structure, all human habitation unbelievably came to an abrupt end. There were a couple of uneven but lush green lots covered with weeds and hyacinth, and then a stretch of inky water almost wholly covered with bright pink water lilies. Looking at this from my living room window, I had the sensation that this indeed must be the end of the earth. Lotus bloomed on the dark water as far as I could see. I was sure that beyond that there could only be nothingness. To my dusty Indian eyes, the colours of everything I saw here were so vivid as to be almost startling. The stars at night were bigger and brighter and the sky an unreal, picture-book blue I had never seen anywhere before. But the Guianese people in the streets, in contrast to their vibrant setting, seemed mild and lackadaisical at first sight. The population was very mixed and I was soon able to distinguish the natives from those who did not really belong. The outsiders were conspicuous because of their higher energy levels and the air of earnestness and anxiety they wore, probably because like me they were in Georgetown for a purpose and had to justify their presence within a defined period.

When we had landed at Atkinson Field airport a couple of months earlier, I had experienced another kind of unreality. I could hardly believe my eyes when I saw a prominently displayed sign that read 'No Singing Allowed'. This was not a mistake as I first thought. The entire building was dotted with the same announcement, in different colours and type sizes. Very intriguing, I thought. But it began to make sense as soon as we took our place at the tail end of a queue. The man ahead of us had a guitar strapped to his waist and started to strum softly, obviously to pass the time while he was waiting his turn. He compulsively moved his hips and shoulders in time to the music in his mind, while his lips soundlessly shaped the words of the song he was obviously itching to sing. This harmless movement triggered off a shot of energy that ran through the length of the queue, and in no time at all electrified everybody, or rather all those who were Guianese or Trinidadian. They all slowly began to sway, tap, gyrate, and undulate in response to the irresistible call of the guitar. The prime mover had started tentatively, chanting the words of a calypso under his breath, but it gradually became a full-blooded song and all those who could, joined in. All official business forgotten, the queue broke up and smoothly turned into a joyful revel. 'Dee bard and dee pijon, Were quite good compaanion', they all sang ecstatically. The official at the window, obviously a local person, pushed his papers aside and looked rapturously on, longing to be a part of the festivities. One frantic outsider repeatedly asked the time of departure of a flight to Chicago but failed to get the official's ear. When he persisted, the official sleepily dislodged an aged schedule from a shelf with the help of a cane, releasing clouds of dust, and murmured reassuringly, 'Afther launch, afther launch, dez right, no hurry!'

I subsequently found that this introduction to the Caribbean temperament was quite faithful. Every day provided some fresh evidence of the people's talent for happiness and their commitment to whatever kind of good life circumstances allowed. I once saw a gathering that started out as a funeral but turned imperceptibly into a rollicking party, just on the strength of human company and liquor. So long as these were assured, it was not unusual for those present to disregard what had brought them there in the first place. This could on occasion also be true of public places of business. After a while, I began to understand the 'No Singing' signs I had seen at the airport.

However, the Guianese of Indian origin seemed to be somewhat different. They were notorious for being focused and hard-working. It was said that even at the time of the Carnival, they hardly lifted their heads from the soil they were tilling on both sides of the road, unaffected by the loud music and the boisterousness of the parades as they went by. They clung to their Indian identity and took great pride in their customs and festivals.

I had made friends with a tomato-seller called Buddhoo who used to go from house to house on a bicycle, dressed in a brown felt hat and Bermuda shorts.

'Tammara is Janamashtami Ma'am. Will you come to the Hindoo church?' he said one day.

This I was not going to miss for anything. The next evening

I dragged my husband to the address Buddhoo had given and for the first time entered a 'Hindoo church'. Nothing could have been less like a noisy Indian temple during Janamashtami. This was a large, white wooden structure with a church-like dome and balustrades. Inside there was awed silence though the space was crowded with people. Men and women sat in separate sections in the pews, humble and expectant. Soon a 'priestess' appeared and made her way down the aisle to the altar. Her head was covered with an orhni that could have come from any village of eastern UP, but she also wore high-heeled shoes and a knee-length Western-style dress. She gave some kind of signal in a dialect I did not understand, and the women, dressed in the same combination of East and West, rose one by one, each with a thali carrying the familiar offering of coconut, banana, red paste, flowers, and a lighted oil lamp. The priestess accepted the thalis on behalf of the divine from each devotee in turn. It was a disciplined ritual, without any scrambling or raised voices.

There was a sudden ripple of excitement. 'De paandhit-jee comin, de paandhit-jee comin', someone exclaimed loudly, as an elderly car rattled to a stop outside the entrance and an extraordinary personage alighted. A wide-brimmed straw hat which seemed several sizes too large for him topped his grave, weatherbeaten face. He wore knee-high gumboots and sported a long, flowing nylon scarf in place of an angavastram. His body language suggested that he should have had a long white beard like Moses or Abraham, although in fact the growth on his face was only a day old, as far as I could judge. With the air of a royal personage, he moved importantly to the altar, looking imperiously left and right. Everyone including the priestess froze in deference.

The self-appointed master of ceremonies who had excitedly

announced the arrival of the panditji now took up another refrain. 'He comin for de ser-mon, he comin for de ser-mon!' The word was pronounced in two separate parts, the first half in a descending tone where the lowest point was held for an instant before the 'mon' part of the word was released as though by a little catapult to ascend to the normal pitch of the voice. The word when pronounced in Guianese style sounded like a caress.

The panditji mounted the pulpit and cleared his throat. There was no microphone and I knew we were in for a spell of serious bellowing.

'Today bein Jan-am-ash-tamee, I tellin ya bout Gita, wat Krishna tellin de whole world. Wat he tellin Arjuna on de baatlefield of Kurukshetra, dat he tellin you and dat he tellin me!' Panditji roared in the manner of a prophet of the Old Testament, his imaginary white beard flowing in the wind.

The audience was rivetted and suitably intimidated, since the manner of the address suggested that doomsday could not be far.

'Wat Krishna tellin Arjuna on de baatlefield of Kurukshetra? Well, wat he tellin Arjuna, dat he tellin you and dat he tellin me. Is Krishna tellin Arjuna "Doan be eatin, doan be drinkin, doan be dancin?" No, no, no. He not tellin Arjuna dat, he not tellin you dat, he not tellin me dat.'

Panditji paused for effect, at which point my husband whose ear was not his strong point whispered: 'What language is he speaking? I think it's a garbled version of Sanskrit.'

He was incredulous when I said it was more likely to be a version of English.

The local prophet had warmed up and was now in full cry, repeating his theme in bhajan style.

'Is Krishna sayin to Arjuna "doan be drinkin, doan be dancin, doan be makin love, doan be enjoyin?" No, no, no! He not tellin

Arjuna dat, he not tellin you dat, and he not tellin me dat! He sayin "enjoy all—food, drink, dancin, makin love!"'

The rhetoric took on a menacing tone as he shook his fist at the cowering congregation.

'Yea, be eatin, drinkin, dancin, makin love!' he thundered. 'Only remember, this all belongin to Krishna and HE GONNA TAKE BAACK WHEN TIME KOM!'

You could have heard a pin drop in the Hindoo church. Doomsday was at hand.

We went home in silence, carrying with us forever the most original interpretation of the Gita ever offered by mankind.

TWENTY-THREE

The Many-Splendoured Harmonium

I could never have believed that at the ripe age of fifty-five I would fall in love with the tone of a harmonium! I had considered the instrument an abomination throughout my life and was not at all prepared for what happened to me one wet evening at the Alternative Museum in New York. My life had suddenly cut me off from Indian music and I was so starved for it that anything that could even remotely remind me of my lost world was welcome. I saw in the newspapers that a Baul singer was to perform at this small centre for experimental art. Even though this was not my kind of music, I hungrily made my way to the address given in the *New York Times* in the hope that I would at least hear some healing sounds.

It was impossible for anyone or anything to be unobtrusive in the space to which I was led by unconventional ushers. Everyone present was an original, in their own fiercely individual way. Funky music addicts with blue-dyed hair, clean-shaven Buddhist monks of European extraction, nostalgic Asians like myself, and regular, curious metropolitan young people interested in 'happenings' mingled self-consciously with one another as they found places to sit, squat, or perch. The walls were plastered with the lurid art of overconfident young rebels which the organization obviously supported. I could not help thinking that it would be difficult to have traditional Indian concerts here, because the paintings were of the screaming variety and would have clashed hopelessly with the mood of almost any raga I could think of. The room was thick with human vibrations and I wondered with motherly concern how the simple Baul singer from Bangladesh would fare.

I need not have worried. The Baul was quite at home. In fact he seemed to be carrying his home with him in his mind and confidently expected his audience to share it. The first plaintive cry of his hoarse voice was so convincing that everyone was transported. The instruments followed suit. The ill-tuned drums began to rumble happily, and the strings twanged and rasped to a compulsive rhythm. It was hypnotic but disturbingly off-key. I consoled myself with the thought that at least the atmosphere was close to what I was longing for, even though there was nothing to soothe my ear.

Just then, a dishevelled member of the Baul's party returned from the washroom, smiled uncertainly, and casually took his place behind a waiting harmonium. He ran his cadaverous fingers over the keys to test the instrument. The melody that emerged took my breath away. It was the most tuneful, beautiful sound I had heard for months. Certainly I had never come across a harmonium that could hold its own like this. The double reeds were perfectly tuned, the tone was like velvet, and the silent breath had incredible range. Undoubtedly the creation of a master craftsman, I thought. The relief from the earlier sounds was overwhelming. I was so grateful to the wielder of this magic box that I rushed to congratulate him at the end of the evening. I was also curious about the instrument-maker whose skill had given me so much unexpected pleasure, but to my amazement the player seemed quite unaware of the quality of what he had just played. 'The *baja* is not ours. We have borrowed it from him', he said pointing to a slightly flabby, clean-shaven man in his early forties. Owning and cherishing an instrument like this had so many implications that I just had to meet the real owner. He was bound to be an extraordinary musical person, exactly the kind of friend I needed just then. I asked to be led to him forthwith.

When I was facing him, I introduced myself, first in English, and then, encouraged by his polite and authentic '*ji*', I slipped comfortably into Hindustani. He was much younger than I was, and was deferential in a way I had become unused to. He was not articulate in English but the *Dilli ka muhavara* I deliberately served up to him evoked a powerful response. He was also from the old city of Delhi but had not spoken or heard good Urdu for twenty years. For ten years he had lived among Punjabis in Lahore, and then had escaped to the USA to settle down in Queens in the state of New York. He was yearning for a cultural reconnection with his roots. He told me his name was Shahid Akhtar Khan and we were soon chatting like long-lost friends. He glowed and blushed when I complimented him on his wonderful harmonium. 'Yes, it is in great demand in the Tri-state area', he said with that special mixture of modesty and pride that only people from our subcontinent know how to use. The Baul party had returned the harmonium to him by now and it rested on a nearby chair draped in a laced dark green velvet cover that looked a hundred years old. He stroked and patted it lovingly as though it were a prize racehorse.

Now it was time for him to say something nice to me. Civilities snowballed as they often do in oriental settings. Shahid complimented me on my speaking voice and my accent which reminded him of his mother, his favourite aunt, the mohalla of Ballimaran that he had grown up in, and everything else that was dear to him. Would I please go on talking to him in Urdu? Would I also please agree to talk to his elder sister on the telephone? She would be very grateful. She was married to a Polish businessman and lived in a state of pathological homesickness in New Jersey with no relief in sight. I asked Shahid whether he himself was a musician. No, he said, though he adored music. I gathered in slow stages that his area of activity was as far from music as it could possibly be. He worked as a loader with Pakistan International Airways at Kennedy Airport. This I was not prepared for.

The life injections by telephone became a daily occurrence after this encounter, a sort of game. Sometimes the homesick sister would also participate. We would all deliberately try to speak a formal, flowery, overly polite, almost courtly Urdu of long ago that could not possibly have meant anything in our frenetic New York existence. Shahid was going to be my humble servant forever. The opportunity to be of use to an incomparable artist like myself was his great good fortune and he would pray to the Almighty that the privilege should never be denied him. He had decided that I was a great musician without ever having heard me perform. I protested, but he just knew because this was something God had told him personally. He clinched the argument by saying I was like his mother and the Holy Book said that heaven lay under the mother's feet. I countered his avalanches repeatedly with equally stately rejoinders. I was not worthy of such devotion. I had done nothing to deserve it. God had shown me His mercy by leading me to Shahid through his harmonium. And so on. Anyhow, we got mildly addicted to this sort of exchange and began to use it as an intoxicant fairly regularly. Meanwhile both Shahid and I continued to toil at our respective roles in the city of New York, both more secure in the knowledge that a reliable new supporter was now only a phone-call away.

When the ardour of our first exchanges subsided a little, I asked Shahid how he had acquired his harmonium. It could not have too many peers. I had once seen something like it in Lucknow in the possession of Begum Akhtar. I remembered her telling me that she had personally supervised every stage of its construction and assembly with a famous craftsman of Calcutta, and that it had taken two years to complete and another three for its tone to 'take on colour'. I knew that Shahid himself could not have had the resources or ability to make the same kind of effort. He told me frankly that the instrument belonged to Farida Khanum, a celebrated ghazal singer of Pakistan who was the mother-in-law of a friend of his who also lived in Queens. She had not been able to carry it back with her after a concert tour in the States and had left it in the indefinite custody of her son-in-law to be transported at a future date. Meanwhile, the son-in-law had been transferred to Atlanta, Georgia, and had left his clutter with his friend. Ten years had passed and nobody seemed to be doing anything about restoring the harmonium to its owner. As far as Shahid was concerned it was like a stray cat who had sneaked into his house and decided to live with him. The harmonium was his by default. Even though he was not directly aware of its virtues, its performance as a magic carpet that could fly him almost anywhere slowly convinced him that he had come by a treasure.

I had known Shahid for about two months when I got my first chance to perform in New York city. A wealthy American patron of Indian dance and music organized an evening for interested people in his large apartment in Manhattan and invited me to give a vocal recital. I accepted at once and excitedly rang up Shahid. At last I could be on stage along with his fabulous harmonium! Would he accompany me? Yes, yes, of course, there was no question! He would go with me to the ends of the earth! He would take leave from his job, stand on his head, do whatever was needed. It would be an unprecedented honour for him, this worthless *nacheez,* to be associated with my wonderful music. Clearly, it was all settled.

On the appointed evening he came to our apartment in a flashy maroon car to take me and my large tanpura to the scene of action. He was dressed in an impressive Pakistani salwar suit and smelt of musk or something equally overpowering. When I introduced him to my husband and elder son, he was courtesy itself. But my family wasn't quite sure how to react, specially since I could not tell them where we were going and for how long. Shahid was taking care of the details and I was quite happy to be in his hands. 'If you are not back by midnight, I'm going to the police', my son stage-whispered fiercely as we left.

The fashionable Fifth Avenue apartment which was our destination had been turned into a baithak fit for an Indian cultural evening. Diyas flickered in antique brass lamps. Most of the American guests were turned out in ethnic Indian fabrics, beads, and chunky silver jewellery which proclaimed their interest and support. An Indian dancer who lived in New York had brought a huge bowl of kheer 'for afterwards' and smilingly garnished it with red rose petals as she set it on the table meant for refreshments. Shahid and I settled down decorously on the Irani carpet with our instruments. Someone quickly checked the sound system and the recording apparatus. I gave the final touches to the tuning of my tanpura. Shahid unveiled the harmonium and rested his fingers on the keys. His eyes were fixed expectantly on my face. At last the moment had come.

I started by singing a long note to introduce the raga. Even before I could hear myself properly, Shahid burst into a volley of applause. '*Wah, wah! Kya kehne! Kya baat hai, kya awaaz hai*!' he expostulated, startling and mystifying everyone including me. Two things were clear. One, that he had no ear for music, otherwise he would have waited till I had really done something with my voice before exploding like that. Second, his enthusiasm had no connection with my calibre as a singer. He was determined to lionize me for some complicated psycho-cultural reasons of his own that I could not quite fathom. I was nonplussed but plodded on with the recital. At this point I noticed that no sound was emerging from the harmonium although Shahid was constantly emitting sounds of appreciation for my efforts from his throat. He concentrated his attention on the smallest whisper I might produce but his fingers lay inert on the keys. I gestured to him several times to begin playing but absolutely nothing happened. He did not even know what to do with the bellows. He gestured back helplessly, and to my utter disbelief mouthed the words 'I don't know how to *play*', as though this was just a minor detail.

To Shahid, the harmonium was an important object in a serious ritual and he was the designated attendant. He saw nothing incongruous in the situation. Even while I was singing, it came to me in a flash that to him it was not so much a musical instrument as an insurance against loneliness. Because of it, he was in great demand too and on its wings was regularly able to escape from the dreariness of his suburban American existence. For him it was a credit card, an entrance ticket to a warmer and more friendly world, a priceless possession which lent him value and eminence. I thought of the accident which had left the harmonium in his care. A strange sympathy for him and his utter ignorance of the ways of the music world welled up in me. However, this did not faze him in the least and he continued to greet the smallest musical phrase I uttered with loud cries of appreciation and encouragement, like a fervent spectator at a bull fight. There was no way out of my embarrassment. I could hardly pretend that I had nothing to do with him. We were clearly a duo, joined at the waist so far as the audience was concerned and the sum total of the sound input this evening was squarely my responsibility.

At last my ordeal ended and the host invited the guests to ask any questions they wished. There were a number of innocuous ones which were neither here nor there. But then came a question that profoundly affected my own understanding of the music I had been practising for years. An earnest American lady from the Asia Society furrowed her brow with concentration and said in slow, measured tones that she wanted a clarification. 'The gentleman sitting to your left seemed to be saying a *lot* of things all through the concert. I want to know what that was. Was it a part of the song? Or the music? I must say the gentleman's constant participation didn't sound much like music but it seemed to fit right in!'

Nothing could have been more true. It set me thinking about some fundamental things. Yes, it was a part of the music in an organic sense, an inalienable part without which the intended communication in Indian music cannot really happen. Neither Shahid nor the lady from the Asia Society can have any idea how many doors they accidentally opened for my mind that evening.

TWENTY-FOUR

The New Face of Listening

Here I am. Now do something to please me, the eager young eyes seem to say, as their owner fussily subsides in the seventh row, a little to the left, better view, you see, and the best seats, sound-wise. It's a sort of party, so there are three others in tow. Two of them have to go out to dinner later; so they hope, very loudly, that the maestro will do his stuff fast, because they simply must leave by eight-thirty. The serious young man in jeans and khadi kurta carries a paperback, a battered Walkman, and an assortment of cassette tapes in a cloth sling-bag, his arrangements for alternative activity just in case the evening doesn't work out.

The performer squints at the footlights and begins to tune up, to prepare psychologically for the ineffable and intimate disclosures that his art is all about. But his audience is no one in particular, just a vast black pit with an unknown animal in it. It might roar or pounce, purr or go to sleep. He has no way of knowing until he is more than halfway through. As he tries to concentrate and establish the first note, there is a hum of rival sounds.

'I think eight-thirty is cutting it too fine, yaar.'

'Don't fuss. It'll be o.k.'

'Look who's here ! Haaaiii! Didn't see you yesterday!'

'Couldn't make it. Was the music good?'

'Faantaastic! There were gorgeous guzzles at the end. I don't understand all the words, but Oordu is such a beautiful language! I just love guzzles!'

'My God, what a smashing outfit! Where do you find such things?'

'Shhh. He's started, I think.'

'Will he do guzzles?'

'Don't be idiotic, yaar. He's dhurpad or something. Really heavy stuff! Now be quiet, for heaven's sake. I've heard he's really cool.'

When the music finally ends, there is uproarious clapping by eight hundred people, a shattering sound without tone or rhythm, a frightening cacophony that can immediately erase the beauty and meaning of what has gone before.

This, more or less, describes the new elements that have entered the scene at public concerts of classical music in any big city in India today. The atmosphere of the music world was fundamentally different only fifty years ago, which is why people of my generation tend to begin every sentence with the tiresome 'When we were young . . .'

For one thing, the perception of silence is now quite different from what it has always been in the past. The century we have just entered is the noisiest one the world has ever known and India is no exception. Connoisseurs of the old school here used to regard silence as the starting point of all music. The portrait of a raga was thought to consist of unbroken melodic lines drawn on the canvas of silence. All traditional Indian music makes use of silence in many other subtle and delicate ways which are all but lost to the musician of today and of course, very sadly, to the listener as well. The gradual erosion of silence by ever-increasing noise levels is to my mind the single most important change that has come about in the music world in the last fifty years. It has irreversibly affected performers and coarsened listeners, producers, presenters, and marketeers of music.

If one were to consider just the physical aspect of the music that is being produced today, one could justifiably say that it is louder and much more strident than it has ever been. This stems from the attitudes of both music-maker and listener. Both have changed drastically in recent years. Music can no longer be the intimate communication that was its original intention. Now it has to be shouted out, not whispered, if it is to be heard at all above the din that pervades life today. To get and hold the attention of the listener, musicians can no longer depend entirely on their art. They have to make a little go a long way and too often have to resort to grandstanding and gimmicks.

The advent of the microphone has ushered in another major change. Along with other electronic aids and the mass media, it has extended the reach of both musician and listener. Of course methods of transmission must change if much larger audiences have to be reached, but must the product itself? Although this could not have been the intention, many examples spring to mind where the need to channel music through the microphone has killed many born singers and created several who would otherwise have been only hummers and crooners. The microphone is the new tyrant of the music world. It demands a kind of modulation which is alien to the direct and intimate idiom of Indian music. Not only that. By offering artificially an unaccustomed range of tonal possibilities, it often becomes an invitation to spurious emoting, posturing, and striving after sound effects, specially for vocalists.

The saving grace for instrumentalists is that many of them are learning to use the potential provided by electronic amplification in a positive manner. In this they are guided by the extraordinary technological improvements that have taken place in almost all Indian instruments over the last fifty years. It is thrilling to hear clearly the echoes of the softest whisper of a string even after it has stopped vibrating. This was not the case in the instrumental music of even the greatest masters of the 1940s and 1950s. The vast expanse of musical space that audio technology has opened up offers to the creative musician limitless opportunities for experimentation. Many have used it with discrimination, and succeeded in introducing a new sophistication and refinement in the body of the old music. In irresponsible and casual hands however the danger of derailment is also immeasurably greater than it was before. Examples of this are also plentiful. In other words, the microphone like the curate's egg has turned out to be good in parts.

Correspondingly, the audience today does not consist of connoisseurs who were brought up to tune in to the mind of the performing musician, but of a vigorous new class of passive listeners who feel entitled to the best that life has to offer and expect it to be served to them without any effort on their part. Today's patrons of music are more powerful than they have ever been in the history of Indian music. Their strength is in their numbers, in their omnipresence, their mobility, their boundless energy, and above all their determination to get the best there is. And access to the best has never been easier. The greatest music can quite affordably be in the hands of anyone who cares to buy a recorded cassette. One can listen at leisure, whenever and wherever one wishes. It has often occurred to me that at least physically every literate music lover can have almost as much in the way of music as the emperor Akbar might have had at the height of his power, and more. Myriad music events take place almost every day, at least in the big cities. Most of them are open to the public and charge no entrance fee, as they are usually sponsored by corporate enterprises engaged in building a more attractive image of themselves. Music and dance schools have sprung up almost at every street corner and it is altogether a most lucrative proposition for institutions to engage in all forms of cultural promotion.

Most serious listening in the not-so-remote past happened within the traditional baithak. Its hushed air of intelligent expectancy was an ideal setting for the delicate and intimate idiom of classical music. Each of the two-hundred-odd in the audience was aware of his or her role as a listener and had his responses finely turned to the extraordinary communication he was about to receive and be a part of, as ready to hear as the musician was to play or sing. The ideal for both was to share each phase of the creative process, to travel together to magic worlds which the musician had seen and was now about to share with admirers anxious to follow him. A performance was an intensely personal affair, with deeply entrenched rules of etiquette which spoke of a real cultural connection with the music. Only peers or elders could be vocal in their appreciation. Successful performances did not end with mechanical bursts of clapping, but human sounds such as *wah, wah! bahut khoob, kya kehne*, and so on. Younger enthusiasts had to hold themselves in. For them to express praise was considered presumptuous, even insolent. To fidget or change your posture while the baithak was in session was the height of bad manners. Eating, drinking, and smoking during the music were taboo except in some degenerate courtly settings. Accompanists who tried to outshine the main performer were frowned upon and considered uncivilized. Of course one always removed one's footwear, but one could never stretch one's legs and point them in the direction of the instruments, as invariably happens today in soirees that claim to simulate the traditional setting. In short, in the old days one entered the presence of music with respect and humility. The musician was not someone who had been paid to deliver something to which the listener was entitled, but a living treasure to be cherished for what he was—a superior being. He was the leader and the listener the follower.

These roles have gradually been reversed because the musician must now please his new, many-headed patrons if he is to survive professionally. His stature no longer depends only on artistic merit. He has also to woo the big stage and cultivate a winning personality which is in keeping with the public's image of the sensitive artist. He must seem to be a superstar even if he has not yet made it. He must also learn to speak the language of organizers and promoters in addition to the wordless language of music. And, most importantly, he must make sure that he sells. These are some of the pressures on the musician today which his predecessors did not have to grapple with.

Electronic aids and the mass media have extended the reach of both the musician and the listener. That the new audiences are now at least a hundred times larger and consist mostly of the rising middle classes and young people in their twenties is undoubtedly a good sign from a social point of view. The treasures that our music has to offer are no longer the preserve of the privileged few. Music is for everyone. It is a commodity that is consumed like any other product in a fast-changing society. This is a sign of development and must be welcomed. But something fundamental, and I suspect valuable, has been lost as a result. Inevitably the targets, the volume, and the methods of transmission must change with progress. But must the product itself?

The germ of the big change has entered the very substance of music and laid a cold finger on its ancient values of restraint and purity. The intimacy of communication which was its life now too often gives place to unsubtle posturing and stagey oratorical styles which are quite alien to its original intention. The audiences of today, far from trying to refine their ear, confidently lay down their demands very explicitly through patterns of response. They want something 'that comes straight from the heart' but are oblivious that they might have a role to play in this exchange. To prove his worth the musician has to function alone. He must hold their attention and impress them somehow. Gimmicks, displays of virtuosity, and spurious emoting are increasingly becoming the norm. This amounts to a passive dilution and vulgarization, a lowering of quality in order to meet the expectations of the mass audience and stay in business. The challenge to the creativity of today's performing maestro is gigantic. He must innovate genuinely and so vigorously that the frontiers of his art stretch to admit the energetic audiences of the new commercial culture. Classical music might then become the most worthwhile, most consumable music even for the new audiences.

The motivations of the public that flocks to concert halls are also more varied than they have ever been. Not everyone who makes the effort to attend is necessarily interested in the music, as used to be the case not so long ago. Many of the young come because they are in search of their lost cultural identity. Jaded politicians come to prop up their image. Socialites come to be seen and because it is a pleasant and possibly rewarding way to pass the time. Snobbery, curiosity, boredom, networking, and entertainment are some other reasons which draw audiences and can sometimes account for nearly half their number. This also confirms that, after Independence, Indian music has gained immeasurably in prestige if not in genuine sources of artistic stimulus.

The ease with which the doors of the music world can now open has naturally brought in an element of casualness even among rising young musicians who seriously wish to excel. The intense devotion and dedication that used to be an inalienable part of the music business have rapidly waned although the level of activity on the music scene has risen to a feverish pitch. The sheer volume of the music that has to be produced to keep up with the demands also contributes to the dilution of quality. So does the rise of the personality cult. The average musician today would rather work at being a superstar than at deepening the material he has inherited or acquired. The press and television often publicize the appearance of a new raga specially crafted for this or that national occasion by some celebrity, while many rare and beautiful ragas that have existed for centuries languish and face extinction from sheer neglect. Most musicians are too busy 'doing' music in some form or other to ever think about it. No one considers *chintan* and *manan* a part of a musician's normal discipline, least of all the performing artists themselves. This is not how it used to be.

Another conspicuous change from the 1950s and 1960s is the loss of innocence among the practitioners of the art of music. Though the masters we admired in our youth were human and undoubtedly indulged their prejudices and jealousies, their art was the centre of their universe, in the same way in which a child's mother is its ultimate, inviolable haven. Once they entered their music, they remained effortlessly true to it and to themselves, regardless of the audience's reaction. They took it for granted that everybody would find it as engrossing as they did themselves. Musicians like Amir Khan and Nikhil Bannerji did not even raise their eyes during a performance because they were so deeply involved with what they were doing and oblivious of everything else. They were sure that nothing significant could possibly exist beyond the frontiers of their world of music. It is in this sense that I call them innocent. There are several anecdotes that illustrate this quality which characterized a whole generation of musicians.

Once, after he had received a state award, Ustad Hafiz Ali Khan found himself sitting next to the President of India. The president politely asked him what in his opinion the government could do to help the cause of music. After thinking carefully for a few moments, he said what can roughly be translated as: 'Sir, Darbari is in a very bad condition. It is a great raga. People are treating it very badly, specially the gandhara and dhaivata. This is a serious matter. Please do something about it.' The president was understandably flustered and is reported to have instructed an attending official to 'look into the matter'.

Then there is the well-known story of Ustad Bundu Khan who, on being told that his scheduled broadcast had been cancelled because Mr Jinnah had arrived unexpectedly and had to be fitted in the same slot, is reported to have said, again roughly translated: 'I have played with every musician in the country, but I've never even heard of this singer. What note does he use as his *sa*?'

Another telling incident is about Krishna Rao Shankar Pandit who was the guest of honour at a glittering function in New Delhi. Rajiv Gandhi happened to drop in since the venue was the house of a family friend. Naturally the hostess first introduced the chief guest. The eighty-year-old maestro beamed graciously at the clean-faced youngster who had come up to meet him. When his hostess murmured that this was the prime minister, he smiled at him and said, 'Oh, then you must be the biggest person in Radio!' This was the first and most important thing that came to his mind!

Mallikarjun Mansur, it is often told, courteously turned down an invitation to perform for the Festival of India in America because the concert schedules interfered with the timings of his daily practice and meditation.

These are attractive and loveable personalities. One can hardly imagine people of this ilk performing with a sheaf of air tickets in their breast pockets in readiness for the flights they have to catch for their other engagements, or imitating the mannerisms and dress styles of megastars of Western jazz and rock music, or working the public relations circuits armed with glossy brochures listing their achievements and the standing ovations they received in this or that foreign country. In the old days no printed bio-data was ever asked for or needed. All publicity was by word of mouth and the grapevine of the music community. The artistes themselves were usually no party to any promotional exercise that involved them personally. The point here is not that they were better people; only that their music reflected their absolute faith in their own world and therefore carried an indescribable depth and conviction which are rarely heard today.

That world has started to break up. The over-confidence which comes with easy access has affected not only audiences but also the new generation of learners. They are a breed apart from the worshipful disciples whose legendary devotion to the master and his art used to be a favourite feature of many a myth in the music world. They are much more canny and have a far more acute awareness of themselves as individuals. Even if they are associated with a particular musical cuisine or gharana, they feel free to graze where they will and pick up whatever suits their repertoire and temperament at a particular phase in their career. Alap in the Kirana style, taan in the Jaipur style, bol baant in the Agra mode, and akar in the manner of singers of the Patiala gharana can and do appear simultaneously in the performances of many young celebrities in the making. The walls of the gharanas are crumbling and have lost the will to keep their specialities to themselves. The newly-acquired license to cater for a variety of tastes gives performers a heady feeling of freedom and power. Nothing is wrong with this except that dishes are being served before the cuisine has attained perfection. And this *is* a pity, as it robs the future of the ripest and richest fruits of single-minded concentration. The intelligent, confident, mobile, vitamin-enriched and uncommitted pupil of today feels he can get results even by sitting at the feet of a tape-recorder if a guru is problematic. In the present set-up of musical education, he does not have to hang on the lips of a guru who is not likely to be available at his convenience if he is available at all. The musical aspirant today feels much more in control of his destiny. His fresh young mind is influenced by the systematic approach of Western researchers who are trained to ask questions and examine everything under a microscope. Unlike his earlier counterpart, he too demands a reason for everything. Armed with his tape-recorder and cassette collection, he is sure that he can imitate any aspect of any gharana he fancies because he can repeat a lesson at will, and as many times as necessary. He does not need to collect carefully, memorize, and cherish every pearl that might drop from the lips of a guru as it might not come his way again. Disciples of earlier generations had to do this as a matter of course.

But it has to be admitted that despite the ouster of devotion as the supreme quality in serious musical aspiration, the results are less disappointing than one feared. Never before have there been so many new 'prodigies' in both the Hindustani and

Carnatic classical traditions. This phenomenon has less to do with population growth in general than with the devising of new learning techniques combined with the much higher level of efficiency and competence among the young. The substitution of devotion by skill, application, and an attitude of 'If anyone can do it, I can too' has been effective in ways that could be very important to the future of music in our country. Most of the new stars, especially in the Carnatic system, are in their teens and early twenties. The 'young' discoveries who were hailed by the world of Hindustani music only fifteen years ago are already presenting their own disciples on the stage! In addition to the crucial tape-recorder, there is a battery of dependable gadgets such as electronic tanpuras and taal-malas which seem to work like seven-league boots for the new celebrities in the matter of their regular practice. The gradual fading of the guru–shishya parampara does not seem to have blocked the phenomenal increase in the number of whiz kids in both classical traditions. Organizers and impresarios no longer have to worry about who to feature in concerts because the possibilities are inexhaustible and still exceed the opportunities.

In this sense too, there has been progress. Something has undoubtedly been gained. At the same time a sense of loss pervades the ears that were young in the 1950s. To them, the intensity and conviction, the directness and innocence of the musicians of the earlier part of this century still have an unsurpassable musical quality which cannot be found in the most sophisticated recordings of today. As an old master put it, the clever new generation of musicians have eyes not only at the back of their heads but also in their armpits. According to him, too much seeing and too little intuition can rob the mind of its real musical potential.

Both the Hindustani and Carnatic systems of classical music

demand a perseverance and concentration that is difficult to achieve in any circumstances. The existing distractions of modern life, for instance the persistent sounds of film music and commercial audio-cassettes offered almost round the clock by television and radio, make things even harder. The music that deluges us consists mainly of innovations devised by Indian composers on synthesizers and uses all the sounds of the world in an effort to present something that is both novel and instantly appealing. The music industry's frantic efforts to ensure that products are being manufactured in enough quantity to match the varied and ever-growing demand has unleashed a new energy which speaks of the inexhaustible vigour and earthiness of our cultural roots even though all the efforts at composition may not qualify as great music. Nonetheless, I would say that of every five hundred unremarkable pieces which are likely to be self-conscious and imitative exercises in musical packaging, there is usually at least one which compels attention because it has been ignited by a genuinely creative imagination.

A desirable fall-out of this churning and exploring has been that musically the North and the South have come closer today than they have been for a long time. The new Indian pop and Hindi film music have performed the signal service of providing a common meeting ground for music directors from both systems. In fact the conservative South has been more enterprising than the North in this respect because the first real fusion trends were the contribution of music directors of Tamil films. It is now commonplace to hear sargams and taalas of the Carnatic system embroidering Hindustani raga-based pieces. The accompanying music of Bharatanatyam and Kathak often merge in depicting modern themes. Vocalists, instrumentalists, and percussionists from both systems frequently appear together on stage in various permutations and combinations which do not fail to thrill the public. New music makers from the South are bestsellers in the North and singers from the South want to master thumri and ghazal. This was unthinkable even fifteen years ago when the two systems were disapproving and wary of each other even though they were tacitly agreed on the traditional promises of classical music—inner joy and the enrichment of the spirit.

Today, the term 'spirit' carries a different meaning altogether, something more akin to enthusiasm and optimism than anything to do with spirituality. People generally prefer to be teased and prodded rather than soothed and elated. This is what the new music-maker caters for. At the centre of his tireless experimentation is a preoccupation with creating new sounds rather than with creating music. Indian folk and tribal music and elements of raga still provide the skeleton of most popular offerings, but the flesh defies identification. One can hear African and South American rhythms, melodies from the Middle East, Western-style delivery of pop songs, the sounds of Western jazz and much else in the music being produced in India today. This in itself is no disaster because Indian music has always absorbed influences from outside and integrated them into the mainstream. But the thread of continuity has always been there like a reassuring heartbeat. This sound is becoming fainter and sometimes cannot be heard at all.

Indian music cannot afford to sever *all* connection with its inherent values of purity and restraint. To the extent that these are diminished, the intrinsic quality of the music, however serviceable it may prove to be socially, suffers. At the same time music has to be the genuine product of an age. It must draw life and sustenance from its environment if it is not to degenerate into a museum piece. And herein lies the dilemma. There is no question that the musical forms and values associated with all traditional Indian music are in a state of flux. There is also no question that this is not the first time in history that this has happened. Change is always painful for the diehards but experience tells us that it does not necessarily imply a negative development. When the khayal first established itself alongside the ancient dhrupad form, around the fifteenth century, it was considered an unworthy upstart and frowned upon by purists in much the same manner as music lovers who were young in the fifties view the innovations in Indian film and pop music today. Yet one has to admit that this unworthy upstart evolved into a rich and highly aesthetic form which is universally hailed as the finest flowering of the Hindustani raga system. It is relevant to remember that khayal in its turn meted out to thumri and dadra the same treatment it had received itself at the hands of dhrupad. Taking a lesson from this example in recent history, we must reserve judgement on the trends that are overtaking music in India today. It is perfectly possible that a new music which will be 'truer' to the times is in the making even as we speak. What seems sometimes to be an assault on ancient musical ears might well be the birthpangs of a new musical vision. The example of the khayal—there are many more—should caution us against instant assessment. The new pop music, whatever else it may lack, certainly is not feeble. On the contrary, it is almost always characterized by vigour, energy, and an intense desire to communicate. Admittedly, these are not enough to qualify sound as music, but there is a fair chance that these could turn out to be positive attributes.

If music concerts are designed for two thousand rather than two hundred people, as indeed they should be, the intimacy of the baithak has obviously to be sacrificed. The change in the physical scene however presents some unforeseen difficulties which are not physical but have to do with the nature of the music that is being produced and presented. First, the ambience of the large auditorium is radically different from anything the musician's training and discipline have prepared him for. He can no longer find the same kind of inspiration from his distant audience as his guru probably could in old-style recitals by simply looking into the eyes of a listener and expressing what was in his heart. I remember a recent concert of Ustad Bismillah Khan in a large hall where he stopped midway and demanded that all the lights be turned on so that at least he could see who he was playing for. He said he wanted to let his shehnai address them directly. Needless to say, there was an immediate thaw in the atmosphere and the music he played after this spiralled to new heights. There are numerous examples where the presence or absence of rapport has made all the difference to the quality of the music at a performance. But the realities of the situation today cannot always accommodate this intrinsic requirement of our music.

Another intrinsic requirement is spontaneity. This too is less and less in evidence because of time constraints which foster an element of premeditation alien to the nature of Indian music. Some artists go so far as to work out exactly what they will do at a played concert, down to the last detail of rhythmic climaxes, fast runs, and other gems in their repertoire which are guaranteed to dazzle their listener. This road is yet another departure from the trodden path of genuine improvisation. In my view it is a threat to quality because the genius of Indian music does not lie in this direction but in the opposite one. The nature of Indian music is such that if it is preset, however roughly, in the manner of Western classical music, it can lose much of its power to infect and persuade, even though it still might fall pleasantly and tunefully on the ear. In this situation the musician has little chance of being able to *share* his spiritual striving with his listener. And this sharing is what our music is really all about. Everyone agrees with this—including the worst defaulters. Whether or not conditions permit intimate rapport and spontaneity, every performer on stage, radio, and television compulsively simulates these characteristics, thereby paying unconscious tribute to these values in our traditional music. Ironically, even the most self-centred audiences are only impressed by the musician who ignores and disregards them because he is completely immersed in his own art.

Even though traditional practitioners try to accommodate their new audiences out of sheer self interest, they find it almost impossible to keep pace with modern electronics. The following advertisement I came across recently in a popular magazine is dramatic evidence of the explosion that has taken place:

> Have you nurtured an unfulfilled desire to become a music director? Now here's your chance. The Miracle Piano Teaching System plugs into a Nintendo games machine or on IBM compatible computer and then works as a keyboard synthesizer. It has over 100 'voices' and has a full musical instrument digital interface (MIDI) compatibility so that it can be hooked on to other synthesizers.
>
> The Miracle can also be a fun way to learn and to give lessons.
>
> The second musical marvel is the Yamaha QY10. Smaller than a video cassette, the QY10 is a miniaturized MIDI sequencer. This means it scores MIDI notes and enables you to edit them, allowing you to work on eight compositions at a time. It has 76 pre-set accompaniments and drum patterns. So if music is the essence of life, here's your chance to play on.

The easy and informal language of the insertion suggests that the young music buff at whom it is aimed is not unfamiliar with the possibilities he is being invited to try out. On the other hand, his counterpart in the older generation is not likely to have the least idea what is being talked about. Never have things moved so far so fast. Along with physical and technological changes, the attitudes and awareness of society in general have also undergone a metamorphosis. A prominent signboard I saw on the façade of a small three-room flat at a street corner the other day announcing lessons in 'Western Dance, Guitar, Sitar, Cassio, Kathak, Painting and Folk' is a symptom of this metamorphosis. Such ambitious and confident enterprises are mushrooming all over the big cities. Among other things this tells us that culture has now become big business and that marketing might be a more important component of this business than art. Since this in turn depends on the number of consumers that can be drawn in, the emphasis has increasingly to be on what everybody understands, recognizes, expects, and wants. It follows that the lowest common denominator which satisfies the innumerable layers of the new urban and rural clientele will have to determine the nature of the product that is offered. This will automatically eliminate most of the subtleties and refinements.

Another area of danger is the growing tendency to concentrate on the physical aspects of sound rather than its meaning. It is an inalienable characteristic of Indian music that the intention of the performer takes precedence over the physical attractiveness of the sound. This is why some of the most sought-after musicians have been people in their seventies. This is also why disturbances such as clearing the throat or pauses for retuning in the middle of a traditional concert do not detract from the value of the music. So basic is this principle that even the uninitiated Indian ear is conditioned to it. A departure from these priorities could cut off a vital source of life.

But there are some hopeful signs. Regardless of their quality, the music videos that are flooding the market all aspire, perhaps unconsciously, to satisfy another central principle of raga, namely the gradual accumulation of musical meaning around a nucleus so as to suffuse the listener. The insistent refrains, the repetitive motif, the pounding rhythms of the videos aim at stimulating the senses into a heightened state of being, much in the same way as happens in keertan, qawwali, bhajan, and even khayal. At the same time the presentation tends to be theatrical, aggressive and garish in a manner inimical to the nature of Indian music—as earlier generations understood it.

We are in the centre of a musical transition in which grace and romanticism, purity and restraint, depth and serenity, which still seem to us the most attractive attributes of Indian classical music, are receding. But music is not. Our lives are more full of sound than ever before. But it will be many years before we can clearly hear what it is saying to us.

PART III
Afterword

Two Obituaries of Sheila Dhar

Dileep Padgaonkar: 'Sheila's Spell'*

A marvellous singer and a spinner of fabulous yarns passed away in Delhi this week. Those who were privileged to hear Sheila Dhar's *gayaki* and listen to her anecdotes about musicians, bureaucrats, academics, and even small fry will remain grateful to her for the joy she gave them in abundance. To be in her company was to enter a world where song and laughter, elegant living and learning borne lightly, reigned supreme.

I got to know the Dhars when I moved to Delhi in the early 1970s. Professor P.N. Dhar then served as one of Prime Minister Indira Gandhi's closest advisors. He and Sheila were possibly the most attractive 'power couple' in the capital during that period. They were an unlikely pair. He tended to be taciturn; she was gregarious. His manner was subdued, somewhat cold and courtly. She was expansive, forceful, entirely natural. His smile was pinched. Her laughter was full, free, *bindaas*. The different temperaments were easily explained. He was a Kashmiri Brahmin. She was a Mathur Kayastha from Delhi. He epitomized the 'life examined' and she the graces of a refined lifestyle. But both shared much in common too. They were fiercely attached to

*First published in *The Sunday Times of India*, New Delhi, 29 July 2001.

their integrity. This is no easy task at the best of times. But in those years, when sycophants ran amok, safeguarding one's integrity required uncommon courage. The Dhars did not hesitate to mix with friends who Indira Gandhi had blacklisted. They expressed their opinions with a candour that seldom failed to surprise us. To be candid during the Emergency, especially when one was placed in a vantage position in the power structure, was to expose oneself to the risks of humiliation, harassment, and worse. They chose to remain true to themselves: liberal, sensible, balanced, and outspoken.

Six years ago, Sheila published a book of her reminiscences which generated enthusiastic reviews. She wrote with verve and humour about the lifestyle of the Mathur Kayasthas in the Delhi of the 1940s and '50s, gave scintillating accounts of her exposure to the great musicians of the time—Bade Ghulam Ali Khan, Kesar Bai Kerkar, Pran Nath, Begum Akhtar, and Siddheshwari Devi among others—and offered delightful vignettes about life in the bureaucracy. I have not read a more pleasant book about musicians before the appearance of this one, or since.

She was sixteen when her father asked her to receive Bade Ghulam Ali Khan at the station, escort him and his accompanists to the house of the host, and fetch them to the concert hall after they had refreshed themselves and had their dinner. The hosts happened to be vegetarians. The maestro could not stomach the sight of this unfamiliar food. He exploded: 'Do you think I can sing the way I do if I have to feed on grasses swimming in fluids of various kinds? Every note I sing has the aroma of kebabs.' Sheila then describes how everyone ran helter-skelter to prepare a meal consisting of a rich chicken curry. That day, she writes, 'hearing him was pure and instant intoxication.'

In these memoirs Sheila displays a huge talent to write about music without the least jargon or pretentiousness. From Pran Nath, for example, she learnt to think about ragas in terms of colours. 'It was natural for him to dive into the dark depths of early morning ragas like Lalit and Bhairava, where there was no sun. Sometimes we would hear the greys and dusky ochres of twilight ragas like Puriya and Marwa, the midnight blue of magical and mysterious ragas like Malkauns, and even the restrained gold of the majestic and courtly Darbari.'

Another gift of Sheila's that stood out in the memoirs was her ability to speak about the fads, eccentricities, and weaknesses of people without a trace of malice. I have read with delight over and over again her chapters on the rivalry between Begum Akhtar and Siddheshwari Devi. Much the same thing can be said about the pages she devotes to her boss in the Publications Division, Mohan Rao, who imposes his overbearing hospitality on Richard Attenborough with a South Indian vegetarian meal. The guest looked visibly uneasy and at one point could not help saying: 'How do you chaps manage to eat this stuff? To me it tastes like stewed armpits!'

Such was Sheila Dhar: a singularly talented woman who sailed through life on the strength of her songs and stories and an inexhaustible capacity to laugh and make others join in her laughter.

Rukun Advani: 'Pungent Melody: The Life of Dheila Dhar'*

Sheila Dhar, the singer of Hindustani classical music who died at the age of seventy-two last month, will not be remembered as

*First published in *The Hindu*, Sunday Magazine Section, 26 August 2001.

much for her singing as for what she wrote about the practitioners and practice of singing. She would have sounded surprised if told—and her passion for music would never have let her admit it—that her real forté was the written word, and that she was actually among the most classically accomplished writers of evocative English prose any Indian has written over the past fifty years. Though she wrote three books—the first one, *Children's History of India*, appeared in 1961, and the second, *This India* (with a foreword by Indira Gandhi), in 1973—the clearest evidence of her art is her third book, *Here's Someone I'd Like You to Meet* (1995). The extended clumsiness of the title, rather like the unwieldiness of her own physique in old age, is completely at odds with the idiosyncratic and idiomatic charm, the vivacity and infectious liveliness that lay inside her capacious body and which has been remarked upon by all who have read this gem of a slim little book.

She was no child Mozart and her early career, though academically first class, did not promise such unusual writerly blossom in late middle age. She was briefly forced by her family to study medicine—'they just needed a doctor at large', she once quipped, 'and since I was already large all that remained was the doctor bit.' But medicine was not music to her ears and she walked out of Lady Hardinge Medical College within a year in disgust: the smell of the laboratories could not be disguised even with furtive cigarettes. Dropping a year, she switched to Hindu College and topped her Delhi University English Honours batch in 1950 with a record-breaking score, married Professor P.N. Dhar the following year, accompanied him on his stint at Harvard, was awarded a *Summa Cum Laude* for her M.A. by Boston University, taught Literature for a short while at Miranda House, and then joined the government's Publications Division where, she said, 'I was immediately given the thrilling task of editing books with titles like "Home Care of the TB Patients" and "Sustainable Development of the Timber Forests in Andamans and Nicobars".' Every time she said something self-deprecating like this her eyes would narrow with suppressed merriment and she would explode into laughs. Every time she said anything at all, you could sense an impatient queue of wicked grins inside her, just waiting to get out and rearrange her face into a hawkish guffaw. She was a ready-made iconoclast, a natural mimic, and the cleverest raconteur of hilarious stories from real life about real people that it is possible to imagine. It was difficult to sit in her company and not be rolling about the floor.

No description of what it felt like to be within her ambience really makes much sense in words because she possessed the kind of intellectual liveliness and emotional warmth that has to be experienced to be believed. Her normal way of talking, of just being ordinarily herself, suggested she was three times as alive as anyone else. It seemed to account for her size. Some of her friends, having sensed this was an extraordinary being who did not so much radiate charisma as encompass it and transcend it at the same time, tried to get her on film, but she was very much a part of the oral tradition, she didn't like the sound and smell of celluloid, she become uncharacteristically morose facing the camera, the film was a flop, and so it is doubly unfortunate that words fail in trying to recapture her.

The nearest thing anyone can now do to get some sense of her living personality, even better than listening to cassettes of her singing, is to read her incredibly sparky prose, in which she manages to mould impeccable, grammatical, and refined English sentences to serve the needs of quintessentially *desi* situations, dialogue, and characters, a feat which defies all but the very best who strive to translate hybrid and locally specific Indian experience into English. She does this even better than Arundhati Roy, whose book she greatly admired for this specific reason. 'That girl', she once memorably said, 'has made English sentences perform Bharatanatyam on a tightrope of coconut fibres.'

Her central interest in all she wrote was to communicate what it really felt like to be alive in the presence of certain people who had captivated her, or taught her to think or sing, or to look at the world from a slightly different angle. In *Here's Someone* these are usually Hindustani musicians and singers, but in *Children's History of India* they are historical personages. In the latter book, she said, the idea was to write history without dates, a notion that standard historians thought senseless but which was a great hit with children. She argued that children are definably children only so long as they want to know just what happened next, not when it happened. The moment they ask 'when did Aurangzeb become emperor?' is when 'they have grown up, and then they should stop reading my book.' Her argument was that children should remain 'prehistoric' and 'timeless', they would be stuffed with dates and facts in any case when they grew up. Nehru, a historian himself, thought this an odd but wonderfully eccentric assumption on which to base a history book for children. He wrote a preface for it, the book became a huge bestseller and went into sixteen impressions (it remains in print to this day), and it was translated into all fourteen Indian languages in the 1960s. Sheila Dhar returned Nehru's favour by editing a very large number of his speeches for him. Later, persuaded by Pupul Jayakar during the first Festival of India, she was instrumental in putting together a Leavisite LP titled 'The Great Tradition: Masters of Indian Music'. Her argument here was that a distinction needs to be made between 'musicians' and 'performers'. The former were those who forged the language of music. These included Zohra Bai, Abdul Karim Khan, Fayyaz Khan, Kesar Bai, Mallikarjun, Amir Khan, Gangubai, and Bade Ghulam Ali Khan. The latter were virtuoso artistes whose accomplishment, no less considerable on a different stage, is mistakenly demeaned by comparison. Among these superlative performers she listed Bhimsen Joshi, Begum Akhtar, and Rashid Khan. Kishori Amonkar, she felt, belonged to both categories, 'depending on her mood on a particular day'. Sheila Dhar's canon of music became available in the shape of the 'Music Today' cassettes and CD's, for it was she who advised the producers and selected the performers.

Sheila Dhar's irreverent and balloon-pricking temperament had to be curbed when she started training to be a singer of Hindustani classical music, for the culture of this musical tradition is feudal and devotional, requiring something between deep respect and unquestioning worship of the ustaad by the shagird. Her years of rigour were, all the same, interspersed with long intervals of relaxed conversation with and observation of the likes of Begum Akhtar, Bade Ghulam Ali Khan, Siddheshwari, and Bhimsen Joshi, all of whom feature within her chapters on musicians in *Here's Someone*. She remarks on the sometimes insufferable narcissism of Indian musicians, pointing out that this is almost a religious tenet within their culture, but also one of its unlovelier aspects. The book mixes iconoclastic observation with an insider's casually deep knowledge of music-making in north India.

There is nothing quite like it. It is intensely alive, each chapter a riveting story, each situation full of the most endearingly peculiar people, the whole book a memorable and treasured possession that enriches one's inner life incalculably and therefore something one keeps wanting to re-read again and again. There is also within it Sheila Dhar's personal trademark of acute perceptiveness about foibles of character, nuances of situational atmosphere, and subtleties of musical culture on the one hand, and an ability to kill us laughing at all of it on the other. Whereas the standard vocabulary of music criticism is completely technical at one end and effusively emotional at the other, hers does a better job than anyone else's in communicating something of the experience of Hindustani music to a lay listener. Using culinary metaphors which convey the 'taste' and 'fragrance' of specific melodies, she brings the tongue and the nose to bear upon the ear and does not hesitate to use the oddest analogies and examples if she believes they serve her literary and analytic purpose. 'My musical utterance inalienably carries within it the flavour of everything that has ever happened to me and of all the emotional landscapes I have traversed', she writes; actually, this is a description of her prose as well. The book also contains the most sociologically sharp evocation of a Kayastha household in pre-independence Old Delhi, a piece of informal literary anthropology which, for those to whom generic boundaries seem irrelevant, ranks with Malgudi and *The Remembered Village*. All this makes her book both an oddity and a masterpiece, though this is by no means the universal opinion on the book: many musicians and music critics who, unlike Sheila Dhar, cannot see that music can simultaneously be worshipped and its makers laughed at, have found her non-conformism unsettling. These are the people she always secretly wished to unsettle.

For she was an Epicurean in the classical mould: she had substituted the ridiculous idea of worshipping unseen gods with a passionate seeking out and sharing of friendship, music, and divine food, much of it cooked by herself. This was her notion of *advaita*. At the time of her death, Sheila Dhar was putting together a small collection of her essays. It will appear shortly, bearing a title which combines the two passions of her life: it is called *The Cooking of Music and Other Essays*. Madhur Jaffrey, one of her distant nieces, acknowledges several of her recipes as having been derived from 'Sheila'. Few know that this Sheila was Sheila Dhar.

Index